Tanzania under Mwalimu Nyerere: Reflections on an African Statesman

Godfrey Mwakikagile

Copyright (c) 2006 Godfrey Mwakikagile
All rights reserved.

Tanzania under Mwalimu Nyerere
Godfrey Mwakikagile

Second Edition

ISBN-10: 0-9802534-9-7
ISBN-13: 978-0-9802534-9-8

New Africa Press
Dar es Salaam, Tanzania
Pretoria, South Africa

No part of this book may be reproduced in any form for commercial purposes without written permission from the publisher.

Contents

Acknowledgements

Introduction

Chapter One:
Tanganyika before Independence

Chapter Two:
Tanganyika after Independence

Chapter Three:
Tanzania in the Seventies and Eighties

Chapter Four:
The Introduction of Multiparty Democracy in Tanzania under Nyerere's Stewardship

Chapter Five:
Life Under Nyerere

Chapter Six:
Tanzania after Nyerere

Appendix I:
Nyerere: Reflections

**Appendix II:
Gerry Helleiner: The Legacies of Julius Nyerere:
An Economist's Reflections**

Chapter Notes

About the Author

Acknowledegments

MUCH OF THIS WORK is derived from my life and experience in Tanganyika, later Tanzania. But a significant portion of it can be attributed to the secondary sources I have cited to complement my analysis.

The people of Tanganyika, and Tanzania after Tanganyika united with Zanzibar, deserve special thanks for inspiring and sustaining this work. It is because of them that I wrote the book. Without them, there would have been no Nyerere as a leader. He led them, but they made his leadership possible.

I must also express my deep gratitude to three individuals who knew and worked with President Nyerere when they were professors at the University of Dar es Salaam in Tanzania.

They are Cranford Pratt, who was the first principal of the University College, Dar es Salaam, from 1961 to 1965. He assumed the post the same year Tanganyika won independence from Britain on 9 December 1961.

He wrote extensively about Tanzania. He also wrote a moving tribute to Mwalimu Nyerere, but one not entirely sentimental. It is an objective appraisal, by a scholar, of Mwalimu's policies and leadership. And I am grateful to him for citing portions of his work to support my arguments.

I am equally grateful to Professor John Saul who, in spite of his ideological affinity with Nyerere as a socialist, assessed Nyerere's work objectively enough without compromising scholarship.

He argued that Tanzania did not achieve economic development because it was not socialist enough. I have benefited from his insights although I don't share his position on that, forcefully articulated in his paper, "Julius Nyerere: The Theory and Practice of (Un)democratic Socialism in Africa."

I am also grateful to Professor Gerry Helleiner whose analysis is reproduced in this work.

All three scholars, who are Canadian, wrote their essays on Nyerere's legacy after Nyerere died. And they continued to be some of the leading authorities on Tanzania in the West where they continued to teach in their home country, Canada.

The rest of the sources I have cited to document my work have been extremely useful and must be equally acknowledged for their contribution to the successful completion of this study whose merits are beyond the scope of my assessment.

Introduction

MANY PEOPLE have written about former President Julius Nyerere since his death. He has been universally acclaimed by his admirers and critics for his personal integrity and selfless devotion, and has been equally condemned for his "disastrous" economic policies.

I hope to strike a medium between the two. As a Tanzanian myself, it may be difficult to make an objective appraisal of his successes and failures. But that is what I have attempted to do in this book. Whether I have succeeded or not, is not for me to say. It is for the readers to decide.

Mwalimu, as he was and still is affectionately called, died when I was out of the country. His death was a shock to me and I am sure to many others in and outside Tanzania because of the type of leader he was. I saw him for the first time in the late 1950s when he was campaigning for independence and he left an indelible mark on me. I was under ten years old then, but I never forgot the day I first saw him, as I explain in the book.

As a mere mortal among mortals, he made mistakes like the rest of us. And he admitted his mistakes unlike most leaders. I discuss this in my book.

He was also unique among leaders in many fundamental respects, a subject I also address in this work.

But my focus is not just on what type of leader he was, but on what kind of policies he pursued especially in the domestic arena which was also his main theatre of operation; although none of this diminished his stature as one of the giants among leaders in history.

In spite of his lofty status, he remained what he was: of humble origin and a peasant at heart, at home with the masses in the villages in the rural areas unlike most leaders. His formidable intellect was equally acknowledged by friends and foes alike.

Why a leader of such high moral integrity and extraordinary intelligence could pursue "wrong" economic policies has baffled his critics, although the answer is very simple. They have never asked *why* he did what he did and under *what* circumstances. Professor Ali Mazrui described Nyerere as the most intellectual of the East African presidents, and one of the two most intellectual presidents Africa has ever produced; the other one being Leopold Sedar Senghor.

An admirer of Nyerere as an intellectual, and also his critic, Mazrui has attempted to explain why Nyerere pursued some of the policies he did; so have others.

It is a subject I also address in this work, complemented by appraisals from some of the people who understood his policies more than most of his critics did, in order to put everything in its proper perspective for a full understanding of Mwalimu.

Those amongst us who admired him, or disagreed with him, would be better advised to look at what he did without preconceived notions, remembering that Mwalimu was a mere mortal with frailties like the rest of us who admitted his mistakes but who also did his best.

I have also done my best to show how life was in Tanganyika, later Tanzania, under Mwalimu in a country where I was born and brought up.

I am also fully aware that I may not have done justice to a leader who was not only one of the giants in the history of Africa but in the history of mankind.

Chapter One:

Tanganyika before Independence

WHAT IS TANZANIA TODAY did not come into existence until Tanganyika united with Zanzibar in 1964 to form one country.
    I was born and brought up in Tanganyika. And it is Tanganyika that I focus on in this chapter as the land of my birth where my personality and identity was shaped during British colonial rule in the fifties and in the first decade of independence in the sixties.
    Tanganyika itself did not exist as a territorial entity until 1885 when it was annexed by Germany. It was created as a colony by the Germans whose claim to the territory was given formal recognition at the Berlin conference during the partition of Africa. The German Colonization Society led by Dr. Karl Peters claimed the territory in 1884. He was supported by his home government under Bismarck and went on to establish the German East Africa Company to rule the territory.
    In 1886 and 1890, the British and the Germans signed agreements which defined their spheres of influence in the interior of East Africa and along the coast previously claimed by the sultan of Oman who had moved his capital from Muscat, Oman, to Zanzibar. In 1891, the German government took over direct administration of the territory from the German East Africa Company and appointed a governor with headquarters in Dar es Salaam, a port city founded by the Arabs and whose name means "haven of peace."
    Our imperial conquerors drew territorial boundaries to define their spheres of influence, creating the countries we have in Africa

today.

In East Africa, the British had Kenya, Uganda and Zanzibar; and the Germans, Tanganyika and Ruanda-Urundi - what is Rwanda and Burundi - which together formed one colony called German East Africa which existed from 1885 to 1919. After that, the British took over what became Tanganyika following Germany's defeat in World War I. The Belgians acquired Ruanda-Urundi which became two separate colonies but administered together with the Belgian Congo.

British formal presence on Tanganyikan soil began in 1914 at the beginning of World War I when the Royal Navy occupied Mafia island in the Indian Ocean a few miles southeast of Dar es Salaam.

During World War I, German East Africa was occupied by the Allied forces including troops from South Africa led by General Smuts. It was - minus Ruanda-Urundi - renamed Tanganyika Territory in 1920 (named after Lake Tanganyika) and placed under the League of Nations mandate.

It was administered by Britain after American President Woodrow Wilson refused to assume responsibility for the former German colony as proposed by British Prime Minister David Lloyd George of the Liberal Party. He was prime minister from 1916 to 1922.

In 1921, the Belgians transferred Kigoma district in western Tanganyika to British administration, making it part of Tanganyika. They had administered the district - together with Ruanda-Urundi - since the Allied occupation of the former German colony in 1916. In 1924, Britain and Belgium signed an agreement defining the border between Tanganyika and Ruanda-Urundi.

Until 1925, Tanganyika was administered in an improvised way and followed German administrative practices. After that, the system of indirect rule was introduced. It was first practised by Lord Lugard in northern Nigeria where he used traditional rulers including emirs to administer a vast expanse of territory.

In 1946, Tanganyika became a UN trusteeship territory; coincidentally, the same year the Nigerian federation was formed out of three massive regions created by the British. The regions were Northern Nigeria dominated by the Hausa-Fulani, Eastern

Nigeria dominated by the Igbo, and Western Nigeria by the Yoruba. Nigeria itself was created in 1914 with the amalgamation of the North and the South which had been administered separately, as if they were two distinct colonies, but by the same colonial power, Britain.

When Europeans came to Africa and established colonies, they never intended to relinquish control and transfer power to Africans. They came to stay permanently and dreamt of transforming at least some of their colonies into permanent extensions of Europe as the British did in Australia and New Zealand, and as they attempted to do in South Africa, Southern Rhodesia - what is Zimbabwe today - and Kenya. In fact, Kenya was declared a "White Man's Country" from the beginning of British occupation of the territory under Lord Delamere.

Neighbouring Tanganyika would have met the same fate had the British colonialists succeeded in establishing a giant federation stretching from Kenya all the way down to South Africa.

In fact, the governors of all the colonies in the region - Kenya, Uganda, Tanganyika, Nyasaland (now Malawi), Northern Rhodesia (Zambia today), and Southern Rhodesia met in Tukuyu, southern Tanganyika, in 1925 to work on a plan to form such a federation. But, years later as political awakening among Africans began to take place, the proposed federation was strongly opposed by African nationalists who feared that the establishment of such a giant political entity would consolidate and perpetuate imperial rule and white domination over Africans who constituted the vast majority of the population throughout the region as much as they did in the rest of the continent.

And it's very interesting to know how the European settlers felt about their new life in the colonies they had established under the tropical sun far away from Europe. In spite of the difficulties they faced living in underdeveloped regions of the world, they were still very much satisfied with their new life. That is why they did not want to leave or relinquish power to Africans until they were forced to do so.

In fact, life couldn't have been better for them, since many of our colonial masters would not have been able to get in their own countries - in Britain and elsewhere in Europe - the kind of jobs they got in colonial Africa.

Since I focus on Tanganyika in this chapter, the examples I cite come from East Africa to illustrate my point. As Erika Johnson, writing about the 1950s in colonial Tanganyika, stated in *The Other Side of Kilimanjaro*:

> Robin [Robin Johnson was a District Commissioner, simply known as D.C. throughout British colonial Africa] maintains that there was no better life for a man in those days than that of a District Commissioner. It was a marvellous combination of an active open air life, coupled with a wide, varied and interesting amount of office work. You did long walking safaris through your area and slept under canvas, and in this way you got to know your parishioners and their problems.
>
> Responsible for a vast area, you were father, mentor and disciplinarian to everyone, sorting out family and tribal disputes. You had to do anything and everything: build roads, dams and bridges, dig wells and be a magistrate and administrator of law and order. Your problems could vary from shooting a rogue elephant despoiling villagers' crops to trying a stock thief in court.
>
> In later years, [Julius] Nyerere once said to a silent Robin that the D.C's had made little contribution other than collecting taxes![1]

The colonial rulers did, of course, have a tendency to exaggerate their own importance because of their condescending and paternalistic attitude towards Africans, called "natives," a derogatory term as it was always used in this context. For example, it is obvious who built the roads, dams and bridges, and who dug the water wells: Africans. Yet Robin Johnson, typical of the colonialists' attitude, claims credit for all that without even mentioning the African labourers who did all the hard work; what the colonialists called dirty work since it was beneath them to soil their hands or stoop to scoop up soil or make bricks or do whatever was required to be done.

That is what prompted Nyerere to say the colonial rulers did nothing except collect taxes. And all that money, collected from the "natives," went to the colonial masters. Hardly any was used to help Africans, the very same people who worked so hard and paid taxes to maintain the colonial system that was oppressing and exploiting them.

In fact, I personally remember seeing African men doing "dirty," hard work, building roads, in the town and outskirts of Mbeya and also working on the road from Mbeya to Chunya, a district north of Mbeya; and in Rungwe district working on the road from Tukuyu to Kyela, 30 miles south of Tukuyu close to the Tanganyika-Nyasaland (now Malawi) border, when I was a little boy under 10 in the 1950s.

They worked for the colonial Public Works Department, what was simply known as PWD, and rode in the back of Bedford lorries; they were British lorries imported from Britain. The lorries also were simply called PWD. I even remember their colour. They were painted green on the sides and white on top. The African labourers worked hard, all day long, often in scorching sun, for a mere pittance. It was, of course, better than nothing. They also needed the money to pay taxes, although quite a few of them also wasted money getting drunk.

That was in the Southern Highlands Province where I grew up. The province was under a British provincial commissioner, called P.C. The town of Mbeya was the provincial capital where my parents and I together with my siblings lived in the early and mid-fifties before we moved to Rungwe district. Our home in Kyimbila in Rungwe district was about four miles south of the town of Tukuyu, the district capital. Tukuyu is 45 miles south of Mbeya.

During those days of colonial rule, Tanganyika was divided into seven provinces: The Southern Highlands Province, the Southern Province, the Central Province, the Western Province, the Lake Province, the Coast Province, and the Northern Province. After independence, the Southern Highlands was divided into Mbeya Region and Iringa Region; so were the rest, also broken down into smaller regional administrative units called regions.

But life in those days was good for the colonial rulers. I also remember British men and women playing golf and tennis in the town of Tukuyu which is about 35 miles from the Tanzania-Malawi border. And they used to give us tennis balls now and then when we passed through the golf course. Many of them came from as far away as Mbeya, the provincial capital, and even from neighbouring Northern Rhodesia, now Zambia.

I was too young then to know what was going on in terms of colonial domination or what it meant to be colonized or ruled by the British or Europeans in general. But I do remember that whenever we saw them, they seemed to be very happy and satisfied with their lives which were made much easier by African servants in almost every European household. The African female servants even helped raise or bring up the white children.

It was unthinkable not to have one, a "house boy" or a "house girl," since almost all whites could afford to pay a pittance to the "native" servants. And remember, Africans had no say in those days in our own countries. They couldn't go against our colonial masters until they started to mobilize forces to campaign for independence.

That was the last thing the colonialists wanted to see, since they were not ready to give up power. They did everything they could to delay independence or stifle nationalist aspirations. In Tanganyika, the British settlers formed the United Tanganyika Party, known as UTP, to stem the nationalist tide that started to sweep across the country, during the same time when British colonial rulers such as Robin Johnson felt that they were doing a wonderful job to help Africans while they were really helping themselves and enjoying themselves in the tropical climate.

One of the areas in which British settlers in East Africa became deeply involved was commercial farming. It happens that for us in East Africa, our blessing has also been our curse. East Africa is endowed with an abundance of fertile land at high altitude with a cooler climate, although still tropical. But it somewhat reminded the Europeans of the temperate climate back home in Europe, at temperatures they were comfortable with.

Much of East Africa is, of course, also hot, in fact very hot; for example along the coast, in the lowlands and in other parts of the region. But it also has more arable land, at higher altitudes, than West Africa does. For example, in an area where I come from called Kyimbila, there is a large tea estate called Kyimbila Tea Estate stretching for miles; we also grow a lot of coffee in our district. Pine trees which grow in a temperate climate are also common in my home area of Kyimbila and other parts of Rungwe district.

Kyimbila Tea Estate is one of the largest in Tanzania, indeed in the whole of East Africa, and was originally established by the Germans. In fact, there was a German settlement at Kyimbila, about a mile and a half from our house, when the Germans ruled Tanganyika as German East Africa – *Deutsch Ostafrika* - and built a large church there, called Kyimbila Moravian Church.

There is also a large grave yard at Kyimbila where Germans are buried. I remember reading the headstones showing the deceased were born in the 1800s; they were born in Germany. After the Germans lost World War I, the British took over the tea estate and continued to reap benefits as the Germans had done before them using cheap African labour.

When the British ran the tea estate when I was growing up, they always had a British manager who lived on the premises. I also remember vividly one tragic incident that happened in 1956 when I was in standard one, what Americans call the first grade. I was six years old then and my schoolmates and I used to take a short-cut, walking past the manager's residence, going to Kyimbila Primary School about two miles from our house. I was the youngest in the group.

Everyday we went by, his dogs, a German Shepherd and a Dalmatian, used to bark at us. They were not always tied, so quite often they used to chase us before being called back by their master or by his African servant who washed clothes and cooked for the British couple and cleaned up the house.

He wasn't very friendly, either, with us, anymore than his master and wife were; typical of the attitude of a "house nigger" fawning and crawling before his master: "Yes, boss; whatever you say, mister white man. You are the boss. Yes, Sir!" That kind of attitude.

One morning on our way to school, both dogs were loose and they started chasing us. Although I was a fast runner, in fact a sprinter even at my tender age, my friends outran me that day. As the dogs kept on chasing us, I turned and looked back and knew I was not going to make it.

So I dove under the tea shrubs, to my right, to take cover. The German Shepherd went past me and kept on chasing the other children. But the Dalmatian saw me where I was hiding and came right under the bush and bit me on my right knee. I still bear a large scar on my knee 50 years later, a bitter reminder of the little regard our European conquerors had for us, even children.

The British manager of the tea estate and his wife knew full well that school children went by their house every morning on the way to school, and every evening on their way home from school. But they didn't care to have their dogs tied simply because we were black children. Had we been white kids, the story, and the outcome, would have been entirely different.

And nothing could be done about it. We were still under colonial rule as British subjects. We were not even citizens in terms of rights even in our own country since it was owned by our colonial masters, as *their* colony, and not by us. Therefore we had no rights, none whatsoever, a white person was bound to respect. We complained about it but our teachers and our parents couldn't do anything about it. It was unthinkable to bring up charges against a white man let alone take him to court or demand compensation for injury.

At such a young age, we didn't know the British couple deliberately turned the dogs loose on us simply because we were African and black. It was not until years later when I was a teenager that I realized why they did this to us, and why I almost lost my leg, and my life, on that day and came perilously closing to meeting the same fate on many other occasions when were being chased by the dogs.

Our subordinate position as a conquered people was demonstrated on another occasion and again in a very personal way when my father was told by the British manager of a Shell British Petroleum (BP) petrol station in the town of Tukuyu that he could not put his lunch on the table used by the manager; it was *chapati* my mother had cooked for him on that day. I remember that very well.

My father was very bitter about the incident and told us what happened when he came back home that evening. That was around 1958 or 1959. My father, having secondary school education, was one of the few people in the area who knew English and was hired as the assistant manager at the petrol station. He went to Malangali Secondary School in Iringa district in the Southern Highlands Province, one of the best schools in colonial Tanganyika and even after independence.

Earlier, he had worked as a medical assistant in many parts of Tanganyika - in Muheza, Tanga, Handeni, Amani, Kilosa, Morogoro - including the town of Kigoma, in western Tanganyika where I was born on 4 October 1949, before returning to our home district of Rungwe from Mbeya in the mid-1950s.

He was trained as a medical assistant in the mid-1940s at Princess Margaret Hospital – later renamed Muhimbili National Hospital - in Dar es Salaam during British colonial rule. He excelled in school and was supposed to go to Tabora Secondary School for further education in standard 11 and standard 12 after completing standard 10 at Malangali Secondary School but couldn't go further because of family obligations, forcing him to seek employment early.

One of his classmates at Princess Margaret Hospital was Austin Shaba who, after completing his studies, went to Tukuyu to work as a medical assistant. He later became minister of local government in the first independence cabinet under President Nyerere.

I remember my father saying Austin - they knew each other well - encouraged him to go into politics but he refused to do so. Both, like other Africans in Tanganyika, had been subjected to indignities of colour bar - another term for racial discrimination here in East and southern Africa- which probably played a major role in encouraging people like Austin Shaba to go into politics and campaign for independence.

Another classmate of my father, at Malangali Secondary School, who also went into politics was Jeremiah Kasambala. The son of a chief, he also became a cabinet member under President Nyerere and served as minister of agriculture and cooperatives in the first independence cabinet. He came from Rungwe District, like my parents did, and he and my father had known each other for years. Kasambala also encouraged my father to pursue a career in politics but, again, he refused to do so.

Considering my father's experience with the British colonial rulers and the indignities he was subjected to, including the incident at the Shell BP petrol station in Tukuyu in the late fifties, it was a miracle he didn't go into politics right away. But that was not his calling.

Still, those are the kind of incidents, and insults, which turn people into militants and revolutionaries as would have the dog incident in my case had I been an adult when I was bitten by that Dalmatian back in 1956. Had there been a Mau Mau in

Tanganyika, I definitely would have supported it, fully, at the very least.

Andrew Nyerere, the eldest son of President Julius Nyerere who was my schoolmate at Tambaza High School in Dar es Salaam from 1969 to 1970, also told me about a similar incident when I was writing a book, *Nyerere and Africa: End of an Era: Expanded Edition*,[2] after I contacted him to find out if he had anything to say that I could add to the book. He did, including the following, as he stated in a letter to me in 2003:

> As you remember, Sheikh Amri Abeid was the first mayor of Dar es Salaam. Soon after independence, the mayor went to Palm Beach Hotel (near our high school, Tambaza, in Upanga). There was a sign at the hotel which clearly stated: 'No Africans and dogs allowed inside.' He was blocked from entering the hotel, and said in protest, 'But I am the Mayor.' Still he was told, 'You will not get in.'
>
> Shortly thereafter, the owner of the hotel was given 48 hours to leave the country. When the nationalization exercise began, that hotel was the first to be nationalized.[3]

These incidents demonstrate, in a very tragic way, how vulnerable and helpless we were at the hands of our colonial masters. They also demonstrate the utter futility in trying to seek justice under a judicial system that did not treat blacks and whites as equals. And many people in East Africa even today can tell similar stories about their bitter experiences with the British and other Europeans who settled in our region in large numbers in order to turn it into a white man's homeland as if we did not even exist. However, we must also understand that not all whites mistreated Africans. In many cases relations were good even if Africans and Europeans did not interact socially.

People in West Africa have similar incidents to talk about, but not as many as we do in East Africa. And probably there is more bitterness in East Africa about the white man's oppression than there is in West Africa for the simple reason that we were subjected to direct humiliation than our brethren were in the western part of the continent because of the daily contact we had with Europeans in a region where they had settled in large numbers. Just remember Mau Mau and what it was all about.

Also remember the Maji Maji uprising in Tanganyika from 1905 to 1907 during German colonial rule. It was a mass insurrection that covered the entire southern half of the country and almost drove the Germans out until they sought immediate reinforcements from Germany to contain and eventually quell the "rebellion."

It was more of a revolution than a rebellion. It transformed the people into true nationalists transcending tribal loyalties. Many tribes took part in the uprising as one people, Africans, fighting alien invaders. The Germans, like the British, also came to East Africa to settle permanently.

I remember what our teachers used to say when they taught us African history in secondary school in the sixties. They used to say the mosquito was the best friend of West Africa because it kept the white man out of there: it stopped Europeans from settling permanently and in large numbers as they did in East Africa, especially in Kenya, and to a smaller degree in Tanganyika.

It was a common saying in Africa, as it probably still is today, especially among people of my generation or older.

When Tanganyika won independence in 1961, it had more than 20,000 white settlers, mostly British; a significant number of Germans, some Dutch including Boers from South Africa and others. And Kenya had about 66,000 whites, mostly British including members of the British aristocracy, at independence in 1963. Kenya also had a significant number of Boers, or Afrikaners, from South Africa who founded the town of Eldoret in the Western Highlands in the Great Rift Valley.

Robin Johnson, whom I mentioned earlier, was typical of the British settlers who had established themselves in East Africa determined to make it their permanent home as civil servants working for the colonial government or as farmers or something else. In fact, a significant number of them were born in Kenya or Tanganyika.

Some came from South Africa and others from as far away as Australia and New Zealand. And many, or their children and grandchildren, are still there today living in different parts Kenya and what is Tanzania today.

Some of the settlers who acquired large tracts of land were members of the British aristocracy, probably the last people who would think of relinquishing power to Africans one day.

Johnson himself gave up his job as a civil servant and took up farming. He was the District Commissioner (D.C.) of Kongwa in the Central Province in Tanganyika during the ill-fated groundnut scheme that was intended to produce groundnuts on a commercial scale. The scheme was a disaster. He was later assigned to Arusha in northern Tanganyika, what was then called the Northern Province:

> Robin himself was becoming increasingly interested in Tanganyika's long-term future. He felt if he became a farmer, like his father before him, and thereby rooted in the soil, he could play a more permanent role in the country's development than permitted to a transitory civil servant.
> He had met David Stirling, the founder of the Capricorn Africa Society, and felt that his policy of common citizenship and a multi-racial form of government might well be the answer for the East African states where Africans, though still backward, must soon begin to move politically, and there was a small settled European and Asian community.
> He resigned from the Colonial Service in 1951 when he was alloted one of the Ol Molog farms [in Arusha in northern Tanganyika]. His colleagues thought he was quite mad. Surely every diligent Administrative Officer only had one goal in life - to be a Governor finally. How irresponsible of Robin carelessly to throw that chance away.[4]

Little did they realize that hard as they were planning to turn East Africa into their permanent home dominated by whites, Africans were at the same time proceeding on a parallel path towards mobilization of the masses in the quest for independence and did not, for one moment, believe that the multiracial government proposed by some of the more liberal members of the settler community would ever include them as equal partners. Universal adult suffrage, a cardinal principle cherished in every democratic society, was totally out of the question in this dispensation.

In Tanganyika, Nyerere admitted in the fifties that the colonial government and the African nationalist movement were headed in the same direction, but at a different pace. As a UN Trust Territory under British mandate, Tanganyika was supposed to be guided towards independence by the colonial government. But the colonial rulers had a different timetable. It would have taken decades before the country won independence. Nyerere and his colleagues wanted independence much sooner.

Many of the settlers were, of course, aware of the political awakening and agitation that was taking place but did not believe that the people of Kenya and Tanganyika under British tutelage would demand or win independence within a decade or so.

The British colonial office suggested that if independence ever came to Tanganyika, it would be in 1985. Britain had to have some kind of time table since Tanganyika was not a typical colony, like Kenya, but a trusteeship territory under UN mandate, with Britain playing the role of "Big Brother" to guide the country towards independence on terms stipulated by the United Nations. Yet the UN itself was not seriously concerned about freedom and independence for Africans without being pushed by our leaders who included Julius Nyerere as the pre-eminent African leader in Tanganyika.

In fact, political awakening among Africans had already been going on for quite some time long before the "halcyon days" of colonial rule in the 1950s. And Julius Nyerere played a critical role, at a very early age, in galvanizing his colleagues into action, despite his humility. As Chief Abdallah Said Fundikira, who became one of the first cabinet members after independence, said about what type of person Nyerere was in those days: "If you want the truth, one did not particularly notice Nyerere."[5]

He was talking about the time when Nyerere entered Makerere University College at the age of 22 after attending secondary school in Tabora in western Tanganyika, the hometown of Fundikira, chief of the Nyamwezi tribe, one of the largest in Tanzania today with more than one million people.

It was when he was at Makerere that his leadership qualities came to be noticed when he formed the Tanganyika Welfare Association intended to help the small number of students from Tanganyika to work together. It was not a political organization but had the potential to become one.

The welfare association soon forged ties and eventually merged with the Tanganyika African Association, an organization founded by African civil servants in Tanganyika in 1929 to address their problems. But they had to operate within prescribed limits as defined by the colonial authorities who said the association could only deal with welfare problems; nothing political.

Nyerere and his colleagues wanted the association to fight discrimination against the African civil servants who were being paid less than their European counterparts. It was a "welfare" problem but with profound implications hardly indistinguishable from political demands.

He later described these "welfare" demands as "the politics of sheer complaints" which did not address the fundamental problem of inequity of power between Africans and Europeans. But he wanted the colonial authorities to pay attention to demands by Africans in order to bring about fundamental change in this asymmetrical relationship that had existed since the colonialists took over Tanganyika before he was born. As he recalled those days:

> When I was born, there was not a single person who questioned why we were being ruled. And if my father had heard that we wanted changes, he would have asked me, 'What do you think you can do, you small silly boy?'[6]

But nothing could dissuade him from his commitment to justice, no matter what the cost. And much as his father would have been apprehensive of the situation had he lived long enough to discuss the matter with his son after he became mature, Nyerere knew that nothing was going to change until Africans themselves did something to bring about change. His mother was equally apprehensive if not more so. She was quoted as saying:

> I began to know about Julius' activities when he was teaching at Pugu College [St. Francis College] in 1952. Everyday, a man called Dossa Aziz came to our house and he would talk with Julius for a long time. One day I overheard them talking about taking over the government from Europeans.
>
> I became afraid. Later I asked Julius if what I heard was true. When he said yes, I became more frightened. I told him what he was doing was bad. God had given him a good job and now he wanted to spoil it. But he said that what he was doing would benefit not only us but everyone in the country.[7]

Nyerere had just returned to Tanganyika in October 1952 after three years at Edinburgh University in Scotland where he was admitted in October 1949. He earned a master's degree in economics and history, and also studied philosophy.

The fifties was a critical decade in the struggle for independence in Tanganyika. It was the decade when TANU

(Tanganyika African National Union), the party that led Tanganyika to independence, was formed. It was also the decade in which the colonial government tried to neutralize TANU as much as the British colonial authorities tried to do to KANU (Kenya African National Union) in neighbouring Kenya when they arrested and imprisoned Jomo Kenyatta in 1952 And it was the last decade of colonial rule in both colonies.

Before the 1958-1959 general election in Tanganyika, the British colonial government launched a harassment campaign to discredit and if possible destroy TANU. Nyerere was banned from making public speeches. He was accused of libel and put on trial and twelve branches of TANU were closed down.

The banning of Nyerere came after a highly successful campaign across the country to get support for TANU and for his campaign for independence. He travelled to all parts of Tanganyika, to every province, in a battered Land Rover which belonged to his compatriot Dossa Aziz who gave the vehicle to TANU to help with the independence campaign and was able to build, with his colleagues, the party's membership to unprecedented levels. Just within a year, TANU had 250,000 members.

It was during one of these campaign trips that I saw Nyerere for the first time when he came to address a mass rally in Tukuyu in the late 1950s; riding in the same Land Rover that had taken him to all parts of Tanganyika before. I remember that day well. He wore a light green shirt and rode standing in the back of the Land Rover, waving at the crowd that had gathered to welcome him when he first arrived to address a mass rally at a football (soccer) stadium in Tukuyu one afternoon.

Although he was committed to non-violence, the colonial authorities claimed that some of his speeches were highly inflammatory. But to the people of Tanganyika, the speeches were highly inspiring. And because of that, he was banned in early 1957 from making public speeches.

Yet he remained unperturbed. As he told a correspondent of *The New York Times* in Dar es Salaam, Tanganyika, on March 31, 1957: "I am a troublemaker, because I believe in human rights strongly enough to be one."[8]

Earlier in the same year, he had written an article published in the *Tanganyika Standard* which two district commissioners (D.Cs, as we called them and as they also called themselves), complained about. They claimed Nyerere had libelled them. Twelve years later, I became a news reporter of the same newspaper in June 1969 when I was still in high school at Tambaza (Form V or standard 13) in Dar es Salaam.

Nyerere also said although TANU was committed to non-violence, the nationalist movement would resort to civil disobedience to achieve its goals; and, by implication, to violence if necessary, should there be no other option left in pursuit of independence.

Now was the time to end all this, the colonial authorities felt, by neutralizing him. They put him on trial.

The trial was a turning point in the history of TANU and of the country as a whole. A reporter of *Drum* magazine was one of the people who covered the trial and had the following to say in the November 1958 edition of the magazine when the proceedings took place in Dar es Salaam, the capital:

> The sun has not yet risen but hundreds of people are already gathered round the small courthouse in Dar es Salaam. Some have come from distant villages, with blankets and cooking utensils as if for a camping holiday. They have been in Dar es Salaam for more than a week at the trial of the president of the Tanganyika African National Union (TANU), Julius Nyerere, on a charge of criminal libel. It was alleged that Nyerere wrote an article in which two district commissioners were libelled.
>
> Police constables line the streets round the court and a riot squad stands ready nearby in case of trouble. As the time draws near for the court to open, the crowds jostle and shove for the best positions.
>
> The trial has been a mixture of exciting arguments, explosive surprises and hours of dullness. Mr. Pritt - Nyerere's counsel - insisted that the two commissioners should be called to give evidence. He accused the government of prosecuting Nyerere without investigating his allegations. The government was telling the world that if anybody said anything against a district commissioner, he could be put into prison for saying what was true.
>
> When Nyerere gave evidence, he took full responsibility for the article and said that he had written it to draw the attention of the government to certain complaints. He was followed by three witnesses who spoke of 'injustices' they had suffered at the hands of the the two district commissioners.
>
> Halfway through the proceedings, the attorney-general appeared in court in person to announce on behalf of the Crown that it would not continue with the counts concerning one of the commissioners.
>
> Now, on the last day of the show, the stars begin to arrive: Mr. Summerfield, the chief prosecutor; Mr. N.M. Rattansey, defence counsel who

is assisting the famous British QC, Mr. D.N. Pritt. Mr. Nyerere, wearing a green bush shirt, follows later. He smiles and waves as members of the crowd cheer him.

The curtain goes up with the arrival of Mr. L.A. Davies, the magistrate. The court is packed. Everyone is tense and hushed. The magistrate sums up then comes to judgement - Nyerere is found guilty!

The magistrate, in passing sentence, says he has formed the impression that Nyerere is an extremely intelligent and responsible man. He fines Nyerere Pounds 150 or six months. The money is raised by locals and the Kenya defence fund.[9]

In the election that followed in 1958 - 1959, TANU won a landslide victory. It won 29 out of 30 seats in the general election. As Nyerere said after the victory, "Independence will follow as surely as the tickbirds follow the rhino."[10] In March 1959, Sir Richard Turnbull, the last governor of Tanganyika, appointed to his 12-member cabinet five TANU members who had been elected to the Legislave Council (LEGCO), the colonial legislature which was established in 1926.

In 1958 Sir Richard Turnbull had succeeded Sir Edward Twining as governor of Tanganyika. He had previously served as chief colonial secretary in Kenya during the Emergency - the Mau Mau uprising - and had witnessed first-hand the violence and bloodshed which resulted from the colonial government's refusal to address the grievances of the masses over land and working conditions and from its unwillingness to accept demands by Africans for freedom and independence. He did not want to see that happen in Tanganyika when he became governor.

Initially, the colonial government in Tanganyika wanted only three ministerial posts to be filled by LEGCO members but Nyerere insisted on having a majority from his victorious party, TANU. During the election, TANU had sponsored an Asian and a European for each seat besides its own African candidates. The two also won. Governor Turnbull conceded and appointed three Africans, one Asian and one European to the cabinet to represent TANU and the majority of the voters who had voted for TANU candidates.

It was also in the same month, March 1959, that Nyerere was interviewed by *Drum* and spoke about the future of Tanganyika after it won independence which was almost three years away:

Tanganyika will be the first, most truly multiracial democratic country in Africa. When we get our freedom, the light of a true multiracial democracy will be put high upon the top of the highest mountain, on Kilimanjaro, for all to see, particularly South Africa and America.

Tanganyika will offer the people of those countries free entry, without passports, to come and see real democracy at work. As long as we do not have a popular government elected by the people on democratic principles, we will strive for freedom from any kind of domination.

We regard the [UN] Trusteeship as part of a scheme to keep Tanganyika under the British Crown indefinitely. The greatest enemy of our vision is the Colonial Office.

But Tanganyika cannot be freed by drawing up resolutions or by tabulating long catalogues of the evils of colonialism. Nor do we find it enough to tell rulers to quit Tanganyika. It will be freed only by action, and likewise the whole of Africa.

Continued colonialism is preventing investment in this country. Germany, for example, cannot invest money as long as the British are still here. I agree that the country lacks technicians. So what? Shall we give the British another 40 years to train them? How many have they trained in the past 40 years?

As far as money for a self-governing Tanganyika is concerned, Tanganyika has not been receiving much money from the British taxpayer at all. For the past 11 years, Tanganyika has only received Pounds 9 million. I can raise 100 times that within a year if it becomes necessary.

I believe that the continued, not existence, but citizenship of the European would be taken for granted had not the white man created a Kenya, a Central Africa [the Central African Federation of Rhodesia and Nyasaland], a South Africa and other similar places and situations.

African nationalism is not anti-white but simply anti-colonialist. When George Washington fought the imperialists, he was fighting for the divine right of Americans to govern themselves; he was not fighting colour.

The white man wants to live in Africa on his terms. He must dominate and be recognised by the rest of the inhabitants of this continent as their natural master and superior. But that we cannot accept. What we are after is fellow citizenship, and that is exactly what is frightening the white man.

The question is not whether we must get rid of whites, but whether they must get rid of themselves. Whites can no longer dominate in Africa. That dream is gone. Africa must be governed by Africans in the future. Whether an immigrant African will have an equal part to play in this free Africa depends upon him and him alone. In Tanganyika, we are determined to demonstrate to the whole of Africa that democracy is the only answer.

We are being held back, not by local Europeans, but by the Colonial Office and, I believe, by Europeans in neighbouring countries, who are frightened of the possibility of success in Tanganyika.[11]

A month later in April 1959, after the interview with *Drum*, Nyerere went to Zanzibar to attend a meeting of the Pan-African

Freedom Movement of Eastern and Central Africa, popularly known as PAFMECA when I was growing up in Tanganyika, and of which he had previously been elected president.

One of the prominent Tanganyikan leaders in PAFMECA was John Mwakangale from my home district, Rungwe. He was also one of the TANU members who was elected as a member of the colonial legislature, LEGCO. Mwakangale was also the leader who was assigned by the government of Tanganyika to receive Nelson Mandela in Mbeya when Mandela came to Tanganyika for the first time in 1962, soon after we won independence from Britain, as Mandela states in his book, *Long Walk to Freedom*.[12]

While in Zanzibar, Nyerere played a critical role in forging unity between some Africans and some Arabs, bringing their political parties closer together in their struggle for independence and for the sake of national unity.

Speaking at a meeting of PAFMECA in Nairobi, Kenya, in September 1959, he made it clear that Europeans and Asians as well as others were welcome to remain in Africa as equal citizens after independence was achieved. The following month, in October, he gave a speech in the Tanganyika colonial legislature (LEGCO) in which he uttered these famous words:

> We will light a candle on Mount Kilimanjaro
> which will shine beyond our borders,
> giving hope where there is despair,
> love where there is hate,
> and dignity where before there was only humiliation.[13]

In December 1959, Britain's new Colonial Secretary Ian McLeod announced that Tanganyika would be given virtual home rule towards the end of 1960 under a constitution that would guarantee an African majority in the colonial legislature, LEGCO. Nyerere criticized the retention of income and literacy qualifications as eligibility criteria for voters and for membership in the legislature. He was also critical of the reservation of a specific number of seats in LEGCO for the European and Asian minorities.

But he saw the concessions by the British colonial rulers, including new constitutional provisions guaranteeing an African-dominated legislature, as a step towards independence in the not-so-distant future.

In the elections of August 1960, TANU again won by a landslide, 70 out of 71 seats, its biggest victory so far and less than a year before independence. Nyerere was sworn in as chief minister of government under a new constitution but the governor, Sir Richard Turnbull, continued to hold certain veto powers, although rarely exercised, if at all, since it was now inevitable that Tanganyika would soon be independent.

Nyerere's status as the leader of Tanganyika was formally acknowledged even outside the colony, for example, when he attended a meeting of British Commonwealth prime ministers in London in March 1961, although Tanganyika was still not independent.

But in his capacity as prime minister of Tanganyika since the colony won internal self-government, hence *de facto* head of government in lieu of the governor, he joined other African leaders in denouncing the apartheid regime of South Africa and its racist policies and declared that if South Africa remained a member of the Commonwealth, Tanganyika would never join the Commonwealth; a position he had articulated earlier in August 1960 when he said: "To vote South Africa in, is to vote us out."

South Africa withdrew from the Commonwealth, and many people attribute this to Nyerere's uncompromising stand on the apartheid regime and his threat to keep Tanganyika out of the Commonwealth had South Africa remained a member.

Following a constitutional conference in in March 1961, Colonial Secretary Ian McLeod announced that Tanganyika would have internal self-government on May 1, and full independence in December.

On 9 December 1961, Tanganyika became independent. A few days later, it was unanimously accepted as the 104th member of the United Nations. Nyerere was 39 years old and, at that time, the world's youngest national leader.

On January 22, 1962, Nyerere resigned as prime minister and appointed Rashidi Kawawa, minister without portfolio, as his successor. He said he resigned to rebuild the party which had lost its focus and to give the country a new purpose now that independence had been won.

With independence came responsibilities. It was no easy task.

So much lay ahead.

Chapter Two:

Tanganyika after Independence

TANGANYIKA was the first country to win independence in East Africa. It was followed by Uganda in October 1962, and by Kenya in December 1963. On May 31, 1962, the government of Tanganyika announced that the country would become a republic in December that year and continue to be a member of the Commonwealth.

It became a republic on December 9, 1962, on the first independence anniversary, and Julius Nyerere who had served as prime minister until then became the country's first president.

A new constitution was adopted and was in many ways similar to that of Ghana under Kwame Nkrumah whom Nyerere admired. In fact, in the first official portrait after independence, Nyerere and some of his cabinet members wore Kente cloth like Nkrumah, his ideological compatriot, and his colleagues did and just like many other Ghanaians still do.

The new constitution of Tanganyika after independence outlawed strikes and greatly increased presidential powers. A preventive detention act aimed at curbing subversive activities had been passed by parliament a few months earlier in the same year, 1962, and greatly enhanced the authority of the government in many areas, although it was viewed with apprehension by some people as an oppressive instrument.

To consolidate national unity, parliament passed a law in 1965 and made Tanganyika a *de jure* one-party state; the year before, in 1964, Ghana also became a one-party socialist state after a

30

controversial referendum and Nkrumah was declared life president, something Nyerere refused to accept when some members of parliament proposed that he should be made life president.

Even before 1965, Tanganyika had been operating as a *de facto* one-party state because it had no opposition in parliament following the devastating defeat of the radical African National Congress (ANC), the main opposition party, in previous elections. The African National Congress was led by Zuberi Mtemvu who left TANU to form the opposition party in pursuit of Africanization which, according to his definition, would virtually exclude non-blacks from the new dispensation as equal members of society.

Soon after independence, Tanganyika faced serious problems in many areas - economic development, education, medical services, civil service, communications and transport, among others - because it did not have enough qualified people to provide much-needed high-level manpower for the young nation. When it won independence, it had only 120 university graduates, among whom were two engineers, two lawyers, and 12 doctors in a country bigger than Nigeria in terms of area, or the size of Texas, Oklahoma and West Virginia combined.

Tanzania is one of the 10 largest countries in Africa in terms of area and population; yet one of the poorest even in Africa itself, and one of the 25 poorest in the world, with a population of about 40 million people in 2006 roughly the same as Canada's.

To solve some of the country's problems, Nyerere instituted a self-help programme and preached self-reliance as national policy under which people volunteered to build roads, bridges, schools, clinics and work on other projects to develop the nation. Teams of volunteers worked across the country and succeeded in completing many of these projects.

The campaign also included adult literacy. People who could read and write volunteered to teach others. The adult literacy campaign was so successful that within a few years, Tanganyika, later Tanzania, had the highest literacy rate in Africa and one of the highest in the world, over 90 percent. Yet it remained poor, very poor.

To tackle poverty, Nyerere introduced the policy of *ujamaa*, a

Kiswahili word which means familyhood. It was a policy of socialism with a human face, unlike that of the Marxist brand.

People established communal villages to work on communal farms and other projects but without much success. It was, in fact, a disaster in economic terms and retarded Tanzania's economic growth for more than a decade since its introduction in 1967.

But it also had notable success in many areas. People lived closer together, making it easier for the government to provide them with social services including clinics and schools. The people also built primary schools in their own areas and other facilities which could not have been built had they lived miles apart before *ujamaa* was introduced.

The policy also help to instill egalitarian values and ideals which played a critical role in keeping the people united without accentuating cleavages so typical of capitalist societies which propagate elitism as a virtue, leading some people to feel that they are better than others.

Without such egalitarianism achieved under *ujamaa*, Tanzania would not be what it is today as a stable, peaceful country where the majority of the people treat each other as brothers and sisters on equal basis in spite of grinding poverty among millions of them. Under Nyerere, ostentatious display of wealth was shunned and even despised. And everything possible was done to reduce the gap between the rich and the poor.

I remember how life was under Nyerere. All of us were involved in development projects, one way or another, sometimes working without being paid. People worked as volunteers on many public projects including farming, the mainstay of the economy. Others were involved in adult education, teaching adults in towns and villages how to read and write. And those of us who had just finished secondary school or high school went into National Service which was mandatory for us in order to participate in development projects instead of simply waiting to get office jobs or go for further education.

We were not paid when we were in National Service. But we were provided with all the basic necessities - food, shelter and clothing. Our induction into National Service was one of the most successful policies which fostered egalitarian values among the elite, including us, many of whom felt they were better than the poor and illiterate peasants and workers, the very same people who paid for our education with their tax money.

I went to Ruvu National Service in January 1971, about 25 miles from Dar es Salaam, and underwent rigorous training which included military training. Other trainees included volunteers from different parts of the country. Most of the volunteers had very little formal education or none. Yet we lived together in the same tents and ate together at the same table without discrimination.

I remember there were some young men and women, fresh from secondary school and high school, who felt that they were better than the illiterate volunteers. They also resented the fact that our participation in National Service was mandatory. But they were a minority. The majority of us accepted the poor and illiterate young men and women from the rural areas as equal to us and we worked together on different projects without any problems.

From Ruvu, I was sent to Bulombora National Service camp in Bukoba district in northwestern Tanzania for further training. The camp was located very close to the shores of Lake Victoria, only a few minutes' walk.

Altogether, the training in National Service camps lasted for six months.

After that I went to Dar es Salaam to work for the ministry of information and broadcasting as an information officer in July 1971 and then went back to the *Daily News*, where I had worked before. I stayed at the ministry of information and broadcasting only for a short time.

Our participation in National Service continued after we left the training camps. We were required to wear National Service uniforms at work, and a large chunk of our salaries, I think about 40 to 60 percent, was deducted to go towards national development projects as mandated by the government.

It was a two-year programme, from the time we first went in, and it taught us discipline and helped instill in us not only egalitarian values but a strong sense of patriotism. We already loved our country. But we were at the same time constantly reminded that there were enemies within, working with enemies outside, to try to destroy our country, sabotage our economy and independence, and we should always be on guard against such fifth columnists. "Be vigilant," we were always reminded in speeches and patriotic songs.

Some of the patriotic songs we sang in National Service training camps concerned apartheid South Africa and other white minority regimes in southern Africa and in Portuguese Guinea in West Africa. They were pretty violent songs, ready to irrigate our land with the blood of the enemy, reminding ourselves that we were on the frontline of the African liberation struggle and should be ready to defend our country, anytime, and at any cost, and be prepared to fight alongside our brothers and sisters still suffering under colonialism and racial oppression anywhere on the continent.

And all that had to do with the leadership of President Julius Nyerere as a staunch Pan-Africanist and strong advocate of African unity who took an uncompromising stand on those issues. And he remained that way until his death.

Apartheid South Africa was the primary target as the most powerful white minority regime on the continent and as the most stubborn. And it evoked some of the strongest feelings among us because of the diabolical nature of the regime and its abominable institution of apartheid.

The Portuguese colonial rulers in Mozambique, our neighbour on the southern border, were not saints, either, and triggered an equally hostile response from us; our anger fuelled by attacks on our country including aerial bombings and planting of deadly mines on our soil by the Portuguese colonial forces because of our uncompromising support for the liberation struggle in Mozambique led by FRELIMO - a Portuguese acronym for Front for the Liberation of Mozambique - waging guerrilla warfare against the colonial forces.

All this was done because of Nyerere's strong commitment to the liberation of Africa and to the independence of Tanganyika, later Tanzania, as a self-reliant nation whose prosperity depended on the people themselves: us.

His Pan-African commitment galvanized him into action probably more than anything else. As he stated in an interview with the *New Internationalist*: "I have always said that I was African first and socialist second. I would rather see a free and united Africa before a fragmented socialist Africa."[1]

The humiliation of Africa by our European conquerors also played a major role in shaping his attitude towards them. As he told Rolf Italiaander, the author of *The New African Leaders* (1961), "I have learned to be a moderate through observing the inflexible behaviour of the Europeans."[2]

He made those remarks shortly before independence and they defined his policies after we won independence when he welcomed Europeans and others to stay and live on the basis of equality with us. Jomo Kenyatta expressed similar sentiments shortly after he came out of prison in 1961 but in more strident a tone. As he stated on October 14th the same year: "Non-Africans who still want to be called 'Bwana' should pack up and go, but others who are prepared to live under our flag are invited to remain."[3]

On January 28, 1962, Kenyatta went a little further, with the stipulation that it is non-Africans who now had to learn to call Africans, "Bwana." The literal translation of "Bwana" is "Mister." But it has deeper meaning, implying "Sir," and someone above you, our European conquerors, for example, in our case.

And that is exactly what Jomo Kenyatta meant when he said on that day in January that Europeans and other non-Africans should not only stop expecting to be called "Bwana" by Africans but should, from now on, learn to call Africans "Bwana." As he put it: "I want Europeans, Asians and Arabs to learn to call Africans 'Bwana.' Those who agree to do so are free to stay."[4]

Nyerere argued along similar lines saying the first thing we got when we won independence was dignity. But he also warned against retaliation by Africans now that we were free. It was obvious that many of them including some leaders were in a vindictive mood. As he stated: "Many of the leaders suffered from discrimination themselves, and some have been unable to achieve that degree of objectivity which would enable them to direct their hatred towards discrimination itself instead of at the racial group which the discriminators represented."[5]

He saw Europeans who remained in Tanganyika and other non-black citizens such as Arabs and Asians as an integral part of the nation not only in terms of equal rights but also in terms of participation in national development and in other areas of national life on equal basis; unlike in neighbouring Kenya where they were marginalized and relegated to the periphery of the mainstream after black Africans assumed power following independence. As the leader of Tanganyika, later Tanzania, Nyerere wanted to see the country develop but without compromising its independence and losing its African personality and culture by becoming a carbon copy of Europe.

Without development, nothing else - fighting poverty, ignorance and disease - could be achieved. And development demanded hard work and a lot of sacrifice; hence the Swahili slogan, *Uhuru na Kazi*, meaning Freedom and Work, Nyerere and other leaders used constantly to exhort us to achieve our nation's goals as one people regardless of race, tribe, colour, creed or national origin. We were all Tanganyikans, later Tanzanians, and we were all Africans. Indians were in India, Europeans in Europe. Those in Africa were African like us. And they still are.

But Nyerere also believed that the country could not develop if its economy and resources were controlled by foreigners. If they did, then they would continue to dictate policy to us as we also continued to delude ourselves into believing that we were truly independent and masters of our own destiny. We just couldn't be independent if our country was controlled by foreigners.

And no country can claim to be truly independent if its economy, not just its government, is controlled or dominated by others. In fact, you can't even have an independent government if you are not economically independent or are told what to do by outsiders. That is why in the mid-sixties Nyerere asked West Germany to withdraw all of its aid from Tanzania when it made such aid conditional. He could not accept anyone dictating terms to us. I remember that time. We lost the assistance that we needed but it was worth the sacrifice.

One of the main reasons Nyerere was able to get the support he needed to implement his policies was his determination to ensure mass participation in the political process from the grassroots level all the way to the top leaving out nobody. And this helped to make even the poorest, illiterate peasants in the remote interior feel that they were a part of the decision making process which affected their lives and that of the entire nation. Thus imbued with a sense of patriotism, millions across the country were prepared to make great sacrifices when asked to do so, or did so simply on their own when they felt that something had to be done in their communities or for the benefit of the country as a whole.

They came to embrace a national cause as their own and felt that whatever they did at the local level was also for the good of the country. And they did so because they sincerely believed that Nyerere who encouraged them to do so was deeply committed to their well-being and that of the entire nation. And he was.

The Tanganyika I knew after independence was one of extraordinary peace and tranquility in spite of poverty; and one of caring for the least endowed amongst us. I remember the free education, the free medical service, and the free transport we were provided with as students going to and coming from our boarding schools.

We did not pay one cent. For example, I remember the warrant we were given to go to Songea Secondary School and back home during holidays (vacation) in the months of June and December every year from 1965 to 1968. A warrant was a free bus ticket given collectively to a group of students going to the same destination. Those of us from Rungwe district were given one for the round trip to and from school, with one student being responsible for keeping it; students from Mtwara district were given theirs, as were the others.

If you went alone in one direction, you were also given yours. For example, I was given one when I travelled from Tukuyu to Dar es Salaam in 1969 to go to Tambaza High School and continued to get it until I finished Form VI, or standard 14, in 1970.

The first decade of independence under Nyerere was also noted for its euphoria and optimism among the people across the country. Most had not yet enjoyed the fruits of independence but there was a sense of hope and strong belief that we now at least had the freedom and opportunity to do what we wanted to do as a free people. That is something we had not been able to do before when we were under colonial rule.

Besides getting free medical service, many schools including the University of Dar es Salaam were also built during the first decade of independence in the sixties; universal primary education was vigorously pursued, and the people in villages and towns were brought into the political process to participate in decision making to ensure justice and equality for all on a scale unprecedented anywhere else in Africa. As Nyerere said back in the late 1950s about his commitment to equality: "Our struggle has been, still is, and always will be a struggle for human rights....Our position is based on the belief in the equality of human beings, in their rights and their duties as citizens."[6]

Rights came with responsibilities, and responsibilities entailed discipline. I remember when President Nyerere visited our school, Songea Secondary School, one evening in 1966. He had been touring Songea district and came to speak to us before flying back to Dar es Salaam that night. He did not have much time and spoke for only a few minutes after he was introduced by our headmaster, Paul Mhaiki who, only a few years later, became head of adult education in Tanzania.

The one and only thing the president emphasized in his speech to us that evening was discipline. He told us, we could not succeed in school, or do anything else constructive or be productive in life, without discipline. And just before he left, he said, "You must have discipline. Always remember discipline." And he knew exactly what he was talking about, not only as the leader of our country but as a former secondary school teacher himself before he went into politics to lead Tanganyika to independence. As he once said, he was a teacher by choice and a politician by accident.

The first decade of independence for Tanganyika, later Tanzania, under President Nyerere witnessed some of the most dramatic changes in the direction of our country which had an impact beyond our borders. Probably the most memorable ones, and the most profound in terms of impact, were the adoption of the one-party system and the promulgation of socialist policies enunciated in the *Arusha Declaration* whose implementation led to nationalization of the country's major assets and to the establishment of *ujamaa* villages.

One interesting thing about the *Arusha Declaration* is that many of the people who criticized it had not even read the document; not only Tanzanians but others as well, including some African students from other parts of Africa whom I went to school with at Wayne State Universit, in the United States in the early and mid-seventies. Because they did not like socialism and *ujamaa* villages, they automatically dismissed the *Arusha Declaration* as a deeply flawed document in all its aspects. Some of them, if they get the chance to read this book, may have second thoughts after they read the Declaration reproduced here in its entirety:

THE ARUSHA DECLARATION: SOCIALISM AND SELF-RELIANCE

Part One: The TANU Creed

The policy of TANU is to build a socialist state. The principles of socialism are laid down in the TANU constitution and they are as follows:

Whereas TANU believes:
(a) That all human beings are equal;
(b) That every individual has a right to dignity and respect;
(c) That every citizen is an integral part of the nation and has the right to take an equal part in government at local, regional and national level;
(d) That every citizen has the right to freedom of expression, of movement, of religious belief and of association within the context of the law;
(e) That every individual has the right to receive from society protection of his life and of property held according to law;
(f) That every individual has the right to receive a just return for his labour;
(g) That all citizens together possess all the natural resources of the country in trust for their descendants;
(h) That in order to ensure economic justice the state must have effective control over the principal means of production;
     and
(i) That it is the responsibility of the state to intervene actively in the economic life of the nation so as to ensure the well-being of all citizens, and so as to prevent the exploitation of one person by another or one group by another, and so as to prevent the

accumulation of wealth to an extent which is inconsistent with the existence of a classless society.

Now, therefore, the principal aims and objectives of TANU shall be as follows:
(a) To consolidate and maintain the independence of this country and the freedom of its people;
(b) To safeguard the inherent dignity of the individual in accordance with the Universal Declaration of Human Rights;
(c) To ensure that this country shall be governed by a democratic socialist government of the people;
(d) To co-operate with all political parties in Africa engaged in the liberation of all Africa;
(e) To see that the government mobilizes all the resources of this country towards the elimination of poverty, ignorance and disease;
(f) To see that the government actively assists in the formation and maintenance of co-operative organizations;
(g) To see that wherever possible the government itself directly participates in the economic development of this country;
(h) To see that the government gives equal opportunity to all men and women irrespective of race, religion or status;
(i) To see that the government eradicates all types of exploitation, intimidation, discrimination, bribery and corruption;
(j) To see that the government exercises effective control over the principal means of production and pursues policies which facilitate the way to collective ownership of the resources of this country;
(k) To see that the government co-operates with other states in Africa in bringing about African unity;
(l) To see that the government works tirelessly towards world peace and security through the United Nations Organization.

Part Two: The Policy of Socialism

(a) *Absence of Exploitation.*
A truly socialist state is one in which all people are workers and in which neither capitalism nor feudalism exists. It does not have two classes of people, a lower class composed of people who

work for their living, and an upper class of people who live on the work of others. In a really socialist country no person exploits another; everyone who is physically able to work does so; every worker obtains a just return for the labour he performs; and the incomes derived from different types of work are not grossly divergent.

In a socialist country, the only people who live on the work of others, and who have the right to be dependent upon their fellows, are small children, people who are too old to support themselves, the crippled, and those whom the state at any one time cannot provide with an opportunity to work for their living.

Tanzania is a nation of peasants and workers, but it is not yet a socialist society. It still contains elements of feudalism and capitalism - with their temptations. These feudalistic and capitalistic features of our society could spread and entrench themselves.

(b) *The major means of production and exchange are under the control of the peasants and workers.*

To build and maintain socialism it is essential that all the major means of production and exchange in the nation are controlled and owned by the peasants through the machinery of their government and their co-operatives. Further, it is essential that the ruling party should be a party of peasants and workers.

The major means of production and exchange are such things as: land; forests; minerals; water; oil and electricity; news media; communications; banks, insurance, import and export trade, wholesale trade; iron and steel, machine-tool, arms, motor-car, cement, fertilizer, and textile industries; and any big factory on which a large section of the people depend for their living, or which provides essential components of other industries; large plantations, and especially those which provide raw materials essential to important industries.

Some of the instruments of production and exchange which have been listed here are already owned or controlled by the people's government of Tanzania.

(c) *The Existence of Democracy.*

A state is not socialist simply because its means of production and exchange are controlled or owned by the government, either wholly or in large part. For a country to be socialist, it is essential that its government is chosen and led by the peasants and workers themselves. If the minority governments of Rhodesia or South Africa controlled or owned the entire economies of these respective countries, the result would be a strengthening of oppression, not the building of socialism. True socialism cannot exist without democracy also existing in the society.

(d) *Socialism is a Belief.*

Socialism is a way of life, and a socialist society cannot simply come into existence. A socialist society can only be built by those who believe in, and who themselves practise, the principles of socialism. A committed member of TANU will be a socialist, and his fellow socialists - that is, his fellow believers in this political and economic system - are all those in Africa or elsewhere in the world who fight for the rights of peasants and workers. The first duty of a TANU member, and especially of a TANU leader, is to accept these socialist principles, and to live his own life in accordance with them. In particular, a genuine TANU leader will not live off the sweat of another man, nor commit any feudalistic or capitalistic actions.

The successful implementation of socialist objectives depends very much upon the leaders, because socialism is a belief in a particular system of living, and it is difficult for leaders to promote its growth if they do not themselves accept it.

Part Three: The Policy of Self-Reliance

We are at War.

TANU is involved in a war against poverty and oppression in our country; this struggle is aimed at moving the people of Tanzania - and the people of Africa as a whole - from a state of poverty to a state of prosperity.

We have been oppressed a great deal, we have been exploited a great deal and we have been disregarded a great deal. It is our weakness that has led to our being oppressed, exploited and disregarded. Now we want a revolution - a revolution which brings to an end our weakness, so that we are never again exploited, oppressed, or humiliated.

A Poor Man does not use Money as a Weapon.

But it is obvious that in the past we have chosen the wrong weapon for our struggle, because we chose money as our weapon. We are trying to overcome our economic weakness by using the weapons of the economically strong - weapons which in fact we do not possess. By our thoughts, words and actions it appears as if we have come to the conclusion that without money we cannot bring about the revolution we are aiming at. It is as if we have said, 'Money is the basis of development. Without money there can be no development.'

That is what we believe at present. TANU leaders, and government leaders and officials, all put great emphasis and dependence on money. The people's leaders and the people themselves, in TANU, NUTA (National Union of Tanganyika Workers), Parliament, UWT (Umoja wa Wanawake wa Tanzania - Union of the Women of Tanzania), the co-operatives, TAPA (Tanzania Parents' Association), and in other national institutions think, hope and pray for MONEY. It is as if we had all agreed to speak with one voice, saying, 'If we get money we shall develop, without money we cannot develop.'

In brief, our Five-Year Development Plan aims at more food, more education, and better health; but the weapon we have put emphasis upon is money. It is as if we said, 'In the next five years we want to have more food, more education, and better health, and in order to achieve these things we shall spend 250,000,000 (British) pounds.' We think and speak as if the most important thing to depend upon is MONEY and anything else we intend to use in our struggle is of minor importance.

When a member of parliament says that there is a shortage of water in his constituency and he asks the government how it intends to deal with the problem, he expects the government to reply that it is planning to remove the shortage of water in his constituency - WITH MONEY.

When another member of parliament asks what the government is doing about the shortage of roads, schools or hospitals in his constituency, he also expects the government to tell him that it has specific plans to build roads, schools and hospitals in his constituency - WITH MONEY.

When a NUTA official asks the government about its plans to deal with the low wages and poor housing of the workers, he expects the government to inform him that the minimum wage will be increased and that better houses will be provided for the workers - WITH MONEY.

When a TAPA official asks the government what plans it has to give assistance to the many TAPA schools which do not get government aid, he expects the government to state that it is ready the following morning to give the required assistance - WITH MONEY.

When an official of the co-operative movement mentions any problem facing the farmer, he expects to hear that the government will solve the farmer's problems - WITH MONEY. In short, for every problem facing our nation, the solution that is in everybody's mind is MONEY.

Each year, each ministry of the government makes its estimates of expenditure, i.e. the amount of money it will require in the coming year to meet recurrent and development expenses. Only one minister and his ministry make estimates of revenue. This is the minister for finance. Every ministry puts forward very good development plans. When the ministry presents its estimates, it believes that the money is there for the asking but that the minister for finance and his ministry are being obstructive. And regularly each year the minister for finance has to tell his fellow ministers that there is no money. And each year the ministries complain about the ministry of finance when it trims down their estimates.

Similarly, when members of parliament and other leaders demand that the government should carry out a certain development project, they believe that there is a lot of money to spend on such projects, but that the government is the stumbling block. Yet such belief on the part of ministries, members of parliament and other leaders does not alter the stark truth, which is that government has no money.

When it is said that government has no money, what does this mean? It means that the people of Tanzania have insufficient money. The people pay taxes out of every little wealth they have; it is from these taxes that the government meets its recurrent and development expenditure. When we call on the government to spend more money on development projects we are asking the government to use more money. And if the government does not have any more, the only way it can do this is to increase its revenue through extra taxation.

If one calls on the government to spend more, one is in effect calling on the government to increase taxes. Calling on the government to spend more without raising taxes is like demanding that the government should perform miracles; it is equivalent to asking for more milk from a cow while insisting that the cow should not be milked again. But our refusal to admit that calling on the government to spend more is the same as calling on the government to raise taxes shows that we fully realize the difficulties of increasing taxes. We realize that the cow has no more milk - that is, that the people find it difficult to pay more taxes. We know that the cow would like to have more milk herself, so that her calves could drink it, or that she would like more milk which could be sold to provide more comfort for herself or her calves. But knowing all the things which could be done with more milk does not alter the fact that the cow has no more milk!

What of External Aid?

One method we use to try and avoid a recognition of the need to increase taxes if we want to have more money for development, is to think in terms of getting the extra money from outside Tanzania. Such external finance falls into three main categories.

(a) *Gifts*: This means that another government gives our government a sum of money as a free gift for a particular development scheme. Sometimes it may be that an institution in another country gives our government, or an institution in our country, financial help for development programmes.

(b) *Loans*: The greater portion of financial help we expect to get from outside is not in the form of gifts or charity, but in the form of loans. A foreign government or a foreign institution, such as a bank, lends our government money for the purposes of development. Such a loan has repayment conditions attached to it, covering such factors as the time period for which it is available and the rate of interest.

(c) *Private investment*: The third category of financial help is also greater than the first. This takes the form of investment in our country by individuals or companies from outside. The important condition which such private investors have in mind is that the enterprise into which they put their money should bring them profit and that our government should permit them to repatriate these profits. They also prefer to invest in a country whose policies they agree with and which will safeguard their economic interests.

These three are the main categories of external finance. And there is in Tanzania a fantastic amount of talk about getting money from outside. Our government and different groups of our leaders, never stop thinking about methods of getting finance from abroad. And if we get some money, or even if we just get a promise of it, our newspapers, our radio, and our leaders, all advertise the fact in order that every person shall know that salvation is coming, or is on the way. If we receive a gift we announce it, if we receive a loan we announce it, if we get a new factory we announce it - and always loudly. In the same way, when we get a promise of a gift, a loan, or a new industry, we make an announcement - even though we do not know the outcome of the discussions. Why do we do all this? Because we want people to know that we have started discussions which will bring prosperity.

DO NOT LET US DEPEND UPON MONEY FOR DEVELOPMENT

It is stupid to rely on money as the major instrument of development when we know only too well that our country is poor. It is equally stupid, indeed it is even more stupid, for us to imagine that we shall rid ourselves of our poverty through foreign financial assistance rather than our own financial resources. It is stupid for two reasons.

Firstly, we shall not get the money. It is true that there are countries which can, and which would like, to help us. But there is no country in the world which is prepared to give us gifts or loans, or establish industries, to the extent that we would be able to achieve all our development targets. There are many needy countries in the world. And even if all the prosperous nations were willing to help the needy countries, the assistance would still not suffice. But in any case the prosperous nations have not accepted a responsibility to fight world poverty. Even within their own borders poverty still exists, and the rich individuals do not willingly give money to the government to help their poor fellow citizens.

It is only through taxation, which people have to pay whether they want to or not, that money can be extracted from the rich in order to help the masses. Even then there would not be enough money. However heavily we taxed the citizens of Tanzania and the aliens living here, the resulting revenue would not be enough to meet the costs of the development we want. And there is no World Government which can tax the prosperous nations in order to help the poor nations; nor if one did exist could it raise enough revenue to do all that is needed in the world. But in fact, such a World Government does not exist. Such money as the rich nations offer to the poor nations is given voluntarily, either through their own goodness, or for their own benefits. All this means that it is impossible for Tanzania to obtain from overseas enough money to develop our economy.

GIFTS AND LOANS WILL ENDANGER OUR INDEPENDENCE

Secondly, even if it were possible for us to get enough money for our needs from external sources, is this what we really want? Independence means self-reliance. Independence cannot be real if a nation depends upon gifts and loans from another for its development. Even if there was a nation, or nations, prepared to give us all the money we need for our development, it would be improper for us to accept such assistance without asking ourselves how this would affect our independence and our very survival as a nation. Gifts which increase, or act as a catalyst, to our own efforts are valuable. But gifts which could have the effect of weakening or distorting our own efforts should not be accepted until we have asked ourselves a number of questions.

The same applies to loans. It is true that loans are better than 'free' gifts. A loan is intended to increase our efforts or make those efforts more fruitful. One condition of a loan is that you show how you are going to repay it. This means you have to show that you intend to use the loan profitably and will therefore be able to repay it.

But even loans have their limitations. You have to give consideration to the ability to repay. When we borrow money from other countries it is the Tanzanian who pays it back. And as we have already stated, Tanzanians are poor people. To burden the people with big loans, the repayment of which will be beyond their means, is not to help them but to make them suffer. It is even worse when the loans they are asked to repay have not benefited the majority of the people but have only benefited a small minority.

How about the enterprises of foreign investors? It is true we need these enterprises. We have even passed an Act of Parliament protecting foreign investments in this country. Our aim is to make foreign investors feel that Tanzania is a good place in which to invest because investments would be safe and profitable, and the profits can be taken out of the country without difficulty. We expect to get money through this method. But we cannot get enough. And even if we were able to convince foreign investors and foreign firms to undertake all the projects and programmes of economic development that we need, is that what we actually want to happen?

Had we been able to attract investors from America and Europe to come and start all the industries and all the projects of economic development that we need in this country, could we do so without questioning ourselves? Could we agree to leave the economy of our country in the hands of foreigners who would take the profits back to their countries? Or supposing they did not insist upon taking their profits away, but decided to reinvest in Tanzania; could we really accept this situation without asking ourselves what disadvantages our nation would suffer? Would this allow the socialism we have said it is our objective to build?

How can we depend upon gifts, loans and investments from foreign countries and foreign companies without endangering our independence? The English people have a proverb which says: 'He who pays the piper calls the tune.' How can we depend upon foreign governments and companies for the major part of our development without giving to those governments and countries a great part of our freedom to act as we please? The truth is that we cannot.

Let us repeat. We made a mistake in choosing money - something we do not have - to be the big instrument of our development. We are making a mistake to think that we shall get the money from other countries; first, because in fact we shall not be able to get sufficient money for our economic development; and secondly, because even if we could get all that we need, such dependence upon others would endanger our independence and our ability to chose our own political policies.

WE HAVE PUT TOO MUCH EMPHASIS ON INDUSTRIES

Because of our emphasis on money, we have made another big mistake. We have put too much emphasis on industries. Just as we have said, 'Without money there can be no development,' we also seem to say, 'Industries are the basis of development, without industries there is no development.' This is true. The day when we have lots of money we shall be able to say we are a developed country. We shall be able to say, 'When we began our Development Plans we did not have enough money and this situation made it difficult for us to develop as fast as we wanted. Today we are developed and we have enough money.' That is to say, our money has been brought by development. Similarly, the day we become industrialized, we shall be able to say we are developed. Development would have enabled us to have industries.

The mistake we are making is to think that development begins with industries. It is a mistake because we do not have the means to establish many modern industries in our country. We do not have either the necessary finances or the technical know-how. It is not enough to say that we shall borrow the finances and the technicians from other countries to come and start industries. The answer to this is the same one we gave earlier, that we cannot get enough money and borrow enough technicians to start all the industries we need. And even if we could get the necessary assistance, dependence on it could interfere with our policy of socialism. The policy of inviting a chain of capitalists to come and establish industries in our country might succeed in giving us all the industries we need, but it would also succeed in preventing the establishment of socialism unless we believe that without first building capitalism, we cannot build socialism.

LET US PAY HEED TO THE PEASANT

Our emphasis on money and industries has made us concentrate on urban development. We recognize that we do not have enough money to bring the kind of development to each village which would benefit everybody. We also know that we cannot establish an industry in each village and through this means effect a rise in the real incomes of the people. For these reasons we spend most of our money in the urban areas and our industries are established in the towns.

Yet the greater part of this money that we spend in the towns comes from loans. Whether it is used to build schools, hospitals, houses or factories, etc., it still has to be repaid. But it is obvious that it cannot be repaid just of money obtained from urban and industrial development. To repay the loans we have to use foreign currency which is obtained from the sale of our exports. But we do not now sell our industrial products in foreign markets, and indeed it is likely to be a long time before our industries produce for export. The main aim of our new industries is 'import substitution' - that is, to produce things which up to now we have had to import from foreign countries.

It is therefore obvious that the foreign currency we shall use to pay back the loans used in the development of the urban areas will not come from the towns or the industries. Where, then, shall we get if from? We shall get it from the villages and from agriculture. What does this mean? It means that the people who benefit directly from development which is brought about by borrowed money are not the ones who will repay the loans. The largest proportion of the loans will be spent in, or for, the urban areas, but the largest proportion of the repayment will be made through the efforts of the farmers.

This fact should always be borne in mind, for there are various forms of exploitation. We must not forget that people who live in towns can possibly become the exploiters of those who live in the rural areas. All our big hospitals are in towns and they benefit only a small section of the people of Tanzania. Yet if we have built them with loans from outside Tanzania, it is the overseas sale of the peasants' produce which provides the foreign exchange for repayment. Those who do not get the benefit of the hospitals thus carry the major responsibility for paying them. Tarmac roads, too, are mostly found in towns and are of especial value to the motor-car owners. Yet if we have built those roads with loans, it is again the farmer who produces the goods which will pay for them. What is more, the foreign exchange with which the car was bought also came from the sale of the farmers' produce. Again, electric lights, water pipes, hotels and other aspects of modern development are mostly found in towns. Most of them have been built with loans and most of them do not benefit the farmer directly, although they will be paid for by the foreign exchange earned by the sale of his produce. We should always bear this in mind.

Although when we talk of exploitation we usually think of capitalists, we should not forget that there are many fish in the sea. They eat each other. The large ones eat the small ones, and the small ones eat those who are even smaller. There are two possible ways of dividing the people in our country. We can put the capitalists and feudalists on one side, and the farmers and workers on the other. But we can also divide the people into urban dwellers on one side and those who live in the rural areas on the other. If we are not careful we might get to the position where the real exploitation in Tanzania is that of the town dwellers exploiting the peasants.

THE PEOPLE AND AGRICULTURE

The development of a country is brought about by people, not by money. Money, and the wealth it represents, is the result and not the basis of development. The four prerequisites of development are different; they are (i) People; (ii) Land; (iii) Good Policies; (iv) Good Leadership. Our country has more than ten million people (1967 census showed 12.3 million people) and its area is more than 362,000 square miles.

AGRICULTURE IS THE BASIS OF DEVELOPMENT

A great part of Tanzania's land is fertile and gets sufficient rain. Our country can produce various crops for home consumption and for export.

We can produce food crops (which can be exported if we produce in large quantities) such as maize, rice, wheat, beans, groundnuts, etc. And we can produce such cash crops as sisal, cotton, coffee, tobacco, pyrethrum, tea, etc. Our land is also good for grazing cattle, goats, sheep, and for raising chickens, etc.; we can get plenty of fish from our rivers, lakes, and from the sea. All of our farmers are in areas which can produce two or three or even more of the food and cash crops enumerated above, and each farmer could increase his production so as to get more food or more money. And because the main aim of development is to get more food, and more money for our other needs, our purpose must be to increase production of these agricultural crops. This is in fact the only road through which we can develop our country - in other words, only by increasing our production of these things can we get more food and more money for every Tanzanian.

THE CONDITIONS OF DEVELOPMENT

(a) *Hard Work*

Everybody wants development; but not everybody understands and accepts the basic requirements for development. The biggest requirement is hard work. Let us go to the villages and talk to our people and see whether or not it is possible for them to work harder.

In towns, for example, wage-earners normally work for seven and a half or eight hours a day, and for six or six and a half days a week. This is about 45 hours a week for the whole year, except for two or three weeks' leave. In other words, a wage-earner works for 45 hours a week for 48 or 50 weeks of the year.

For a country like ours these are really quite short working hours. In other countries, even those which are more developed than we are, people work for more than 45 hours a week. It is not normal for a young country to start with such a short working week. The normal thing is to begin with long working hours and decrease them as the country becomes more and more prosperous. By starting with such short working hours and asking for even shorter hours, we are in fact imitating the more developed countries. And we shall regret this imitation. Nevertheless, wage-earners do work for 45 hours per week and their annual vacation does not exceed four weeks.

It would be appropriate to ask our farmers, especially the men, how many hours a week and how many weeks a year they work. Many do not even work for half as many hours as the wage-earner does. The truth is that in the villages the women work very hard. At times they work for 12 or 14 hours a day. They even work on Sundays and public holidays. Women who live in the villages work harder than anybody else in Tanzania. But the men who live in villages (and some of the women in towns) are on leave for half of their life. The energies of the millions of men in the villages and thousands of women in the towns which are at present wasted in gossip, dancing and drinking, are a great treasure which could contribute more towards the development of our country than anything we could get from rich nations.

We would be doing something very beneficial to our country if we went to the villages and told our people that they hold this treasure and that it is up to them to use it for their own benefit and the benefit of our whole nation.

(b) *Intelligence*

The second condition of development is the use of intelligence. Unintelligent hard work would not bring the same good results as the two combined. Using a big hoe instead of a small one; using a plough pulled by oxen instead of an ordinary hoe; the use of fertilizers; the use of insecticides; knowing the right crop for a particular season or soil; choosing good seeds for planting; knowing the right time for planting, weeding, etc.; all these things show the use of knowledge and intelligence. And all of them combine with hard work to produce more and better results.

The money and time we spend on passing on this knowledge to the peasants are better spent and bring more benefits to our country than the money and great amount of time we spend on other things which we call development.

These facts are well known to all of us. The parts of our Five-Year Development Plan which are on target, or where the target has been exceeded, are those parts which depend solely upon the people's own hard work. The production of cotton, coffee, cashew nuts, tobacco and pyrethrum has increased enormously for the past three years. But these are things which are produced by hard work and the good leadership of the people, not by the use of great amounts of money.

Furthermore the people, through their own hard work and with a little help and leadership, have finished many development projects in the villages. They have built schools, dispensaries, community centres, and roads; they have dug wells, water-channels, animal dips, small dams, and completed various other development projects. Had they waited for money, they would not now have the use of these things.

HARD WORK IS THE ROOT OF DEVELOPMENT

Some Plan projects which depend on money are going on well, but there are many which have stopped and others which might never be fulfilled because of lack of money. Yet still we talk about money and our search for money increases and takes nearly all our energies. We should not lessen our efforts to get the money we really need, but it would be more appropriate for us to spend time in the villages showing the people how to bring about development through their own efforts rather than going on so many long and expensive journeys abroad in search of development money. This is the real way to bring development to everybody in the country.

None of this means that from now on we will not need money or that we will not start industries or embark upon development projects which require money. Furthermore, we are not saying that we will not accept, or even that we shall not look for, money from other countries for development. This is NOT what are saying. We will continue to use money; and each year we will use more money for the various development projects than we used the previous year because this will be one of the signs of our development.

What we are saying, however, is that from now on we shall

know what is the foundation and what is the fruit of development. Between MONEY and PEOPLE it is obvious that the people and their HARD WORK are the foundation of development, and money is one of the fruits of that hard work.

From now on we shall stand upright and walk forward on our feet rather than look at this problem upside down. Industries will come and money will come but their foundation is THE PEOPLE and their HARD WORK, especially in AGRICULTURE. This is the meaning of self-reliance. Our emphasis should therefore be on:

(a) The Land and Agriculture
(b) The People
(c) The Policy of Socialism and Self-Reliance, and
(d) Good leadership.

(a) *The Land*

Because the economy of Tanzania depends and will continue to depend on agriculture and animal husbandry, Tanzanians can live well without depending on help from outside if they use their land properly. Land is the basis of human life and all Tanzanians should use it as a valuable investment for future development. Because the land belongs to the nation, the government has to see to it that it is used for the benefit of the whole nation and not for the benefit of one individual or just a few people.

It is the responsibility of TANU to see that the country produces enough food and enough cash crops for export. It is the responsibility of the government and the co-operative societies to see to it that our people get the necessary tools, training and leadership in modern methods of agriculture.

(b) *The People*

In order properly to implement the policy of self-reliance, the people have to be taught the meaning of self-reliance and its practice. They must become self-sufficient in food, serviceable clothes and good housing.

In our country work should be something to be proud of, and laziness, drunkenness and idleness should be things to be ashamed of. And for the defence of our nation, it is necessary for us to be on guard against internal stooges who could be used by external enemies who aim to destroy us. The people should always be ready to defend their nation when they are called upon to do so.

(c) *Good Policies*

The principles of our policy of self-reliance go hand in hand with our policy on socialism. In order to prevent exploitation it is necessary for everybody to work and to live on his own labour. And in order to distribute the national wealth fairly, it is necessary for everybody to work to the maximum of his ability. Nobody should go and stay for a long time with his relative, doing no work, because in doing so he will be exploiting his relative. Likewise, nobody should be allowed to loiter in towns or villages without doing work which would enable him to be self-reliant without exploiting his relatives.

TANU believes that everybody who loves his nation has a duty to serve it by co-operating with his fellows in building the country for the benefit of all the people of Tanzania. In order to maintain our independence and our people's freedom we ought to be self-reliant in every possible way and avoid depending upon other countries for assistance. If every individual is self-reliant the ten-house cell will be self-reliant; if all the cells are self-reliant the whole ward will be self-reliant; and if the wards are self-reliant the district will be self-reliant. If the districts are self-reliant, then the region is self-reliant, and if the regions are self-reliant, then the whole nation is self-reliant and this is our aim.

(d) *Good Leadership*

TANU recognizes the urgency and importance of good leadership. But we have not yet produced systematic training for our leaders; it is necessary that TANU headquarters should now prepare a programme of training for all leaders - from the national level to the ten-house cell level - so that every one of them understands our political and economic policies. Leaders must set a good example to the rest of the people in their lives and in all their activities.

Part Four: TANU Membership

Since the party was founded (in 1954) we have put great

emphasis on getting as many members as possible. This was the right policy during the independence struggle. But now the National Executive (of TANU) feels that the time has come when we should put more emphasis on the beliefs of our party and its policies of socialism.

That part of the TANU constitution which relates to the admission of a member should be adhered to, and if it is discovered that a man does not appear to accept the faith, the objects, and the rules and regulations of the party, then he should not be accepted as a member. In particular, it should not be forgotten that TANU is a party of peasants and workers.

Part Five: The Arusha Resolution

Therefore, the National Executive Committee, meeting in the Community Centre at Arusha from 26.1.67 (26 January 1967) to 29.1.67 (29 January 1967) resolves:

(a) *The Leadership*
1. Every TANU and government leader must be either a peasant or a worker, and should in no way be associated with the practices of capitalism or feudalism.
2. No TANU or government leader should hold shares in any company.
3. No TANU or government leader should hold directorships in any privately owned enterprise.
4. No TANU or government leader should receive two or more salaries.
5. No TANU or government leader should own houses which he rents to others.
6. For the purposes of this resolution the term 'leader' should comprise the following:

Members of the TANU National Executive Committee; ministers; members of parliament; senior officials of organizations affiliated to TANU; senior officials of para-statal organizations; all those appointed or elected under any clause of the TANU constitution; councillors; and civil servants in the high and middle cadres. (In this context 'leader' means a man, or a man and his wife; a woman, or a woman and her husband).

(b) *The Government and Other Institutions*

1. Congratulates the government for the steps it has taken so far in the implementation of the policy of socialism.

2. Calls upon the government to take further steps in the implementation of our policy of socialism as described in Part Two of this document without waiting for a Presidential Commission on Socialism.

3. Calls upon the government to put emphasis, when preparing its development plans, on the ability of this country to implement the plans rather than depending on foreign loans and grants as has been done in the current Five-Year Development Plan. The National Executive Committee also resolves that the Plan should be amended so as to make it fit in with the policy of self-reliance.

4. Calls upon the government to take action designed to ensure that the incomes of workers in the private sector are not very different from the incomes of workers in the public sector.

5. Calls upon the government to put great emphasis on actions which will raise the standard of living of the peasants, and the rural community.

6. Calls upon NUTA, the co-operatives, TAPA, UWT, TYL (TANU Youth League), and other government institutions to take steps to implement the policy of socialism and self-reliance.

(c) *Membership*

Members should get thorough teaching on Party ideology so that they may understand it, and they should always be reminded of the importance of living up to its principles.[7]

That is the Arusha Declaration.

Throughout the document, one theme constantly comes up. And that is Nyerere's deep concern for the well-being of the poor, the peasants and the workers, especially the peasants, who constitute the vast majority of the population of Tanzania and those of other African countries and others in the Third World.

The Arusha Declaration earned Nyerere a reputation as one of the most prominent socialist thinkers in the world and one of the most articulate spokesmen of the poor and the oppressed. It was also one of the most important political and economic documents to come out of the Third World.

In the context of Tanzania, it had far-reaching consequences. Almost everybody in Tanzania was affected by the *Arusha Declaration*. And its impact is still felt today even after it was abandoned and virtually repudiated in this era of globalization and free market policies.

But the masses and the poor will always remember the *Arusha Declaration* as a political manifesto and an economic blueprint whose implementation enabled them to be accorded dignity as equal citizens entitled to the same rights as the rich; made it possible for them to get a lot of benefits including free education and free medical service provided by the government; and, in the case of workers in factories and elsewhere including government offices, they were guaranteed job security under the guidance of workers' committees - which monitored and sometimes even disciplined employers - without fear of being summarily dismissed or terminated without just cause.

In fact, in the late 1990s and beyond, many people demanded a return to the status quo ante when the *Arusha Declaration* was in force because of the neglect they now suffered in a free market economy.

The one-party system was also renounced after the adoption of capitalism. But, like the *Arusha Declaration*, it also played a critical role in maintaining national unity by instilling egalitarian ideals and providing equal access to the political process for all citizens under one umbrella which would have been impossible under divisive politics so typical of multiparty democracy in the African context where political parties are no more than interest groups formed on tribal and regional basis to promote the interests of their members and supporters at the expense of the nation.

Tanzania under Nyerere was spared the agony of civil wars and ethnic conflicts which have devastated many African countries because of the inclusive nature of the one-party system under his leadership.

After multiparty democracy was introduced in 1992, the country was rocked by violence a few years later, even if only on a limited scale, because of the partisan nature of the political parties appealing to ethnoregional allegiances to the detriment of national unity, peace and stability; with each striving to get the biggest chunk of the national pie.

In terms of social justice, it was a golden era under Nyerere. It is a by-gone era we will never see again.

Chapter Three:

Tanzania in the Seventies and Eighties

TANZANIA SUFFERED severe economic problems in the seventies and eighties caused by several factors.

By the late sixties, which was not long after independence, it was still one of the world's poorest countries. And like many other developing countries, it suffered from a heavy burden of foreign debt, a decrease in foreign aid, and a decline in the price of its export commodities; problems which continued in the seventies and eighties.

Nyerere tried to tackle these problems by implementing a series of measures which included large-scale nationalization and establishment of *ujamaa* villages to boost agricultural production, although his policy of *ujamaa*, what has been called African socialism, was influenced by his strong belief in the merits of the traditional African communal way of life from which he drew inspiration when he enunciated his socialist ideology, and would have introduced the policy even if the country did not have serious economic problems.

The focus was on rural development where the vast majority of the people lived and whom he believed, because of their strong traditional way of life, would be able to extend their communal way of living and kinship responsibilities to the large communities of *ujamaa* villages and eventually embrace the entire nation. He described *ujamaa* villages in the *Arusha Declaration* as socialist organizations.

But the policy was not successful in economic terms for a

number of reasons.

The majority of the people did not want to work on communal farms because they had traditionally worked on their own farms owned by themselves or by individual families. The people did not work hard in *ujamaa* villages as much as they did on their own farms because they did not feel that the farms belonged to them but to the community. There were no incentives to production in *ujamaa* villages one would expect to have when working on one's private farm.

People expect to get profit from their investment in terms of labour and capital. They could not get that by working on communal farms. Everything belonged to the community. That was one of the biggest dis-incentives to production, and there was no way *ujamaa* villages were going to be successful with that kind of attitude among the people.

As long as they did not get profit for themselves from their labour investment, they were not going to work hard. In fact, millions resented being resettled in *ujamaa* villages and there were violent confrontations with the authorities in many cases when people refused to be moved into those settlements.

The government finally realized that the policy was not working. But it was too late by then. Agriculture had virtually come to a standstill. As Nyerere said, in retrospect: "You can socialize what is not traditional. The *shamba* (farm) can't be socialized."[1]

But there were a number of other factors which also had a profound impact on Tanzania's economy in the seventies and eighties which had nothing to do with the country's economic policies besides the unwillingness and refusal by Western countries to provide substantial aid to Tanzania because the country was pursuing policies they did not like. As capitalist nations, they did not want to finance socialist projects to help Tanzania achieve its goal of building a socialist society. Therefore curtailment of foreign aid did have an adverse impact on Tanzania' economy, but it was by no means the only factor, among external factors.

But even the others factors, except drought, were inextricably linked with the West. Prices for export commodities from Tanzania and other Third World countries dropped precipitously in the seventies and eighties. It is Western countries which control the world market; therefore it is Western countries which set the prices for commodities from developing countries. The producers have virtually no say in setting prices for their commodities under an international system they don't control. And that was one of the tragedies for Tanzania and other African countries and the rest of the Third World in the seventies and eighties as much as it is today.

And it has been that way all the time because of their weakness. They are at the mercy of the powerful industrialized nations of the West who dominate the world economy. Some of the Western powers are the very same ones which colonized Africa. And they continue to exploit Africa today.

The sharp increase in the price of oil beginning with the Arab oil embargo since the Arab-Israel war in October 1973 also had a big impact on Tanzania's economy. It was not an exclusively Western factor but the increase in oil by OPEC members including African ones such as Nigeria who formed the oil cartel was in response to external pressure mainly by the West exerted on their economies.

In the case of the Arab oil-producing countries, it was also in response to negligence by the West, especially American bias towards Israel, of the plight of the Palestinians who were being oppressed by the Israel, the strongest ally of the West in the Middle East.

But whatever the reasons were for sharply increasing the price of oil, the decision severely affected the economies of non-oil-producing countries such as Tanzania, draining much-needed foreign exchange which went towards purchasing oil at an exorbitant price.

There was also the war with Idi Amin which affected the economy of Tanzania, a country already in a precarious position as one of the poorest and least developed countries in the world. The six-month war, which started at the end of October 1978 and ended in April 1979, cost Tanzania more than $500 million, draining national coffers.

The large-scale nationalization programme in pursuit of Tanzania's policy of socialism and self-reliance in order to break away from the economic stranglehold exerted by the West and other external forces was another major factor in the decline of the country's economy.

Nationalization was carried out in a hurried manner and without the expert management and technical expertise needed to make it successful; a problem that was compounded by corruption by the very same people who were supposed to implement the country's economic policies of socialism and self-reliance. That was an additional problem.

Besides corruption, it also meant that Tanzania was trying to build socialism and achieve self-reliance by using people who were not committed to socialism and to the policy of self-reliance, except to one thing: enriching themselves at the expense of the nation.

Therefore, while there may have been valid criticism of Tanzania's economic policies and the manner in which they were being implemented, thus compounding the problem, external factors also played a critical role in pushing Tanzania to the brink of economic collapse and to the point where the country not only abandoned its policy of socialism and self-reliance but became heavily indebted and even more dependent on the very same powers, Western countries and financial interests, it was trying to break away from in order to be free to pursue its national interests and promote the well-being of its people, especially the poor masses, without being dictated to by the West.

One of the people who have provided a balanced picture of Tanzania under Nyerere is Professor Cranford Pratt, at this writing an emeritus professor of political science at the University of Toronto. He was the first principal of the University College, Dar es Salaam, from 1961 to 1965. After returning to Canada, he continued to visit Tanzania until 1982, about three years before Nyerere stepped down from the presidency, and wrote extensively about Tanzanian politics and economic issues and personally knew Nyerere with whom he also worked.

One of Professor Pratt's most well-known and influential works about Tanzania is his book, *The Critical Phase in Tanzania, 1945 to 1968: Nyerere and the Emergence of a Socialist Strategy* published in 1976.[2]

He further discussed Tanzania's socialist policies and development strategy in another book, *Towards Socialism in*

Tanzania, co-edited by Professor Bismarck Mwansasu of the University of Dar es Salaam and published in 1979, twelve years after the *Arusha Declaration*. As he stated in his assessment of Nyerere and his policies after Nyerere died in "Julius Nyerere: The Ethical Foundation of His Legacy":

> While many of Nyerere's policy initiatives failed, they rested on an ethical foundation and on an understanding of the challenges which Tanzania faced, which were vastly more insightful than anything offered by his critics. Perhaps, ordinary Tanzanians have always recognized this truth....
>
> The critical view of Nyerere's socialist policies taken by the international financial institutions, by western governments and by most North American development economists goes beyond criticisms of specific initiatives, to an impatient rejection of the very idea that Third World governments should seek actively to intervene in their economies either to advance social justice or to control the direction of their economic development.
>
> Others today will, I am sure, address the intellectual crudity and ideological nature of this neo-liberal view of the international economic policies that would best serve Tanzania's interests.
>
> What I want to underline is this parallel argument - western judgments of Nyerere's domestic legacy have reflected political values that in contrast to his, attach little importance to communities, are largely un-concerned with equality and are overwhelmingly preoccupied with economic growth.
>
> This perspective is also crude and has had consequences as disastrous for very poor countries as has the dominance of neo-liberal international economic policies.
>
> As a result, those concerned with the welfare of the peoples of the poorest states, are increasingly identifying as centrally important, the creation of democratic controls and a robust public ethic that really do work and the pursuit of development strategies that will equitably share throughout the whole society the material benefits they bring.
>
> These tasks, certainly, are not as straightforward as Nyerere had initially hoped. But we need to remind ourselves that it was not the World Bank, the IMF, the aid agencies of the industrialized states or mainstream western economists who had, a decade ago, identified these central development challenges to the world's poorest countries. It was Julius Nyerere.[4]

And what's interesting is that these very same economic experts from the industrialized West who claimed to know so much about development economics and about the best strategy for the economic development of the world's poor countries, failed to answer Nyerere when he challenged them on the validity of their assumptions.

Tanzania, like many other Third World countries,

implemented austerity measures mandated by the International Monetary Fund (IMF) and by the World Bank as conditions for aid. Yet the structural adjustment programmes (SAPs) imposed on the poor countries failed to produce results anticipated by the donor countries and their economic experts and development strategists.

In his last interview with the *New Internationalist* published in December 1998 about one year before he died, Nyerere was asked why his alternative strategy for development had failed. He responded this way:

> I was in Washington last year. At the World Bank these people asked me to speak. Then they asked me the questions.
>
> The first question they asked was how did you fail? I responded that we took over a country with 85 per cent of its adult population illiterate. The British ruled us for 43 years. When they left, there were 2 trained engineers and 12 doctors. This is the country we inherited.
>
> When I stepped down, there was 91-per cent literacy and every child of school age was in school. We trained thousands of engineers and doctors and teachers.
>
> In 1988 Tanzania's per capita income was $280. Now, in 1998, it is $140.
>
> So I asked the World Bank people what went wrong. Because for the last ten years Tanzania has been signing on the dotted line and doing everything the IMF and the World wanted. Enrolment in school has plummeted to 63 per cent and conditions in health and other social services have deteriorated.
>
> I asked them again: "What went wrong?"
>
> These people just sat there looking at me. Then they asked what could they do? I told them have some humility.
>
> Humility - they are so arrogant![5]

Tanzania's transformation from a one-party state to multi-party democracy, and from a socialist state to a capitalist-oriented one, was a fundamental change with a lasting effect on the lives of the people, rich and poor, educated and uneducated. And it changed the direction of the country irrevocably because of the impact of globalization in this post-Cold War era.

The opening up of the economy to the private sector in most areas entailed disposition of state assets for acquisition by local and foreign investors, and rigid compliance with IMF-imposed conditions in order to continue getting assistance from this financial institution and other aid agencies and donor countries. The same conditions apply today.

And private investment in the public sector continues unabated, as the country continues to dispose of its assets still under state control in spite of resistance from the old guard in the ruling party, *Chama cha Mapinduzi* (CCM), or The Party of the Revolution, who don't want to dismantle state monopoly of some of the public enterprises.

But the change is irrevocable and was even endorsed by Nyerere, although not without misgivings, who remained the dominant figure on the political scene in Tanzania until his death in October 1999.

Ten years after he retired from the presidency in November 1985, Mwalimu Nyerere looked back at his leadership during which he led Tanzania for almost three decades since independence from Britain in December 1961.

They were years of successes and failures, also of hope and despair. Probably the biggest failure was in the economic arena where the government, as opposed to the private sector, dominated the economy and played the most decisive role as the owner of the country's major assets. It also imposed severe restrictions on income and private ownership of property in order to achieve social equality, thus robbing the people of the incentive to work, good intentions notwithstanding.

All this, combined with the interplay of forces beyond Tanzania's control as we saw earlier, led to serious economic problems and virtual collapse of the economy; prompting Nyerere, in a rare concession among leaders, to state publicly in his farewell speech in November 1985 when he stepped down from the presidency: "I failed. Let's admit it."[6]

By that time, agricultural production, the largest share of the nation's gross domestic product, had declined considerably; industries were producing at half capacity, and the transport system was in tatters, with the road network - the hub of the transport system - in desperate need of repair. The infrastructure had virtually collapsed because of failed economic policies.

But Nyerere also left behind a record of great achievements. He was able to maintain peace and stability in Tanzania throughout his leadership, while many other African countries descended into chaos, torn by civil wars, ethnic conflicts, military coups, and state-sponsored violence unleashed by security forces against countless innocent civilians.

Very few African leaders can claim to have maintained peace and stability for almost 30 years straight as Nyerere did in Tanzania. The only exceptions during that period were Zambia, Botswana, Swaziland, Ivory Coast, and Gambia.

And while other African countries imposed one-party dictatorships, Tanzania's one-party system allowed mass participation in the political process on democratic basis and held elections at regular intervals in which even some cabinet members who were also members of parliament lost their seats, humbled at the polls by their opponents who were just ordinary citizens.

Under Nyerere's leadership, Tanzania also made great progress in heath and education, unlike many other African countries endowed with more resources. In fact, it was during Nyerere's tenure that Tanzania became one of the countries which made the greatest advances in combating illiteracy. Because of that, Tanzania had a higher literacy rate than India; yet India is a major country, fairly developed, with some of the most educated people in the world including the third largest pool of scientists after the United States and the former Soviet Union.

Nyerere will also always be remembered for other great achievements. His support for the African liberation movements - all of which were based in Tanzania - in their struggle against colonial rule and white racist regimes, is unequalled by that of any other leader on the continent.

It cost Tanzania a lot, tens of millions of dollars from the national coffers in a desperately poor country, yet without flinching. In fact, the country's involvement in the liberation struggle on such a large scale was not only highly expensive for a poor country but had a direct negative impact on the economy in terms of money spent to support the campaign. It was an enormous sacrifice.

Ghana under Nkrumah in the sixties did the same, also at an enormous cost; a point also underscored by John Kufuor, in an interview, after he became Ghana's president years later in 2000 in which he said Nkrumah spent a lot of money to support the liberation struggle in Africa, a sacrifice which had a direct impact on Ghana's financial position.

Nyerere's commitment to African unity also produced tangible results unmatched anywhere else in Africa. It was on his initiative that the union of Tanganyika and Zanzibar was formed, the only union of independent countries that has ever been formed on the continent and which still exists today as the United Republic of Tanzania.

Even with his failed economic policies, all those achievements, and much more, shall endure as a monument to his great leadership.

And in the economic field, he said more than ten years after his retirement that he would do many things differently if he could turn back the clock. But he remained unshaken in his belief in socialism until his death. As he stated in an interview with *The New York Times* in his home village of Butiama in northern Tanzania in September 1996 where he returned after he retired from the presidency in November 1985: "I would still write the *Arusha Declaration*. I believe in it. It is right."[7]

On another occasion, he said the only thing he would change was a few words and phrases here and there in the Swahili version of the *Arusha Declaration*, leaving the rest of the document intact, without in any way compromising its essence.

But Nyerere acknowledged that socialism never mixed well with the traditional way of life in African villages in terms of property ownership, especially of the farm.

It is possible, he said, to have farmers own a tractor collectively, or cooperate in buying fertilizer or selling grain. But he said that in hindsight, it was a big mistake to collectivize the individual farms, or *mashamba* in Kiswahili, which families had owned for generations.

He also said it was a mistake to nationalize sisal - one of the country's major export crops which is grown on large plantations owned by private companies before being nationalized - and other industries, especially in the manufacturing sector, as well as banks.

But he still defended mobilizing the masses into *ujamaa* - collectivized - villages. It was the right thing to do, he said, if only to make the most of the schools, roads and health clinics the government had built and others it could afford to build.

Yet that is also what caused some of the country's biggest problems. Many people resented being put together into *ujamaa* villages, a move which led to low morale and low productivity. Tanzania, with her meagre resources, also spread herself too thin by providing free services in all those areas: education was free, medical service was free, water was free, as were many other social amenities, for everybody. People didn't have to pay a cent for all those services including those with enough money who could easily afford to pay for that.

Free service was provided across the country in all those areas and others. And it was justified on the grounds that the vast majority of the people were desperately poor and could not afford to pay for education and medical service - or for any other social services - on their own.

That was one of the reasons why Tanzania's taxes were among the highest in the world: to help pay for all those services in a country which also was, and still is, one of the poorest in the world.

And that was indeed the case. Most Tanzanians could not afford education and medical service on their own. Therefore providing them free was the right thing to do; it was social equity and no one quarrelled with that. But it also proved to be very costly and contributed to the country's economic ruin despite good intentions.

Abolishing *ujamaa* villages would have boosted production on family-owned or individual farms because private ownership leads to higher productivity; it is an incentive to production. And traditionally, African farms are, for the most part, privately owned. As Nyerere himself admitted, "The *shamba* (farm) can't be socialized."

Therefore *ujamaa* villages should have been abolished back in the seventies when there was widespread resistance by the peasants against forced removal from their traditional farms to be relocated in collective settlements of *ujamaa* villages.

People tend to work harder for themselves than they do for groups. And they care more about their own property than they do about communal property. With peasants and farmers earning more income on family and individual farms, and paying lower taxes, they would have been able to pay at least something for the social services being provided by the government. The poorest should have been asked to pay a token fee or nothing, based on their income; and the rest should have been assessed a fee, also based on their income, for whatever service they got.

There would have been no need for the government to impose high taxes on the people to pay for the services they themselves would have been able to afford or pay at least something for them.

Relocating people into *ujamaa* villages and making them pay high taxes when they were not producing much due to low morale as result of being forced to live in those collective settlements were some of the biggest dis-incentives to production Tanzania suffered since the policy of *ujamaa* was introduced in 1967.

By 1995, according to a World Bank report, Tanzania ranked 172nd out of 174 countries in world income tables; her per capita income was a mere $100; her international debt burden was overwhelming and unbearable - it was more than 200 percent of GDP (Gross Domestic Product) in 1996; and half the government's budget depended on foreign aid[8] which dwindled under the new world order following the collapse of the Soviet Union and the end of the Cold War.

The world's major powers were no longer interested in propping up client states, nurtured during the ideological rivalry between the East and the West in the Cold war era; nor were they interested in buying the friendship of small poor countries with financial aid and other inducements to keep their adversaries out of those countries. And that is what is going on today.

Therefore, Tanzania's failed economic policies cost the country enormously. *Ujamaa* villages might have been successful if the people moved into those settlements willingly, attracted by their benefits as an inducement, and if they were allowed to move out of them if they were not satisfied with the results and life in there; also if they did not have to pay high taxes.

But even such voluntary collective settlements would probably not have provided catalytic change in the economic transformation of Tanzania because their main attraction would have been social services - schools and clinics - provided by the government, and not profit. This incentive, profit, comes from family and individual farms where farmers work hard for themselves, and even harder if they pay lower taxes, because they are able to keep for themselves most of what they earn.

Ujamaa villages did not generate that kind of income and

profit for individuals and families living in those collective settlements where they were also burdened with high taxes on meagre earnings; the problem compounded by corruption among the officials overseeing the socialist transformation programme. The result was economic failure from which Tanzania has not fully recovered and which may take many more years to overcome.

Yet with great achievements in health and education, and provision of social equity, Tanzania's economic policies cannot be said to have been a total failure. But they had to be replaced with free market policies in this era of globalization because of the fundamental changes that have taken place in the international system since the triumph of capitalism over communism towards the end of the twentieth century.

There is no question that in most cases, bad economic policies and bad leadership ruined Africa in the post-colonial period. The continent lost an entire generation in terms of development.

International donors and lenders, tired of seeing their money go down the drain but also determined to exercise hegemonic control over the continent for their own benefit more than anything else, played a critical role in changing the economic policies of African countries.

They instituted a shock-therapy programme for Africa and other Third World regions, demanding imposition of austerity measures to rejuvenate the economies through financial discipline, adoption of free-market policies, and maximum sacrifice from the people of those countries. They were draconian measures known as structural adjustment programmes.

Structural adjustment programmes (SAPs) had a devastating impact on the lives of tens of millions of people, causing severe hardship for families and individuals. And they still do. As Chinua Achebe stated in his Presidential Fellow Lecture before the World Bank Group in 1998:

> I believe it was in the first weeks of 1989 that I received an invitation to an anniversary meeting - the twentieth-fifth year, or something like that - of the Organization for Economic Cooperation and Development (OECD) in Paris....
>
> They talked in particular about the magic bullet of the 1980s, structural adjustment, specifically designed for those parts of the world where economies had gone completely haywire. The matter was really simple, the experts seemed to be saying; the only reason for failure to develop was indiscipline of

all kinds, and the remedy was a quick, sharp administration of shock treatment....The most recurrent prescriptions for this condition were the removal of subsidies on food and fuel and the devaluation of the national currency....

Then the governor of the Bank of Kenya made his presentation. As I recall the events, he was probably the only other African at that session. He asked the experts to consider the case of Zambia, which according to him had accepted, and had been practising, a structural adjustment regime for something like 10 years, and whose economic condition was now worse than it had been when they began their treatment. An American expert who seemed to command great attention and was accorded high deference in the room, spoke again. He repeated what had already been said many times before: 'Be patient, it will work in time, trust me,' or words to that effect....

I signaled my desire to speak and was given the floor. I told them what I had just recognized. I said that what was going on before me was a fiction workshop, no more and no less!

'Here you are, spinning your fine theories to be tried out in your imaginary laboratories. You are developing new drugs and feeding them to a bunch of laboratory guinea pigs and hoping for the best. I have news for you. African is not fiction. Africa is people, real people. Have you thought about that?

You are brilliant people, world experts. You may even have the very best intentions. But have you thought, really thought, of Africa as people? I will tell you the experience of my own country, Nigeria, with structural adjustment.

After two years of this remedy, we saw the country's minimum wage fall in value from the equivalent of 15 British pounds to 5 pounds a month. This is not a lab report; it is not a mathematical exercise. We are talking about someone whose income, which is already miserable enough, is now reduced to one-third of what it was two years ago. And this flesh-and-blood man has a wife and children. You say he should simply go home and tell them to be patient. Now let me ask you this question: Would you recommend a similar remedy to your own government? How do you sell it to an elected president? You are asking him to commit political suicide, or perhaps get rid of elections altogether until he has fixed the economy.

Do you realize that's what you're doing?'[9]

None of the experts could give a good answer to any of those questions. They are the same questions raised by many people, including leaders, in Africa and in other parts of the Third World.

One of those leaders was Nyerere who had a tempestuous relationship with the IMF and the World Bank because of the refusal of the economic experts at these leading financial institutions to see Africa's problems from the perspective of the victims, the poor masses who were living in abject poverty and suffering miserably; yet who were told to sacrifice to get out of their miserable condition as if they had something to offer in sacrifice. Desperately poor people have nothing to sacrifice except their lives.

The leading international financial institution, besides the World Bank, in this new revival has been the IMF (International Monetary Fund), although its stringent conditions for aid have not always been valid in all contexts; one of them being Tanzania which differed with the IMF over the country's economic policies.

In 1984 when Nyerere was still president, he explained in detail Tanzania's stand on the IMF proposals as they related to the country's development and economic plight. He said the major difference between Tanzania and the IMF was not based on the conditions demanded by the latter but the extent to which such conditions could be applied in Tanzania.

In an interview with local and foreign journalists at the State House in Dar es Salaam on November 22, Nyerere said that none of the IMF packages ranging from massive devaluation, reduction of government deficits to liberalization of imports, had helped any Third World economy. As he explained:

> They (international financial institutions) advised us to liberalize imports in 1977 when we had surplus in foreign reserves and we did. But we have been in trouble ever since.[10]

He went on to say that imposition of the ready-made prescriptions on poor countries as a condition for aid was unacceptable:

> Any serious Third World government will ask serious questions. I cannot sign an agreement (with the IMF) and then have riots on the streets. You may be the economic experts but I am the political expert - allow me at least to say how much the people can take.[11]

Nyerere further explained that blind acceptance of the IMF packages would force the government to turn the police force against the people. The president said the government was flexible in its economic policies and had taken a number of measures similar to those recommended by the IMF; and went on to stress:

> We don't say we don't change but we say how much should we change. Every government will have to ask that. Every government asks that.[12]

He said Tanzania needed the financial aid offered by the IMF but insisted that the negotiations must be balanced. Commenting on government involvement in running the economy, Nyerere said all governments, including that of the United States, had to make decisions dealing with the economy. He cited as an example the deliberate decision by the American government to maintain "huge deficits" in its annual budget:

Those deficits are a government decision and it pervades the total economy.[13]

Nyerere said the higher degree of government control of the economy in Tanzania was basically historical because most of the economic infrastructure, including industry, was created by the government, pointing out that little was inherited from the colonial powers (first, Germany, and then Britain). As he put it:

In Tanzania we do a little bit more than they (other countries) do. It is partly historical, partly ideological...but mostly historical.[14]

But he insisted that Tanzania would continue to pursue socialism and self-reliance as the only means to achieve development. However, he told the press conference that collectivization in the rural areas would continue to be voluntary:

It has never been the intention to force collectivization in Tanzania.[15]

It is true that forcing people to build, move into, and live in *ujamaa* villages, had never been the policy of the government under Nyerere. But many overzealous officials who implemented that policy resorted to intimidation and other tactics to forcibly mobilize the people into those collective settlements.

There was excessive use of force and abuse of power. Peasant farming was collectivized between 1973 and 1976, triggering riots and retaliatory violence against government agents enforcing the policy of collectivization.[16] And a number of people were killed on both sides.

President Nyerere reported that by mid-1975, over 9 million Tanzanians - then close to about half the entire population - had been moved into more than 6,000 *ujamaa* villages.

In 1976, the government launched a massive sweep of Dar es Salaam, the capital and the country's largest city, and rounded up thousands of the unemployed and sent them to rural areas to work in their home villages or in new settlements.[17] And by 1980, 91 percent of the people in the rural areas lived in *ujamaa* villages. It was a feat of social engineering without precedent anywhere else in Africa.

But, in spite of his commitment to socialism, Nyerere never ruled out capitalist involvement in the socialist transformation of Tanzania. In fact, the *Arusha Declaration* which he wrote almost single-handedly welcomed such participation and foreign involvement. As he explained in the interview in 1984 almost exactly one year before he retired from the presidency, Tanzania would continue to invite foreign private firms to invest in the country under mutual agreements which did not compromise the principles of either party.

He told a questioner that this was not a capitalistic tendency. He said Tanzania had been willing to cooperate with private companies all along, citing the General Tyre (East Africa) Company formed jointly with an American firm shortly after the *Arusha Declaration* was issued in February 1967. As he told the reporters and others at the press conference:

> I have been advised that it is correct to use capitalists to develop socialism.[18]

But socialism failed to develop Tanzania's economy despite some success in import-substitution industrialization, an achievement which is sometimes overlooked when people talk about the country's failed economic policies. But the failure was disastrous, and no amount of clever sheet-balancing can mitigate its effects.

However, it is critical to understand the context in which the *Arusha Declaration* was formulated and why Nyerere found it necessary to start *ujamaa* villages and exhort Tanzanians - and other Africans in general - to be self-reliant.

It was the nature of the international system - political and economic - whose creation after the end of World War II was predicated on the preservation and promotion of the national and geopolitical interests of the major powers which determined the nature of the response from weak and poor countries such as Tanzania to the domination of the world by the industrialized nations.

They would have to try to protect themselves or accept such domination. Tanzania under Nyerere chose to find a way out of this predicament by charting out a new course towards political and economic independence. It could not even start thinking about protecting its interests if it was not truly independent. As Cranford Pratt stated in *Southern Africa Report*:

> Nyerere shared the preoccupation with economic development with almost all of the Third World leaders of his generation. From Nehru to Nkrumah to Manley; all were determined that their peoples should more fully enjoy the improvements in personal welfare that economic development should entail.
>
> His...central concern that Tanzania not surrender control of the direction of its economic development to international capitalist interests or international agencies dominated by the major industrialized states - reflected not only nationalist aspirations but also a profound sense that integration into the international economic system would bring little advantage, especially to the poorest countries, if they were unable to manage skilfully and selectively their relationships with the major capitalist countries.
>
> This remained a central concern to Nyerere thought throughout his life. It contributed to the decision to launch the socialist initiatives in 1967 and it drove his desperate and finally unsuccessful efforts in the early 1980s to break free of the policy directives of the World Bank and the IMF.
>
> His attempts first with the South Commission and then the South Centre to build a powerful counter-weight to OECD, were essentially an internationalization of his continuing conviction that the Third World had to find ways to avoid being dominated by the developed countries.[19]

One of the earliest successes of this policy of self-reliance as enunciated by Nyerere was, as we saw, in the area of import substitution. Besides some achievement in this area, there was also a strong emphasis on food production in order for the country to be self-sufficient instead of begging other countries for food to feed its people.

But such self-sufficiency was also emphasized at the expense of export-crop growth on which the country depended to earn desperately needed foreign exchange as it still does today. And it was a noble objective. People can't eat cotton, coffee or tobacco.

Food comes first before export crops. However, even food production declined due to lack of incentives as did the production of export crops for the same reasons including corruption and high taxes.

As production declined, budget deficits grew.

The end of the coffee boom of the 1970s and soaring oil prices also had a devastating impact on Tanzania's fragile economy, especially in 1979, the same year the country fought a full-scale war against Idi Amin"s forces. The expenses incurred in this conflict were an astronomical amount for a poor country like Tanzania. And the country's poor economic performance continued to take its toll.

The infrastructure crumbled during that period. Roads were in desperate need of repair; intermittent supply of electricity affected industrial production; communications and transport were in disarray, and with only a few vehicles on the road compared with the country's needs. The Tanzania-Zambia Railway (TAZARA) virtually collapsed. Buses did not run on regular basis. Fuel became scarce and too expensive. The currency was devalued. Farmers suffered a lot because some of the policies being implemented by government officials were biased against them. And corruption became rampant as the economy continued its downward spiral. As Professor Harvey Glickman who spent some time in Tanzania studying the country's economy stated in his article, "Tanzania: From Disillusionment to Guarded Optimism," in *Current History: A Journal of Contemporary World Affairs*:

> Policy bias against farmers, an overvalued currency that cheapened imports, and a bloated and politicized bureaucracy made gaining the ability to grant licenses, tariff protections, and franchises the chief goal of the ambitious and powerful. A political class acquired a vested interest in controls, which strangled enterprise. From 1980 to 1985, per capita income fell by 12 percent.[20]

It was during this period, between 1981 and 1985, that President Nyerere got involved in negotiations with the IMF to help rejuvenate the economy.

They were tough negotiations, with the IMF determined to dictate terms to Tanzania and other countries, prompting Nyerere to publicly ask who elected the IMF to be the finance ministry for every country in the world.

That also marked the beginning of the end of Tanzania's socialist policies. It was a fundamental change Nyerere was not enthusiastic about; which explains why he was so opposed to some of the IMF proposals - the extent to which liberalization of the economy should be carried out - and entered into those negotiations only reluctantly.

However, Tanzania had no choice but to comply with the IMF conditions if the country was to reverse its economic decline. As Adebayo Adedeji, an internationally renowned Nigerian economist who was then the executive secretary of the UN Economic Commission for Africa (ECA), stated in 1983 when the negotiations between Tanzania and the IMF were still going on:

> The donor countries and institutions have the last word, rather than the governments themselves, such as in the recent controversy between the IMF and Tanzania. I think, in the final analysis, that the IMF won.
>
> This is the grueling reality of poverty. When you are poor, you can never be right. It is the rich country that is right, because it is the only one that can help you out.[21]

Like all the other African countries, Tanzania had to adopt stringent austerity measures as a condition for financial aid from the IMF and donor nations of the industrial West. The measures included structural adjustment programmes which demanded reducing controls on marketing and currency exchange rates as well as cutting overall public expenditure, thus causing severe hardship on the people who saw a drastic reduction in the provision of social services and education without a corresponding rise in income. Also implementation of these draconian IMF-imposed measures led to recession, instead of the reverse being the case as anticipated by the proponents of the austerity programmes.

When Ali Hassan Mwinyi succeeded Nyerere as president in November 1985, he continued to implement the IMF structural adjustment programmes and agreed to further austerity measures. One of those was the Economic Recovery Programme of 1986 - it was implemented well into 1992 with IMF backing as the Economic and Social Action Programme - which produced some positive results, especially in freeing foreign exchange, reducing tariffs, and breaking down crop-marketing cooperatives which exercised almost absolute control over the farmers in terms of price control.

Implementation of those measures led to some improvement in the economy. Farmers growing export crops, traders, and small manufacturers benefited from this economic growth, but most of the people in Tanzania experienced exactly the opposite.

There was not enough improvement. Public sector salaries dropped, and social services declined as did school enrolment. And the incentive to produce remained low.

The country still has a long way to go before it achieves significant economic growth. Socialism has been replaced by capitalism but millions of Tanzanians, especially the poor, remember the Nyerere era with nostalgia and wish those days were here again.

But they are gone forever in this era of globalization dominated by the industrial West, Nyerere's nemesis.

Chapter Four:

Introduction of Multiparty Democracy in Tanzania
under Nyerere's Stewardship

PRESIDENT JULIUS NYERERE was the architect of the most successful monolithic state under one-party rule in Africa. Yet, he became one of the most vocal and strongest proponents of multiparty democracy to dismantle the very institution he had created in the first years of independence.

It was Nyerere who initiated the debate on the functional utility, and irrelevancy, of the one-party system in Tanzania even before the wind of change started blowing after the collapse of communism and the end of the Cold War which ushered in a new era of liberazation and free-market policies which swept round the globe in the early nineties.

He fired the first salvo against the one-party monolith back in 1986 - four years before the collapse of the Soviet Union - not long after he voluntarily stepped down from the presidency in November 1985, questioning its relevancy in the context of Tanzania and, indeed, of Africa as a whole, after years of complacency by the national leadership so securely anchored in power without fear of being questioned or challenged by anyone regardless of how badly they performed in office. As he stated in an interview years later when he looked back at his presidency, not long before he died:

I really think I ran the most successful single-party system on the continent. You might not even call it a party. It was a single, huge nationalist movement....

I don't believe that our country would be where it is now if we had a multiplicity of parties, which would have become tribal and caused us a lot of problems.

But when you govern for such a long time, unless you are gods, you become corrupt and bureaucratic....So I started calling for a multiparty system.[1]

Multiparty democracy was introduced in Tanzania seven years after Nyerere left office, and thirty years after the one-party state was established in Tanganyika in 1962 about two years before Tanganyika united with Zanzibar in 1964 to form the United Republic of Tanzania.

The introduction of multiparty politics had the full support of former President Nyerere who said the ruling party had lost its focus and was out of touch with the people. When he called for this fundamental change, he was chairman of the ruling party, CCM, a position he held when he was president and which he continued to hold after his retirement until August 1990 when he gave up the post.

It was also in the same year, actually from 1989, that Tanzania began to move gradually towards multiparty democracy, although the transformation was not formally launched by parliamentary legislation until June 1992. But the change had begun and there was no turning back.

The political transformation was also an integral part of the democratization process that was taking place across Africa and in other parts of the world including former communist countries, given impetus by demands made by the International Monetary Fund (IMF), the World Bank, and donor nations that developing countries - as well as others in the former Eastern bloc - must adhere to "universally" accepted standards of good governance as mandatory conditions for financial aid and other forms of assistance from the industrialized world, especially the West.

It was the equivalent of a new imperial order with the West stipulating conditions for aid and dictating terms to African countries reminiscent of the colonial era when Europeans conquered and carved up the continent for themselves as if we did not even exist - in fulfillment of "the white man's burden" to civilize primitive Africa; since it was they, Europeans, who knew what was best for us.

The propagation of Western values and free-market policies in the post-Cold War era again dominates the agenda for a new world order about which weak countries can do nothing to stop even if they wanted or tried to do so.

But there is also something that many, if not most, of these developing countries find appealing in the Western-dominated agenda for the world. One of those things, besides free-market policies, is democracy. Neither is exclusively western or alien to Africa. For centuries, people in traditional African societies have engaged in trade selling items - food and other commodities - in the open market as individuals or families.

They have also always engaged in a free exchange of ideas, debating issues which affect their lives, as members of the community to which they belong; the equivalent of democratic practices in Western countries.

Therefore, democracy as a concept and as a practice was really nothing new to us; and when Nyerere vigorously supported the introduction of multiparty politics in Tanzania, he was upholding a traditional value, only articulated in a different context in modern life because of the involvement of political parties which did not exist in traditional African societies as well-defined institutions; although the existence of groups of individuals with opposing views in traditional societies could be said to be the equivalent of the modern political parties we have across the continent today.

While Nyerere's support for multiparty politics emboldened Tanzanians who had always wanted pluralistic contests in the political arena, while at the same time invoking as a complementary strategy the mantra of good governance espoused by donor countries and multilateral lending institutions, the leaders of the ruling party were caught off-guard by Mwalimu's frontal assault on their bastion of power and privilege and tried their best to maintain the status quo.

Tanzania made a smooth transition from one-party rule to multiparty democracy precisely because Nyerere played a central role in facilitating this transition; also because of the peace and stability the country continued to enjoy and which had been achieved under under the one-party system.

The one-party system embraced everybody regardless of tribe, race, or class. No one was left out. Everybody was treated as an equal, and everybody was free to participate in the political process - of mass participatory democracy - which was more democratic than what went on in other African countries including those which practised multiparty democracy; nothing but tribal politics in most cases.

And Tanzania achieved all that because of the leadership provided by Nyerere. Therefore, when he called for a national debate on multipatry politics and the one-party system in February 1990, people listened; and his move had a profound impact on the political landscape.

He started the debate with the comments he made in an interview with senior Tanzanian journalists in Dar es Salaam on February 21, 1990. He made it clear in the interview that the ruling party, CCM, was no longer a vanguard party. He went on to say that one-party rule was justified because it was of paramount importance in the quest for national unity.

But now, national unity no longer required a one-party state whose continued existence would only encourage and foster authoritarianism that already existed in the ruling party. As he put it in elaborating his point: "When a Tanzanian cannot write an article and argue the need for more than one party - and that by doing so he is committing treason - then at that stage we shall have gone too far."[2]

In saying so, Nyerere clearly implied that the ruling party had overstepped the bounds of its authority and was abusing its power as much as the communist parties of Eastern Europe and elsewhere did. He went on to say: "Tanzanians should not be dogmatic and think that a single party is God's wish."[3]

That may have surprised some people, especially hearing such harsh criticism coming from one of the main architects of one-party rule in Africa, indeed in the whole world. But throughout his political career, Nyerere never thought or felt that the one-party state he instituted, or any other anywhere else, was an infallible institution. That is why he admitted his mistakes; and that is also why when he and his colleagues established the one-party state in 1965 under a new constitution, he never said it was going to be a permanent institution but a necessary one to maintain and consolidate national unity in pursuit of economic development.

But he also admitted that it was possible a multiparty system could threaten national unity. Therefore if CCM, the ruling party, were to allow the establishment of other political parties, the new parties would have to transcend tribal and regional interests and identities to be truly national parties. They would also have to be secular and socialist. He was then still a strong advocate of socialism and in fact died with his socialist beliefs intact.

Soon after Nyerere launched the debate on multipartyism, the country's newspapers were filled with letters and editorials discussing the subject. And besides being revered as the founding father of the nation, his position as chairman of the ruling party, CCM, during the time he started the debate proved indispensable to the gradual transformation of Tanzania from a one-party state to multiparty democracy. And the smooth transition can equally be attributed to his formidable personality as the dominant figure on the political landscape in Tanzania even after he retired from the presidency and chairmanship of the ruling party.

Many people who participated in the debate, including CCM leaders and academics among others, questioned the validity of the one-party system as a truly democratic institution. Others defended it as a participatory democracy and unifying institution transcending tribal identities and other divisive elements. And there were those who admitted that the one-party system had been a disastrous failure economically but a great success in forging and maintaining national unity.

The first unambiguous and official response to Nyerere's call for multiparty democracy came from his successor, President Ali Hassan Mwinyi, in April 1990. He bluntly stated that the multiparty system was not necessary for Tanzania. He said *wananchi*, the people, had given solid support to the one-party system through the years because it had forged and maintained national unity, transcending tribal differences and identities that were so common during the colonial era. He went on to say: "What Africans want is a fair return for their sweat through a new international economic order," and not the establishment of a hundred regionally entrenched parties based on tribal loyalties and identities "which can bring chaos instead of progress."[4]

The minister for foreign affairs, Benjamin Mkapa who himself became president of Tanzania (1995 - 2005) after Mwinyi and served as foreign minister under both Nyerere and Mwinyi, joined the debate in support of one-party democracy. As he stated on May 15, 1990, there was already sufficient political pluralism and accommodation of diverse views in the country's one-party system which was, for all practical purposes, democratic. He further stated that there was "no optimum universally applicable model of entrenching, strengthening, and consolidating those fundamental freedoms which we all cherish and seek."[5]

What this debate clearly showed was that after it became acceptable to openly challenge CCM, opposition to the ruling party became more pronounced, thus vindicating Nyerere in his contention that the CCM leadership had become complacent and that the one-party state was no longer relevant or responsive to the needs of the people. It was a searing indictment against the ruling elite. And in May 1990, not long before he stepped down from the chairmanship of the ruling party, Nyerere emphasized that "we owe our stability to the one-party system, Kiswahili language and the *Arusha Declaration*. The people must decide whether we can retain unity and stability under a multiparty system."[6]

Opposition to Nyerere's call for multiparty politics continued to draw negative responses from the ruling party elite, including Zanzibari President Idris Wakil who said in June 1990 that a "multiparty system will not provide solutions to economic problems Zanzibar is facing at the moment and will, instead, wreck unity, peace and stability in the island." He went on to say that given Zanzibar's revolutionary history, there was a high probability - if it was not a foregone conclusion - that "parties which will be formed will be based along racial, regional and religious lines, something which is not healthy for the community."[7]

It was obvious that CCM in Zanzibar was vulnerable to attacks by the opposition in the political arena and was trying to do everything it could to win more support from the voters in the former island nation.

But even on the mainland itself, the ruling party was coming under increasing attack from members of the opposition, although its position there seemed to be more secure than on the isles as was clearly demonstrated at the polls in subsequent elections when it won by a large margin; its victory in Zanzibar, however, remained questionable.

Whatever the case, Tanzania had embarked on a new course charted out by none other than Nyerere before multiparty democracy was formally launched in June 1992 by the union parliament when it passed a new law allowing formation of political parties but under strict conditions stipulated by the ruling party, CCM.

Among the most prominent Tanzanians to enter, or in his case to re-enter, the political arena as opposition leaders or members was former foreign affairs minister and secretary-general of the ruling party TANU, Oscar Kambona, who had lived in self-imposed exile in Britain since July 1967.

While still in exile, he wrote a letter to the editor of the *Daily News*, which is a government paper where I also worked in the late sixties and early seventies as a reporter, articulating his position on multiparty politics in Tanzania. It was published on August 2, 1990, calling the establishment of multiparty democracy in Tanzania.[8]

The fact that Kambona had been allowed to have his article published in a Tanzanian newspaper, and one owned by the government on top of that, clearly showed that this was the dawn of a new era, of multiparty politics and free-market policies he had always advocated, and which had been anticipated by many people in Tanzania especially since the collapse of communism in the late eighties. For, here was a man who earlier in June 1970 had been convicted in abstentia of masterminding a coup attempt against President Nyerere in 1969, and of plotting to assassinate him, yet who was now being given a forum to air his views when Nyerere was still the most powerful leader in Tanzania in spite of the fact that he had stepped down from the presidency in 1985.

In the article, Kambona identified himself as a member of the Tanzania Democratic Forum, a political party of Tanzanian exiles that until then had been virtually unknown in the country. Then, in his last speech in August 1990 as chairman of the ruling party CCM before stepping down, Nyerere again spoke about the imperative need for a national debate on multiparty democracy, but strongly warned that "if a multiparty system proves unworkable, the most likely thing to follow it will be either a one person dictatorship, or military rule."9

With Nyerere's full endorsement of the transition from one-partyism to multipatryism, a transformation that would also inexorably lead to the renunciation of socialism as the state ideology although against Nyerere's wishes in the latter case, it was clear that Tanzania had entered a new era towards the end of the twentieth century and the beginning of the second millennium; in spite of stiff opposition by the CCM elite and political heavyweights who wanted to maintain the status quo. But because of Nyerere's formidable influence and as the conscience of the nation, indeed of Africa, they finally relented and began to implement measures that would finally lead to the establishment of multiparty democracy.

President Mwinyi appointed the Nyalali Commission, named after Chief Justice Francis Nyalali who served as its chairman, to study the political situation and find out whether or not multiparty politics was a practical proposition and good for the country. The commission was also given the task to examine different views on the subject in different parts of the country before submitting its final recommendation.

In December 1991, the commission presented a report to the president recommending the establishment of multiparty democracy, although there was significant opposition to this shift because some people, besides CCM leaders, were apprehensive of the future since they had lived and known peace and stability under one-party rule for three decades.

The Nyalali Commission also recommended that 40 repressive pieces of legislation should be eliminated to conform to the new dispensation under multiparty democracy, and a constitutional comission should be established to facilitate the transition. Political education in democracy was also highly recommended as a critical component to the successful establishment of a truly democratic society.

Then the implementation phase followed but the ruling party refused to get rid of the repressive legislation the Nyalali Commission said should be repealed.

However, in February 1992, CCM got rid of the provision in its party constitution which stipulated that Tanzania shall be a one-party socialist state; and by doing so, opened the way for competitive politics under the multiparty system when parliament passed the Political Parties Act in June the same year legalizing multiparty democracy.

The legislation stipulates that a party must have at least 200 members from all regions of the country including Zanzibar and Pemba; and should not be formed on ethnic, regional, religious or sectarian basis. The latter has been easily circumvented since there are parties which are clearly identified with particular tribes and regions, and even with religion as in the case of the Civic United Front (CUF) which is overwhelmingly Muslim, and of the Democratic Party led by fundamentalist minister Christopher Mtikila who is openly hostile to non-Christians and non-black Tanzanians and has called for their expulsion from mainland Tanzania.

Mtikila has also called for the re-establishment of Tanganyika as a separate political entity, preferably followed by dissolution of the union for which this maverick politician has very little regard.

After the Political Parties Act was passed, 24 parties sought registration, thus unwittingly weakening themselves as a credible challenge to the ruling party. While the opposition sought to challenge CCM, it ended up weakening itself by having so many parties instead of uniting to form one strong opposition party.

Among the prominent opposition leaders were former cabinet members in the first independence cabinet: Oscar Kambona, who became the leader of the Tanzania Democratic Alliance, and Chief Abdallah Said Fundikira, leader of the Union for Multiparty Democracy.

Kambona died in 1997 after returning to Tanzania in 1992 from exile in Britain. And Fundikira rejoined the ruling party - of which he had been a leading member as a cabinet minister in the sixties - and was appointed a member of parliament by President Benjamin Mkapa.

The Civic United Front, strongest in the isles, was led by Seif Shariff Hamad, former chief minister of Zanzibar who was then also a member of the ruling CCM.

By 1995, the year of the first multiparty elections which were held in October, 13 political parties had qualified for registration.

The other parties were the National Convention for

Construction and Reform (NCCR-Mageuzi) led by a former deputy prime minister, Augustine Lyatonga Mrema, who left the ruling CCM party and became the strongest contender for the presidency among opposition candidates. Another main opposition party was Chama cha Demokrasia na Maendeleo (CHADEMA) - the Party for Democracy and Development - led by its founder Edwin Mtei, former governor of the Bank of Tanzania and minister of finance under president Nyerere.

He resigned from his ministerial portfolio because of the differences he had with Nyerere over IMF policies. He favoured free-market policies unlike Nyerere who remained committed to socialism.

The remaining parties played only a marginal role on the national scene because of their weak support among the voters and remained on the periphery through the years as they still are today. But their existence legitimized multiparty democracy in Tanzania giving concrete expression to the legislation that had been passed by parliament allowing people to form political parties.

In addition to the ones we have looked at, the opposition camp – although fragmented - included the following parties: the Union for Multiparty Democracy (UMD); the National League for Democracy (NLD); the Tanzania People's Party (TPP); the United People's Democratic Party (UPDP); the National Reconstruction Alliance (NRA); the Popular National Party (PONA); the Tanzania Democratic Alliance Party (TADEA); the Tanzania Labour Party (TLP); the United Democratic Party (UDP); the Forum for Restoration of Democracy (FORD); and Demokrasia Makini Haki na Ustawi (CHAUSTA), which is a Swahili name meaning genuine democracy and development.

In 2004, two more parties sought registration while many of the older ones existed only on paper and in briefcases, and whose entire "membership" could easily fit in the back seat of a taxi or on a single bench in a park.

Nyerere's influence in advancing the democratic agenda under the multiparty system even acquired an aura of invincibility when in May 1995 he openly criticized the leadership of the ruling party for its corruption and personal ambitions and made it clear that he would support a candidate of any party for president or for any other office if that candidate was not tainted with corruption.

One of the leading potential candidates for president from the ruling party was John Malecela, former minister of foreign affairs under Nyerere. He also served as prime minister and then as vice president under President Ali Hassan Mwinyi.

Nyerere saw him as someone who was driven by personal ambition in his quest for the presidency and warned the CCM leadership that he would not even attend the party congress if Malecela was on the short list of possible presidential candidates from the ruling party.

Nyerere's support for Benjamin Mkapa proved critical in helping him secure the nomination over his strongest rival, Jakaya Kikwete, who was the favourite among party leaders of the younger generation.

In the early seventies, Mkapa was the editor of the *Daily News* when I worked there as a reporter. He later became President Nyerere's press secretary, high commissioner (ambassador) to Nigeria and Canada, and ambassador to the United States. And besides serving as minister of foreign affairs under Nyerere and Mwinyi, he also held other cabinet posts under Mwinyi at different times.

In terms of consolidation of political parties as alternative forums for the articulation of ideas, the transition has been gradual yet inexorably leading to competitive politics across the ideological spectrum; although with more of a shift towards the right than towards the left in this age of free-market-dominated agendas. Still, there are parties with a social agenda reminiscent of the one-party socialist era of Nyerere even if not in all fundamental respects. Socialism now is an ideology of a by-gone era we may never see again in Tanzania and in much of the rest of the world.

When Nyerere died in 1999, multiparty democracy had, with his full support, been practised fo seven years.

But pluralism has a long way to go before it is institutionalized and becomes fully accepted, in practice, by the vast majority of Tanzanians so used to the one-party system that had maintained peace and stability for decades since independence.

It is highly probable that Tanzania will remain a *de facto* one-party state ruled by CCM for many years to come. It will be very difficult to dislodge CCM from power

The overwhelming electoral mandate it won in the last general election in 2005 is a clear indication that the party which led the country to independence more than 40 years ago may continue to lead Tanzania for a very long time.

Chapter Five:

Life under Nyerere

THE DEATH of Julius Nyerere in October 1999 marked the end of an era in more than one way.

He was one of the pioneers in the struggle to end colonial rule after the end of World War II. He was also one of the first African leaders who led their countries to independence in the late fifties and in the sixties as ne of the last surviving leaders who spearheaded the struggle for African independence; among them, Kwame Nkrumah, Jomo Kenyatta, Nnamdi Azikiwe, Sekou Toure, Modibo Keita, Patrice Lumumba and others. And he outlived most of them.

The only surviving former African presidents who led their countries to independence in the sixties, and who outlived Nyerere, were Leopold Sedar Senghor, a Francophile, who died in France in December 2001 at the age of 95; Ahmed Ben Bella of Algeria, Dr. Kenneth Kaunda of Zambia, and Dr. Milton Obote of Uganda who were also his ideological compatriots like Dr. Nkrumah, Sekou Toure, Modibo Keita, and Lumumba.

It was the era of "Big Men," the founding fathers, and the life of Julius Nyerere as a political leader of international stature epitomized the best among them, despite a number of failures during their tenure.

They will be remembered as the leaders who not only led their countries to independence but who also maintained national unity, especially in the early years after the end of colonial rule, laying the foundation for the nations we have across the continent today.

They will also be remembered as the leaders who - besides Azikiwe and a few others - introduced the one-party system to fight tribalism and consolidate nationhood, and socialism to achieve economic development.

Nyerere will be remembered for both, probably more than any other African leader. His one-party state was probably the most successful in transcending tribalism and maintaining national unity.

Tribalism never became a prominent feature of national life in Tanzania under Nyerere, unlike in other African countries wracked by war and other conflicts.

And besides Nkrumah, he was also the most articulate exponent and theoretician of one-party rule. A firm believer in socialism until his last days, he was also one of the strongest proponents of socialist policies for decades. And he lived and died as a socialist probably more than any other African leader.

Even after his socialist policies failed to fuel and sustain Tanzania's economic growth, he remained a firm believer in socialism, and responded to his critics in rhetorical terms: "They keep saying you've failed. But what is wrong with urging people to pull together? Did Christianity fail because the world isn't all Christian?"[1]

It is not the purpose of this chapter to examine the successes and failures of Nyerere's socialist policies but to look at how life was under Nyerere in one of the poorest and most ethnically diverse countries in Africa and, indeed, in the entire world.

These are my reflections on Tanzania, the land of my birth (it was then called Tanganyika and still a British colony), and on the life and death of Julius Nyerere, a leader my fellow countrymen and I came to know through the years as a patron saint of the masses and as one of the world's most influential leaders in the twentieth century.

His socialist policies were mostly a failure, but not his ideals of equality and social justice. My life in Tanzania, like those of millions of other Tanzanians, was shaped and guided by those ideals. It is these ideals which sustained Tanzania and earned it a reputation as one of the most stable and peaceful countries in Africa, and one of the most united; a rare feat on this turbulent continent. It was Nyerere's biggest achievement, as he himself said. And it was, even more so than the unification of Tanganyika and Zanzibar in 1964, although this also was a feat of singular significance on a divided continent.

Tanzania stands out as the only country in Africa formed as a union of two independent states. No other union has been consummated on the entire continent, setting Nyerere apart. It was he who engineered the union of Tanganyika and Zanzibar. And it was he who played the biggest role in maintaining stability of the union, and even in sustaining the union itself because of his sense of fairness and extraordinary ability in consensus building as a basis for national unity.

Although the union was indeed a big achievement, there was no question that Nyerere had other goals in that area. His biggest failure, he said, was that he did not succeed in convincing his fellow leaders in neighbouring countries to form an East African federation.

But in fairness, it must be stated that it was the other East African leaders who failed to live up to their Pan-African commitment to form the federation. Kenyatta and Obote agreed with Nyerere in June 1963 to form the East African Federation before the end of the year, but never did.

The other two leaders were not as enthusiastic as Nyerere was. Kenyatta was the least enthusiastic. Obote was ideologically close to Nyerere and in his commitment to a political union of the three East African countries and, in fact, went with Nyerere to see Kenyatta and asked him if he was ready to unite. They also told him that he should be the president of the new macro-nation once the three countries united.

But Kenyatta refused, as Nyerere said in an interview with the *New Internationalist*[2] in December 1998 we cited earlier. So, Obote would probably have united Uganda with the other two countries. But internal opposition to his rule, especially from the Buganda kingdom, precluded any possibility of fulfilling his Pan-African commitment to form the East African Federation.

Although failure to form the East African Federation was one of Nyerere's biggest disappointments in the Pan-African sphere and in foreign policy, he also had one major achievement in these two areas as the most prominent and relentless supporter, among all African leaders, of the liberation movements in southern

Africa. And he lived up to his commitment. Tanzania under his leadership became the headquarters of all the African liberation movements and provided material, diplomatic, and moral support to the freedom fighters through the years until the end of white minority rule. But without strong domestic support, Nyerere's efforts to help free southern Africa and pursuit of his foreign policy initiatives would not have been successful.

It was Tanzania's stability and mass support for Nyerere as a national leader, which made the realization of these goals possible. And it is to this domestic arena that we now turn, in my reflections on Tanzania and on the life and death of Julius Nyerere.

My life as an African has a lot in common with the lives of my fellow Africans across the continent. We all live in countries affected by one form of strife or another, differing only in degree. And we all, at least most of us, belong to one tribe or another. I am a Nyakyusa, one of the few tribes in Tanzania - including the Sukuma, the largest, with more than 7 million, the Nyamwezi, the Chaga, the Hehe, the Haya - with more than one million people in a country of 126 different tribes.

Yet I am a Tanzanian first and foremost, transcending my tribal identity. Still, the tribe is an enduring entity and an integral part of Africa. You cannot define Africa without it, or even begin to understand Africa without comprehending its nature and the central role in plays in life across the spectrum in most African countries.

Call it an ethnic group, a term sometimes more acceptable than tribe because of the latter's derogatory connotation applicable mostly in the African context, while deemed inappropriate and irrelevant in Europe despite the existence of tribes there as well, but which Europeans and others prefer to call ethnic groups to set them apart from "primitive" Africa. Or call it a clan like in Somalia. It is still a tribe in all its manifestations in terms of malignancy associated with tribalism.

Therefore countries like Kenya and Nigeria, Rwanda and Burundi, which have had serious ethnic conflicts ignited and fueled by power struggle between different groups, are not unique in this continent of polyethnic societies. They all face basically the same problems, but differ in the way they tackle them, if at all.

In many cases, they do nothing.

But there are a few, in fact very few, exceptions where tribalism has not been a major problem in Africa. Tanzania is one of them.

Growing up in Tanganyika - later Tanzania - in the sixties was a unique experience in this part of Africa where many of our neighbours were going through turmoil, rocked by tribal conflicts and other forms of strife, during the very same time when we were enjoying relative peace and stability in my country.

The Hutu and the Tutsi in neighbouring Rwanda and Burundi were at each other's throat, killing each other, a perennial problem in these two countries. The town of Kigoma, where I was born and which is on the shores of Lake Tanganyika, became a hub for refugee activities; and for decades the entire western region of Tanzania has been a sanctuary for refugees from Rwanda and Burundi as well as Congo.

The former Belgian Congo, another neighbour, was also torn by civil war, ignited and fueled by ethno-regional rivalries, secession, and intervention by outside powers including the United States and other Western countries especially Belgium, France, and apartheid South Africa as well as Rhodesia both of which also belonged to the Western camp. The Soviet Union and the People's Republic of China also intervened in the Congo.

All those highly combustible elements in one of Africa's biggest, potentially richest and most strategically located countries which slid into anarchy soon after independence on June 30, 1960, would have been too much for any leader to handle without solid national support for a strong central government. The Congo had neither.

The country was split along ethno-regional lines, making it impossible for any leader to mobilize national support for central authority. And the central government itself was weak, and national allegiance to it tenuous at best.

I remember listening to short-wave radio broadcasts from Congo's capital, Leopoldville (renamed Kinshasa by Mobutu in 1971), and from Elisabethville (now Lubumbashi), capital of the secessionist Katanga Province under Moise Tshombe which is about 300 miles west from my home province, Mbeya Region, on the Tanzania-Zambia-Malawi border in southwestern Tanzania. I was in Rungwe District then, in the Great Rift Valley, ringed by misty blue mountains in this region in the Southern Highlands of Tanzania.

The broadcasts were in Kiswahili, the national language of Tanzania and one of the languages spoken in Congo, and the war in that country dominated the news in the sixties. The Simba rebellion (*simba* means lion in Kiswahili), the capture of Stanleyville (now Kisangani) by Belgian paratroops with American support; the "disappearance" and subsequent assassination of Lumumba; the Kwilu rebellion led by Lumumba's heir-apparent Pierre Mulele and his subsequent assassination by Mobutu's henchmen (he was reportedly chopped up and his body pieces fed to crocodiles in the Congo River in October 1968); the battle for Katanga between Tshombe's army as well as mercenaries and the United Nations peacekeeping forces; these are some of the most memorable events I can easily recall even if I don't cherish the memory because of the devastation wrought in this bleeding heart of Africa.

Those were the turbulent sixties when the Congo was in the news everyday. Besides the radio broadcasts coming directly from Leopoldville and Elisabethville everyday about the war, we also got ample news about the same events on our national radio, TBC (Tanganyika Broadcasting Corporation), Dar es Salaam, later renamed RTD (Radio Tanzania, Dar es Salaam). The conflict in the Congo was one of the dominant stories even in Tanganyika, almost everyday. But there were other crises in the region.

Uganda, another neighbour of Tanzania and Congo, also had to contend with separatist threats by the Buganda kingdom; although not as serious as those in the Congo but serious enough to prompt Prime Minister Milton Obote to use military force to contain the danger. In May 1966, he swiftly deposed Kabaka (King) Edward Frederick Mutesa II (who was Uganda's president, but only as nominal head) and declared a state of emergency in Buganda kingdom. And in June 1967, he abolished all four kingdoms and declared Uganda a republic. That was when he also became president.

The other traditional centers of power in the kingdoms of Toro, Ankole, and Bunyoro, and in the princedom of Busoga - as well as the region of Teso - had their own well-established political institutions like the Buganda kingdom and were equally suspicious of the national government which wanted to centralize power under a unitary state; thus stripping traditional rulers of authority over their own people. But they did not pose as big a threat to national unity as Kabaka Edward Mutesa did.

Another neighbour, Kenya, under the leadership of Mzee Jomo Kenyatta, had just emerged from Mau Mau, and the Kikuyu were consolidating their position as the dominant tribe across the spectrum at the expense of their rivals, the Luo, and other tribes; culminating in the assassination of 39-year-old Tom Mboya, a Luo and Kenyatta's heir-apparent, in July 1969.

I remember the day he was assassinated in broad daylight in Kenya's capital, Nairobi. It was Saturday afternoon, and I was at work then, as a reporter at the *Standard*, Dar Es Salaam. The assassination is still vivid in my memory because of the magnitude of the tragedy itself. It was also one of the major assassinations in East Africa and, indeed, in the entire continent in the post-colonial era.

Tom Mboya's assassination threatened to plunge Kenya into chaos, a country already rife with ethnic tensions and rivalries. No one knew how members of his tribe, the Luo, and other Kenyans opposed to Kenyatta's leadership and domination by the Kikuyu, would react. Nashon Njenga Njoroge, a Kikuyu and the man arrested and accused of shooting Tom Mboya, said after he was captured: "Why don't you go after the big man?"

The implication of who exactly "the big man" was, besides Kenyatta himself and other Kikuyu political heavyweights of national stature such Mbiyu Koinange who was also close to Kenyatta, added to the confusion as tempers flared especially among the Luo, Mboya's fellow tribesmen. Large-scale violence was a distinct possibility.

Fortunately, nothing of the sort happened, much of this domestic tranquility attributed to Kenyatta's dominant personality as the revered father of the nation and to his tight grip on the nation he ruled with an iron fist.

But from then on, a cloud hung over Kenya, and prospects for peaceful co-existence between the country's two main ethnic groups and their allies remained bleak. The problem was compounded by the mistreatment of Jaramogi Oginga Odinga, another prominent Luo politician of international stature who resigned as Kenya's vice president under Kenyatta and in March 1966 formed the opposition party, the Kenya People's Union (KPU).

But he was effectively neutralized as an opposition leader. His passport was withdrawn, preventing him from going to the United States in 1968 to deliver a lecture at Boston University, entitled, "Revolution As It Affects Newly Independent States." He was also denied permission to go to Tanzania where he had an ideological compatriot, President Julius Nyerere.

On October 27, 1969, Oginga Odinga was put under house arrest following an anti-government demonstration by KPU supporters and, three days later, the KPU was banned, leaving the Kenya African National Union (KANU) led by Kenyatta as the only legal party in the country. And on November 11, 1969, Kenyatta was re-elected to a second term. All this took place only about three months after Mboya was assassinated in July.

Yet, Oginga Odinga was one of Kenya's most revered politicians. He was also one of the most prominent leaders of the independence movement, not only in Kenya but in Africa as a whole. And it was he who led KANU when Kenyatta was in prison and could have very easily become Kenya's first president had he decided not to step aside when Kenyatta was released. It was also Oginga Odinga, together with Tom Mboya, who led the Kenyan delegation to the constitutional talks in London on Kenya's transition from colonial rule to independence.

Many Kenyans and others also remember him as the author of the best-selling book, *Not Yet Uhuru*,[3] meaning "Not Yet Freedom or Independence" (*uhuru* means freedom or independence in Kiswahili), which he wrote after he resigned as Kenya's vice president.

President Julius Nyerere wrote the introduction to the book, as he did years later to that of President Yoweri Museveni who said he considers himself to be a disciple of Nyerere. But although Odinga was silenced, he remained a highly respected leaders in Kenya. And he remains a revered figure in Kenyan politics even today on the same level with Kenyatta.

There were more crises in the region. In Zambia, formerly Northern Rhodesia before independence, just across the border from my home region in the Southern Highlands of Tanzania, violence also erupted on a significant scale. The country had just won independence from Britain on October 24, 1964, highly optimistic of the future under the leadership of Kenneth Kaunda, a former school teacher and an apostle of non-violence and author of a book, *Zambia Shall Be Free*.[4]

Yet, just before and after independence, the country was rocked by violence instigated by members of an anarchist independent church movement known as the Lumpa Church led by a prophetess, Alice Lenshina, which claimed hundreds of lives and disrupted the lives of thousands of people. The church members refused to pay taxes and rejected secular authority. They clashed with the government and fortified their villages, and refused to surrender to security forces. And they invoked the Scriptures to justify their defiance and refusal to submit to temporal authority.

The Lumpa Church and its leader Alice Lenshina became "household" names. And clashes between government forces and the church members was one of the major stories in the early sixties in that part of Africa, with the short-wave radio as an indispensable medium. Zambia also had to contend with separatist threats in the western province, also known as Barotseland, which was and still is a powerful kingdom, and in the southern part of the country, which was also the opposition stronghold of Zambia's main opposition leader Harry Nkumbula of the African National Congress (ANC).

Maluniko Mundia, leader of the United Party (UP), was another prominent opposition figure. He came from Barotse Province - Barotseland - where he was allied with the powerful traditional rulers including the king of the Barotse people. His party was banned in 1968 because of its sectarian politics, threatening national unity.

And just 30 miles from my home in the misty blue mountains of Rungwe District in the Great Rift Valley, across the border in Malawi (known as Nyasaland until July 6, 1966, when it won independence from Britain and changed its name), Life-President Dr. Hastings Kamuzu Banda had instituted a reign of terror, persecuting and killing his former compatriots, including leading cabinet members some of whom sought asylum in Tanzania. They included Yatuta Chisiza, Malawi's former home affairs minister in Banda's cabinet, who was assassinated in October 1967 by security forces. Malawian officials claimed he entered the country from Tanzania in order to subvert the government with the help of the Tanzanian authorities.

Another one was Malawi's Minister of Foreign Affairs Kanyama Chiume who also sought asylum in Tanzania. When I was a reporter at the *Daily News* in Dar es Salaam, Kanyama Chiume was at *The Nationalist*, a daily newspaper owned by the ruling party TANU (Tanganyika African National Union), where he worked as a features writer and editor, together with Ben Mkapa who was the managing editor before President Nyerere appointed him editor of the *Daily News*. Years later, Mkapa himself was elected president of Tanzania fro two five year-terms from 1995 to 2005.

Under Nyerere, Tanzania became a haven for asylum seekers and refugees from many African countries and others; and I attended Songea Secondary School in Ruvuma Region in the southern part of the country with some of the sons and relatives of these exiled cabinet members from Malawi, such as Henry Chipembere, who was minister of education under President Banda.

Other students at the school included the nephews of former Tanzanian Minister of Foreign Affairs Oscar Kambona who came from that region and who himself went into exile in Britain in July 1967 where he continued to be a fierce critic of Nyerere until his death in 1998, following his return to Tanzania in 1992 to form an opposition party after the introduction of multiparty democracy in 1993.

And at our newspaper, the *Daily News*, we also had reporters from other countries including South Africa, Rhodesia (renamed Zimbabwe at independence in April 1980), Zambia, Kenya, Nigeria (from former Biafra), and Britain.

Dr. Banda also claimed substantial parts of Tanzania, including my home district - Rungwe - and the rest of Mbeya Region in southwestern Tanzania, as Malawian territory. He also claimed the entire Eastern Province of Zambia, provoking a curt response from Zambia's president, Dr. Kenneth Kaunda, who challenged Banda to "Go ahead and declare war on Zambia."[5]

And President Nyerere dismissed Banda's claim to large chunks of Tanzanian territory as "expansionist outbursts, which do not scare us, and do not deserve my reply." The outlandish claim also drew a sharp response from Nyerere who said Dr. Banda was "insane." But, he warned, "Dr. Banda must not be ignored; the powers behind him are not insane."[6]

So, that was the situation in these neighbouring countries in the sixties when I was in my teens, and thereafter.

The situation in Mozambique, another neighbour, was somewhat different but equally explosive. Mozambique was still a Portuguese colony, and, because Tanzania gave full support to the freedom fighters who used our country as an operational base and headquarters of their liberation movement FRELIMO (Portuguese acronym for Mozambique Liberation Front), the Portuguese attacked parts of southern Tanzania, especially Mtwara Region, as well as Ruvuma Region where I attended Songea Secondary School from 1965 to 1968.

But the attacks only strengthened our resolve to support the freedom fighters; an unwavering commitment that continued until Mozambique finally won independence on June 25, 1975, after almost 500 years of Portuguese colonial rule.

One of the casualties of this liberation struggle was Dr. Eduardo Mondlane, founder and first president of FRELIMO, who was assassinated in Dar es Salaam in February 1969 when he opened a parcel, rigged with a bomb and mailed to him from Japan. The bomb, hidden in a book of Russian essays, was traced back to the Portuguese secret police in Lisbon. I was then a student at Tambaza High School (formerly H.H. The Aga Khan High School) in Dar es Salaam. I was in standard 13 (Form V) that year.

Our high school system had two grades, standard 13 and standard 14 (Form V and Form VI), covering two years, what Americans would call grade 13 and grade 14, after completion of secondary school in standard 12. This is roughly equivalent to what Americans call junior college, but with a concentration in three subjects, after which you went to university if you passed the dreaded final exams in standard 14. It was patterned after the British school system we inherited from our former colonial masters.

Many students, including myself, attended Mondlane's funeral at Kinondoni Cemetery within walking distance from our high school. President Nyerere was at the grave site, together with Mondlane's widow Janet and their two little children, a boy and a girl. Leaders of all the African liberation movements based in Dar es Salaam and members of the diplomatic corps also attended the funeral, one of the saddest moments in our history.

But the assassination of Dr. Mondlane did not in any way interfere with the liberation struggle. President Nyerere, who had asked Mondlane to come to Tanganyika and establish an operational base in our country for the liberation of Mozambique when the two met at the United Nations where Mondlane worked and when Nyerere argued our case for Tanganyika's independence (he went to the UN for the first time in February 1955), vowed to continue supporting the freedom fighters until Mozambique was finally free.

Mondlane returned to Africa in 1962 and settled in Dar es Salaam, Tanganyika, where he went on to unite the various Mozambican nationalist groups to form FRELIMO, one of the most successful liberation movements in colonial history. Nyerere's invitation to the freedom fighters was typical of him. As he stated in his address to the Tanganyika Legislative Council (LEGCO) on October 22, 1959, even before our country became independent:

> We the people of Tanganyika, would like to light a candle and put it on top of Mount Kilimanjaro which will shine beyond our borders giving hope where there is despair, love where there is hate, and dignity where before there was only humiliation.[7]

And he went on to fulfill that pledge. Without Tanzania functioning as a rear base and as a conduit for material support to the freedom fighters, Mozambique would probably not have won independence when it did, and the liberation of other countries in southern Africa including the bastion of white rule on the continent, South Africa, would have been equally affected, only in varying degrees.

In spite of her poverty as one of the poorest countries in the world, Tanzania still contributed a significant amount of resources to the liberation struggle far more than many other and richer

African countries did.

Many people used to say that Tazania contributed far more than its share; let other countries play their part. For instance, I remember talking to a Malawian surgeon, Dr. Geoffrey Mwaungulu, in Detroit, Michigan, in the United States when I was a student there in the early seventies, who said "Tanzania is doing too much," overburdening herself, while many other African countries - including his, Malawi - are doing nothing or very little to support the liberation struggle in southern Africa and Portuguese Guinea (Guinea-Bissau) in West Africa.

A graduate of Temple University in Philadelphia, Pennsylvania, he worked at Ford Hospital in Detroit and was one of a large number of African immigrants living in Detroit, including professors, lawyers, engineers and other professionals in the city and other parts of the metropolitan area.

There were even some people in Tanzania who said President Nyerere was devoting himself too much to the liberation struggle and pursuits of other foreign policy goals while overlooking domestic problems.

Yet there was no contradiction between the two. His commitment to the well-being of Tanzania was not in any way compromised by the active role he played in the international arena. And he could not have succeeded in the pursuit of his foreign policy objectives - including support of the liberation movements - without the unwavering support of the vast majority of Tanzanians. As David Martin, a renowned British journalist with *The Observer*, London, who was the deputy managing editor of the *Standard*, Tanzania, and the one who first hired me as a reporter in June1969 when I was still a high school student, stated in December 2001, two years after Nyerere died:

> I arrived in the Tanzanian capital of Dar es Salaam as a journalist on 9 January 1964. Three days later there was a revolution in Zanzibar by the African majority against the Arab minority put in power by the retreating British colonialists just one month earlier. An African-driven union between Tanganyika and Zanzibar followed three months later and the country's name was changed to Tanzania. Despair, hate and humiliation had begun the painfully slow process of retreating.
>
> Dar es Salaam in those days was the headquarters of the Organization of African Unity (OAU) Liberation Committee. Living in the city were the leaders of the liberation movements of southern Africa such as the ebullient Eduardo

Mondlane from Mozambique, more taciturn poet, Dr. Agostinho Neto, and a host of others. Nyerere was their beacon of hope.

He was uninhibited by the paranoid attitudes that gripped the east and west at the height of the Cold War. And although he was not adverse to using westerners to achieve his vision, he sought for the continent to have African solutions created by African people. He did not tolerate fools and was a masterly media manager. He could go for months without seeing the press. But, whe he had something to say, as he did in 1976 during two visits by the US Secretary of State, Dr. Henry Kissinger, he astutely ensured that his version of events got across.

I remember one day sitting in his office questioning that a number of African countries had not paid their subscriptions to the OAU Liberation Committee Special Fund for the Liberation of Africa. He looked at me for some moments, thoughtfully chewing the inside corner of his mouth in his distinctive way. Then, his decision made, he passed across a file swearing me secrecy as to its contents. It contained the amount that Tanzanians, then according to the United Nations the poorest people on earth, would directly and indirectly contribute that year to the liberation movements. I was astounded; the amount ran into millions of US dollars.

It was the practice among national leaders in those days to say that their countries did not have guerrilla bases. Now we know that Tanzania had many such bases providing training for most of the southern African guerrillas, who were then called 'terrorists' and who today are members of governments throughout the region.... Tanzania was also directly attacked from Mozambique by the Portuguese. But, in turn, each of the white minorities in southern Africa fell to black majority political rule and Nyerere saw his vision for the continent finally realized on 27 April 1994 when apartheid formally ended in South Africa with the swearing in of a new black leadership.[8]

Mozambique was the first country in the region to win independence by armed struggle, six years after Dr. Mondlane was assassinated. His assassination in February 1969 was one of the two major political killings in the region that year, followed by the assassination of Tom Mboya only a few months later in July, about a month after I was first hired as a news reporter of the *Standard*, renamed *Daily News* in 1970. I started working full-time on the editorial staff in 1971 after completing high school and National Service.

As a reporter, I used to go to the headquarters of the Mozambique Liberation Front, FRELIMO, on Nkrumah Street in Dar es Salaam for the latest developments on the guerrilla war in Mozambique and to pick up press releases. The office of the African National Congress (ANC) of South Africa was also on the same street, on the opposite side, not far from FRELIMO's, just a few minutes' walk, probably not more than five minutes. The person I always spoke to when I went to FRELIMO's office was Joaquim Chissano who became president of Mozambique after the tragic death of President Samora Machel in a plane crash in October 1986.

President Machel and his entourage were on their way back to Mozambique from Harare, Zimbabwe, when the plane crashed just inside the South African border not far from Maputo, the Mozambican capital. The South African government was immediately implicated in the crash, and subsequent investigations showed that the "accident" was an act of sabotage by the apartheid regime.

The South African government was also behind the assassination of Swedish Prime Minister Olof Palme on February 28, 1986. Palme, who was shot by a gunman as he was walking home with his wife from a movie theater, was a strong supporter of the African liberation movements in southern Africa, as was his country, which - especially under his leadership - reportedly contributed more than $400 million to the liberations struggle in terms of financial and non-military support.

Chissano was in charge of the FRELIMO office in Dar es Salaam, and became Mozambique's minister of foreign affairs after his country won independence. He held the same ministerial post until he became president after Samora Machel was killed. Marcelino dos Santos who also used to live in Tanzania during the struggle for Mozambique's independence, remained vice president, under Chissano, as he was under Samora Machel.

Our interaction with the FRELIMO office in Dar es Salaam as reporters was facilitated by Chissano because he also spoke English, besides Portuguese. He also learned and spoke Kiswahili, our national language.

So, it was easy for us to communicate with him, as much as it was with most of the freedom fighters from other countries at their headquarters in Dar es Salaam who also spoke English, and some of them Kiswahili.

Dar es Salaam during those days was the center of seismic activity on the African political landscape and beyond. The list of the names of those who came to the city, who lived there, and those who just passed through during the liberation wars, is highly impressive to say the least. It was here, in Tanzania, where Nelson Mandela first came in 1962 to seek assistance for the liberation struggle in South Africa. And Nyerere was the first leader of independent Africa he met. Tanganyika was also the first country in the region to win independence, in 1961.

Mandela also had his first taste of freedom after he arrived in Mbeya, a border town in southwestern Tanzania (then Tanganyika) and the capital of the Southern Highlands Province (later split into Mbeya and Iringa Regions) where, as he states in his autobiography *Long Walk to Freedom*, he was not - for the first time in his life - subjected to the indignities of color bar as he automatically would been in his native land.[9]

Almost all the leaders in southern Africa who waged guerrilla warfare to free their countries from white minority rule, lived or worked in Tanzania at one time or another.

Thabo Mbeki, who became vice president and then president of South Africa, first sought asylum in Tanganyika when he fled the land of apartheid in the early sixties. So did others, including many leaders in South Africa today besides Mbeki. They include the Speaker of the South African Parliament Dr. Frene Ginwala who once was editor of our newspaper, the *Daily News*, appointed by President Nyerere before Sammy Mdee replaced her. She lived in Tanzania for many years and is the person who received Mandela in Dar es Salaam when he first came to Tanganyika in 1962.

President Robert Mugabe also lived in Tanzania and Mozambique during Zimbabwe's liberation war. So did Dr. Agostinho Neto, the first president of Angola, and Sam Nujoma, president of Namibia, and many of their colleagues in government.

I remember interviewing Sam Nujoma in 1972 at the office of his liberation movement, the South West African People's Organization (SWAPO), on Market Street in Dar es Salaam, only a few minutes' walk from our newspaper office on Azikiwe Street and from the offices of three other liberation movements: Zimbabwe African National Union (ZANU), Popular Movement for the Liberation of Angola (MPLA), and the Pan-Africanist Congress (PAC) of South Africa. I talked to Nujoma just before he left for New York to address the United Nations

Decolonization Committee and speak in other forums in his quest for Namibian independence.

Looking very serious, and highly articulate on the subject, he was very optimistic about the future. He was, of course, vindicated by history. But little did he or anybody else back then know that it would be almost 20 years before Namibia would be free.

Many other leaders found sanctuary in Tanzania. They include those from the Seychelles and the Comoros, two island nations on the Indian Ocean east and southeast of Tanzania, respectively; and President Yoweri Museveni of Uganda who attended the University of Dar es Salaam and lived in Tanzania for many years and who - after he became president - continued to express profound respect and admiration for Nyerere whom he acknowledged as his mentor.

When he was a student at the University of Dar es Salaam, Museveni was a member of a study group led by Dr. Walter Rodney. Mwalimu Nyerere even wrote an introduction to one of President Museveni's books, *What Is Africa's Problem?*[10]

The late President Laurent Kabila of the Democratic Republic of Congo also lived in Tanzania for more than 20 years since the sixties after the assassination of Patrice Lumumba, his hero, and even owned houses in Dar es Salaam where he was also known by different aliases, prompting his neighbours and other people to suspect that he was a government agent. His son Joseph Kabila who succeeded him as president was raised and attended school in Tanzania.

In fact, many Congolese refused to accept him as their leader when first became president because they saw him as a foreigner, a Tanzanian, who did not even speak Lingala or French, the main languages spoken in Congo, but instead spoke only English and Kiswahili, Tanzania's national language, although Kiswahili is also widely spoken in Congo.

Even President Kenneth Kaunda of Zambia forged ties with Tanzania early in his life. He spent some time in Mbeya in the southwestern part of what was then Tanganyika, and with his friend Simon Kapwepwe who also spent some time in Mbeya and later became his vice president, used to dream of the day when Northern Rhodesia (Zambia) would be free one day.

The two were childhood friends in Chinsali - their hometown and district in the Northern Province - in Northern Rhodesia renamed Zambia.

The list of people who found asylum in Tanzania goes on and on. They include many who became leaders in Rwanda, Burundi, Ethiopia, Eritrea, Somalia, Sudan, Ghana, Nigeria, Guinea, Congo, Zambia, besides those in southern Africa - Mozambique, Zimbabwe, Angola, Namibia, South Africa - and other countries.

Even Che Guevara spent months in Tanzania. He was in Dar es Salaam for about four months from November 1965 to February 1966, besides the time he spent in the western apart of the country during his Congo mission. And it was when he was in Dar es Salaam that he wrote his famous book, the *Congo Diaries*,[11] while staying at the Cuban embassy during those critical months.

In fact, before he embarked on his Congo mission, it was Che Guevara himself who recommended Pablo Ribalta - his friend and compatriot since their guerrilla war days in the Sierra Maestra during the Cuban revolution - to be Cuba's ambassador to Tanzania because he felt that Ribalta's African ancestry would facilitate his mission to the Congo. And during his military engagement in the Congo, Che sometimes used Kigoma in western Tanzania as one of his sanctuaries.

But he had a very low opinion of Laurent Kabila - whom he said had no leadership qualities and lacked charisma - and other Congolese nationalist leaders including Gaston-Emile Sumayili Sumialot. He accused them of abandoning their troops in eastern Congo preferring, instead, to live in comfort in Dar es Salaam.

But in spite of the fact that Tanzania was the headquarters of all the African liberation movements, and a place which attracted many liberals and leftists from many parts of the world including black militants from the United States such as the Black Panthers (among them Black Panther leader Pete O'Neill and his wife Charlotte who have lived in Tanzania since 1972), and Malcolm X who also visited Tanzania and had a meeting with President Nyerere and attended the OAU conference of the African heads of state and government in Cairo, Egypt, in July 1964 (where he almost died when his food was poisoned, probably by CIA agents who followed him throughout his African trip); our country still enjoyed relative peace and stability, not only during the euphoric sixties soon after independence, but during the seventies as well, when the liberation wars were most intense in southern Africa, with Dar es Salaam, our capital, as the nerve center.

Therefore, besides the raids by the Portuguese from their colony of Mozambique on our country; a sustained destabilization campaign by the apartheid regime of South Africa whose Defence Minister P.W. Botha said in August 1968 that countries which harbor terrorists - freedom fighters in our lexicon - should receive "a sudden knock,"[12] a pointed reference to Tanzania and Zambia, and by the white minority government of Rhodesia (Prime Minister Ian Smith called Nyerere "the evil genius" behind the liberation wars), all of whom had singled out Tanzania as the primary target because of our support for the freedom fighters; the influx of refugees from Rwanda, Burundi, and Congo into our country; and Malawian President Banda's claims to our territory; in spite of all that, Tanzania was, relatively speaking, not only an island of peace and stability in the region but also an ideological center with considerable magnetic pull, drawing liberal and radical thinkers from around the world, especially to the University of Dar es Salaam which became one of the most prominent academic centers in the world with many internationally renowned scholars who strongly admired Nyerere and his policies.

Among the scholars drawn to Tanzania was the late Dr. Walter Rodney from Guyana who first joined the academic staff at the University of Dar es Salaam in 1968 and, while teaching there, wrote a best-seller, *How Europe Underdeveloped Africa*;[13] the late distinguished Professor Claude Ake from Nigeria who died in a mysterious plane crash in his home country in 1996; Professor Okwudiba Nnoli, also from Nigeria (secessionist Biafra); Professor Mahmood Mamdani from Uganda and one of Africa's internationally renowned scholars; Nathan Shamuyarira who - while a lecturer at the University of Dar es Salaam - was also the leader of the Dar-es-Salaam-based Front for the Liberation of Zimbabwe (FROLIZI) headed by James Chikerema, a Zimbabwean national leader.

Shamuyarira went on to become Zimbabwe's minister of foreign affairs, among other ministerial posts.

Many other prominent scholars from many countries around the world, and from all continents, were also attracted to the University of Dar es Salaam. C.L.R. James from Trinidad & Tobago, one of the founding fathers of the Pan-Africanist movement who knew Kwame Nkrumah when Nkrumah was still a student in the United States, and who introduced him to George Padmore when he went to Britain for further studies before returning to Ghana (then the Gold Coast) in 1947 with Ako Adjei, was also attracted to Tanzania. So was Kenyan writer Ngugi wa Thiong'o, disenchanted with the Kenyan leadership, and Ghanaian writer Ayi Kwei Armah, an admirer of Nkrumah and Nyerere, who has also called for the adoption of Kiswahili as the continental language just as Wole Soyinka has.

Besides Malcolm X, other prominent black American leaders who came to Tanzania included Stokely Carmichael (originally from Trinidad) who as Kwame Ture lived in Guinea for 30 years until his death in November 1998. When in Dar es Salaam, Stokely used to stay at the Palm Beach Hotel, not far from the Indian Ocean beach and our high school hostel, H.H. The Aga Khan, in an area called Upanga; while Malcolm X and Che Guevara used to go to the New Zahir restaurant. But while Malcolm X was in Tanzania only for days, Che spent about four months in Dar es Salaam.

Angela Davis of the Black Panther Party and others in the civil rights movement including Andrew Young, Jesse Jackson, and Robert Williams who organized some blacks for self-defense in North Carolina, also came to Tanzania.

I also remember when Robert Williams came to our editorial office at the *Daily News* in Dar es Salaam. I saw him again in 1975 when I was a student at Wayne State University in Detroit, Michigan, USA. He came to Detroit and spoke to Wayne State University students who were members of the Young Socialist Alliance (YSA). I was at that meeting as an observer and reminded him of his visit to our newspaper office in Tanzania, which he remembered very well, as we went on to talk about a number of subjects including the influence of President Nyerere in a Pan-African context.

Some of the prominent leaders in the American civil rights movement who lived in Tanzania for a number of years include

Charlie Cobb and Robert (Bob) Moses. They were active in Mississippi and other parts of the Deep South during the turbulent sixties when they almost got killed. Bob Moses was one of those who got a thorough beating in Mississippi for trying to organize blacks to vote. The White Citizens Council, founded in Greenville in Mississippi, the Ku Klux Klan and other racist groups could not tolerate that.

Cobb had similar close calls. Both eventually moved to Africa. After they returned to the United States, they continued to be involved in civil rights activities and organizing communities for their collective well-being.

They co-authored *Radical Equations: Math Literacy and Civil Rights* and developed an algebra curriculum also designed to mobilize communities to achieve common goals. Launched in 1982, the Algebra Project now operates in many cities and communities across the United States, and their book, *Radical Equations*, describes the project's creation and implementation. The project involves entire communities to create a culture of literacy around algebra, a crucial stepping-stone to college math and opportunity, especially for blacks and other minorities who lag behind in preparation for college work because of the low quality of education they get in inner-city schools.

Bob Moses, who was a secondary school teacher in Tanzania, began developing the Algebra Project after becoming unhappy with the way algebra was taught to his teen-age daughter. He saw algebra as a major obstacle for black students trying to go to college.

Charlie Cobb was a field secretary for the Student Non-violent Coordinating Committee (SNNC), once headed by Stokely Carmichael, in Mississippi from 1962 to 1967 where he developed the idea for the Freedom Schools that SNNC operated. The schools taught basic literacy skills to black children and became a model for many new approaches to education still used today across the United States.

He also helped found the National Association for Black Journalists and became a senior writer for allafrica.com, the web site of AllAfrica Global Media. The site posts hundreds of news stories about Africa everyday from more than 80 African media organizations and its own reporters.

The years the two civil rights activists and many others spent in Tanzania helped strengthen ties between Africa and Black America, and is strong testimony to Tanzania's hospitality to oppressed people from around the world who found sanctuary in Tanzania during Nyerere's tenure.

The relationship between Tanzania and Black America has also been demonstrated in many other ways. For example, when Malcolm X returned to the United States from Africa, FBI agents were waiting for him at the airport in New York. He was seen going into a car with a diplomatic license plate which was traced to "the new African nation of Tanzania." The car took him to the residence of the Tanzanian ambassador to the United Nations, trailed by FBI agents the same way Malcolm X was followed by CIA agents throughout his African trip.

President Nyerere also forged ties with Black America soon after independence when he instructed the Tanzanian ambassador to the United States to recruit skilled African-Americans to work in Tanzania to help the country meet its manpower requirements and as act of Pan-African solidarity. There are also schools and other institutions in black communities in the United States named after Nyerere and other African leaders such as Nkrumah, Lumumba and Mandela.

And Kiswahili, Tanzania's national language, is the most popular African language among African-Americans; much of this popularity attributed to the influence and stature of Mwalimu Julius Nyerere as an eminent Pan-Africanist who was embraced by the African diaspora as much as Nkrumah was.

Many African-Americans came to Tanzania because of Nyerere and his policies. Others viewed their trip as a pilgrimage, a spiritual journey, and a return to the motherland in the spirit of Pan-African solidarity.

One of the African-Americans who was among the earliest to settle in Africa was Bill Sutherland, like Dr. W.E.B. DuBois and George Padmore, both of whom he knew and worked with in Ghana where they also lived and died. He came from Glen Ridge, New Jersey, and lived in Tanzania for decades. He knew and worked with Nyerere and was still in Tanzania when Nyerere died. Influenced by Mahatma Gandhi as a youth, he became a pacifist and worked for the Quaker-affiliated American Friends

Service Committee after he graduated from Bates College in Maine. From 1942 to 1945, he was in a federal penitentiary as a war resister.

He first went to Africa in 1953 and settled in Ghana where he worked closely with Kwame Nkrumah. And through the years, he met or worked with many other African leaders including Nyerere, Kaunda, Lumumba, Tom Mboya, Mandela; others in the diaspora such as Frantz Fanon, and Malcolm X whom he interviewed extensively; as well as the leaders of the liberation movements in southern Africa, all of whom were based in Tanzania.

In his book he wrote with Matt Mayer, *Guns and Gandhi in Africa: Pan-African Insights on Nonviolence, Armed Struggle and Liberation in Africa*, Sutherland has a lot to say about Nyerere whom he knew and worked with for more than 30 years. He moved to Tanganyika after he fell out with Nkrumah and left Ghana following his criticism of Nkrumah's increasing dictatorial tendencies and abandonment of nonviolence in the struggle for African liberation.

When he settled in Dar es Salaam, he became involved in politics - as he had always been - and worked in the office of Prime Minister Rashidi Kawawa who became vice president of Tanganyika under Nyerere, and later second vice-president of Tanzania; with the president of Zanzibar, Abeid Karume, serving as first vice-president as stipulated by the constitution of the United Republic of Tanzania.

As with Nkrumah, Bill Sutherland also disagreed with Nyerere on the same subject of non-violence and quotes him in his book. As Nyerere explained his support for armed struggle to liberate southern Africa: "When you win, the morale of the African freedom fighters will go up and the morale of their opponents throughout southern Africa will go down. I said that's what we should do, demonstrate success, which we did." Sutherland also quotes Nyerere as saying that although the struggle for Tanganyika's independence was non-violent, he was not opposed to the use of violence if that was the only way to win freedom.

Therefore his opposition to violence or support of armed struggle was not based on principle but dictated by circumstances. As Nyerere told Sutherland about the non-violent struggle for

Tanganyika's independence: "The nonviolence of our movement was not philosophical at all...My opposition to violence is [to] the unnecessary use of violence."

And Zambian President Dr. Kenneth Kaunda, once a pacifist himself, asked Sutherland and co-author Matt Meyer if they had ever run a country on pacifist principles. As he put it: "Have you tried running a country on the basis of pacifist principles without qualification or modification, or do you know anyone who has?" As Sutherland states in the book, the discussion went well into the night, "but the upshot was that nobody had a clear and definable answer. We were not really able to respond to Kaunda."

I remember talking to Bill Sutherland in Grand Rapids, Michigan, USA, in the summer of 1977 when he spoke about the liberation struggle in southern Africa. He also talked about other African subjects including Idi Amin, saying Amin did what he did in many cases just "for a little bit of publicity," as he put it. He also happened to know well some of the people, including national leaders, I knew in Tanzania.

I was still a student then, in the United States, following closely the events in Africa including the liberation wars in southern Africa. We agreed on almost everything except the armed struggle. I supported it.

But even he as a pacifist was ambivalent about it, especially in the context of southern Africa.

He understood the necessity of armed struggle but, as a pacifist, could not as a matter of principle support the use of violence. I saw it as the only viable option; a concession he grudgingly made in conversations with the freedom fighters in Tanzania and elsewhere, and even with Nyerere and Kaunda, although they also agreed to diasgree.

Yet he also realized that he could not really oppose the use of violence in southern Africa, considering the nature of the situation. Nor could he justify the use of non-violence in a situation where the oppressor did not have the slightest compunction shooting and killing unarmed, defenseless, and innocent men, women and children for no other reason than that they were demanding basic human rights, including the sanctity of life pacifists themselves invoke to justify non-violence.

Yet, he was a dedicated Pan-Africanist who made Tanzania his home, a country which became the most relentless supporter of armed struggle in southern Africa. And he settled in Tanzania because of Julius Nyerere who was already, even back then in the 1950s, becoming increasingly influential in African affairs, especially in the liberation of our continent from colonialism and imperialism.

A number of revolutionary thinkers from Latin America, Europe, and Asia were equally drawn to Tanzania and lived in Dar es Salaam which was the center of ideological ferment and provided an environment conducive to cross-fertilization of ideas stimulated by Nyerere's policies and ideological leadership.

And Tanzania's prominent role in the African liberation struggle and world affairs because of Nyerere's leadership put the country in a unique position on a continent where few governments looked beyond their borders, with most of them content to pursue goals in the narrow context of "national interest," which really meant securing and promoting the interests of the leaders themselves.

Tanzania was therefore an anomaly in that sense, on the continent, as a haven and an incubator for activists and revolutionaries from around the world. And it remained that way as a magnet throughout Nyerere's tenure. It was also his leadership more than anything else, which played a critical role in forging and shaping the identity of our nation and in enabling Tanzania to play an important role on the global scene, far beyond its wealth and size, especially in promoting the interests of Africa and the Third World in general.

The fact that Nyerere himself was chosen as chairman of the South Commission, a forum for action and dialogue between the poor and the rich countries on how to address problems of economic inequalities in a global context, is strong testimony to that. And it was in this crucible of identity, a country that would not be what it is today had it not been for Nyerere that my own personality was shaped.

In some fundamental respects, it is an identity and an ethos like no other on the continent: an indigenous national language, Kiswahili, transcending tribalism and not claimed by any particular ethnic group as its own - all the tribes and racial minorities contributed to its creation and growth, a unique phenomenon; social equality as an egalitarian ideal implemented by Nyerere through the decades; national unity - and stability - that has virtually eliminated tribalism and racism as major problems in national life, and in a country where speaking tribal languages in front of other people who don't understand those languages is frowned upon.

Kiswahili helped Tanzania's 126 different tribes and racial minorities - Arab, Asian, mostly of Indian and Pakistani origin, and European - to develop a sense of national unity and identity which has remained solid through the years regardless of what the country has undergone since independence in 1961. And the egalitarian policies of President Nyerere reduced social inequalities across the nation and guaranteed equal access to health, education, and other services on a scale unequalled anywhere else on the continent.

But probably more than any other asset, it was Nyerere's leadership which proved to be most useful at a time when we needed it most to forge a true sense of national identity, maintain national stability, and consolidate our independence; as much as Mandela's magnanimity and wisdom proved to be an indispensable asset in South Africa's transition from apartheid to democracy at a time when the country could have exploded, engulfing it in a racial conflagration. The pundits and laymen alike who predicted this were proved wrong largely because of Mandela's astute leadership, like Nyerere's.

Therefore it's not surprising that they are the only two African leaders who are favourably compared to each other with equal international and moral stature - hence Nyerere's honorific title, "The Conscience of Africa." There is nobody else in their league.

I remember Nyerere well. Cordially known as Mwalimu, which means Teacher in Kiswahili, he led by example; his humility equalled by his commitment to the well-being of the poorest of the poor, yet without ignoring the rights of others. And he asked all to make sacrifices for our collective well-being. As he put it, "It can be done. Play your part." His dedication and identification with the masses, and his passion for fairness, were evident throughout his tenure as the nation's leader.

When he became president, he worked and lived with them in their villages, slept in their huts, and ate their food. He spent days, and weeks, working with them in the rural areas in all parts of the country. He mingled with the peasants so well that you wouldn't even know who the leader was in the group, let alone be able to identify him as president of a country if you didn't know how he looked like.

I know this because I worked as a news reporter in Tanzania. No other African leader lived the way he did, and worked in the rural areas as much as he did, clearing and tilling the land for hours with ordinary peasants. He was one of them and, they said, "He's one of us." Not a detached, arrogant leader and intellectual who felt it was beneath him to soil his hands like the poor, illiterate peasants did.

I also know how humble he was, because of what I witnessed years before I even became a national news reporter, first at the *Standard*, next at the Ministry of Information and Broadcasting as an information officer, and then at the *Daily News*.

I remember Nyerere when he was campaigning for independence. It was in the late 1950s when I first saw him. He had already been to the United States, and even appeared on American television with Eleanor Roosevelt in 1956 when he was interviewed by Mike Wallace, a prominent American television journalist and interviewer who was still on the air in 2003 and beyond, although in his eighties.

Nyerere went to the United States to present our case for independence at the United Nations where he appeared more than once in the late fifties, and before American audiences including academic gatherings such as the one at Wellesley College in Massachusetts in 1960 where he participated in a symposium and delivered a lecture, "Africa and the World."

I was just a little boy then, under ten, when he came to our home district in the late fifties more than once. I first saw him around 1958. He was about 36 years old. But in spite of my age - I was born on 4 October 1949 - what I saw then remains vivid in my memory as if it happened only yesterday. I was a pupil at Kyimbila Primary School, about two miles from Tukuyu. Founded by the German colonial rulers and named Neu Langenburg, Tukuyu was our district headquarters for Rungwe District. The town was destroyed by earthquakes in 1910 and 1919 but was rebuilt. It had been the district headquarters since the German colonial rulers built it when they first came to the area in the early 1890s.

When the British took over Tanganyika - then known as German East Africa which included Rwanda and Burundi as one colony - after the Germans lost World War I, they continued the tradition and kept the town (whose name was changed from Neu Langenburg to Tukuyu) as the headquarters of Rungwe District headed by a British District Commissioner, simply known as DC, who lived there.

Nyerere came to Tukuyu one afternoon and our head teacher, who also happened to be a relative of mine, led us on a trip from our school to Tukuyu to listen to him. As life was then, and as it still is today across Africa for most people including children, we walked the two miles to Tukuyu to hear him speak; a man who, we were told, was our leader and who was going to be president of Tanganyika in only about three years, replacing the British governor.

I was then too young to understand the complexities of politics and political campaigning all of which to us at that age seemed to be expressed in esoteric terms. Yet we were old enough to understand what Nyerere was saying in general; a message delivered in his usual simple style everybody, including children my age, was able to understand. And he knew there were children at the rally. He saw us.

He arrived in an open Land Rover, standing in the back, waving at the crowd. The people were just as jubilant. He stepped out of the Land Rover and walked to the football (soccer) field to address the mass rally. He wore a simple short-sleeved light-green shirt and a pair of long trousers (pants), and started speaking, using a megaphone.

It was a cloudy afternoon and, after he spoke for only a few minutes, it started raining. The leading local politician of the Tanganyika African National Union (TANU), Mr. Mwambenja, a formidable personality and relentless campaigner for independence, who welcomed Nyerere at the rally tried to hold an umbrella over him. But he refused to accept it and continued to speak.

He even joked about himself implying that he was a non-entity, an insignificant personality, and said something to the effect that the colonialists and other detractors were now, with all that rain saying, "Just let him get soaked and washed away." The subtle message in this self-deprecating humor was that he was not going to fade into oblivion and give up the struggle for independence. And it kept on raining. But the rain did not dampen his spirits.

We also stayed as almost everybody else did, impressed by his humility and simplicity despite his status as the most prominent and acknowledged leader of Tanganyika, besides the British governor Sir Edward Twining who was later succeeded by Sir Richard Turnbull, the last governor. He got soaked in the rain just like the rest of us and continued to speak until he finished addressing the rally.

It was such humility, devotion and simplicity, which remained the hallmark of his life and leadership. And it was evident even among some members of his family. I attended school with his eldest son, Andrew, at Tambaza High School, the former H.H. The Aga Khan High School which had been exclusively for students of Asian origin, mostly Indian and Pakistani, almost all of whom were Tanzanians. There were also some Arab students.

And there were only a few of us, black students. We were among the first to integrate the school as mandated by the government under Nyerere. In fact, Mwalimu himself had experienced racial discrimination, what we in East Africa - and elsewhere including southern Africa - also call color bar. As Colin Legum states in a book he edited with Tanzanian Professor Geoffrey Mmari, *Mwalimu: The Influence of Nyerere:*

> I was privileged to meet Nyerere while he was still a young teacher in short trousers at the very beginning of his political career, and to engage in private conversations with him since the early 1950s.
> My very first encounter in 1953 taught me something about his calm authority in the face of racism in colonial Tanganyika.
> I had arranged a meeting with four leaders of the nascent nationalist movement at the Old Africa Hotel in Dar es Salaam. We sat at a table on the pavement and ordered five beers, but before we could lift our glasses an African waiter rushed up and whipped away all the glasses except mine.
> I rose to protest to the white manager, but Nyerere restrained me. 'I am glad it happened,' he said, 'now you can go and tell your friend Sir Edward Twining [the governor at the time] how things are in this country.' His manner was light and amusing, with no hint of anger.[14]

Simple, yet profound. For, beneath the surface lay a steely character with a deep passion for justice across the color line and an uncompromising commitment to the egalitarian ideals he espoused and implemented throughout his political career, favouring none.

Years later his son, Andrew Nyerere, told me about an incident that also took place in the capital Dar es Salaam shortly after Tanganyika won independence.

Like the incident earlier when Julius Nyerere was humiliated at the Old Africa Hotel back in 1953, this one also involved race. As Andrew said in a letter to me in 2003 when I was writing this book: "As you remember, Sheikh Amri Abeid was the first mayor of Dar es Salaam. Soon after independence, the mayor went to Palm Beach Hotel (near our high school, Tambaza, in Upanga). There was a sign at the hotel which clearly stated: 'No Africans and dogs allowed inside.' He was blocked from entering the hotel, and said in protest, 'But I am the Mayor.' Still he was told, 'You will not get in.' Shortly thereafter, the owner of the hotel was given 48 hours to leave the country. When the nationalization exercise began, that hotel was the first to be nationalized."

Such insults were the last thing that could be tolerated in newly independent Tanganyika. And President Nyerere, probably more than any other African leader, would not have tolerated, and did not tolerate, seeing even the humblest of peasants being insulted and humiliated by anyone including fellow countrymen. And his passion for equality was legendary. For example, he sent his son Andrew to a local school - with the sons of peasants and workers - when he could have sent him abroad, as was customary among most leaders across the continent. They either sent their children to exclusively private and expensive schools within their own countries, or flew them overseas, and still do.

All this was in keeping with his commitment to social equality for all Tanzanians. He said we are not going to build a society based on privilege; we are going to narrow the gap between the haves and the have-nots, and abolish classes which accentuate cleavages and define some human beings as better than others. At our high school, many people knew that President Nyerere's eldest son was one of the students. Yet he got no special favours.

He was treated just like the rest of us, and we saw him as just another student like us.

And he saw himself that way, and acted that way. You wouldn't even know he was the president's son because of the way he behaved and carried himself, just as an ordinary student, and the way the rest of us treated him. We lived in the same hostel, most of whose students were Tanzanians of Asian origin; ate the same food at the same table, and worked on the farm together, tilling the land, as true sons of a nation of peasants and workers.

Our school in Dar es Salaam had a farm near Muhimbili National Hospital where we were required to work to instill egalitarian values in our minds. We walked to the farm, about two miles round trip, carrying hoes and sickles and other agricultural implements; a strong reminder that we were no better than ordinary peasants and workers simply because we had acquired some education and were destined to become part of the nation's elite.

And Nyerere's son also walked around the city with fellow students and other friends, just like the rest of us, when many people would probably have expected him as the president's son to ride in a Mercedes Benz. But that was not the kind of society based on class and privilege President Nyerere was trying to build. And to his son's credit, he was just as humble and friendly with everybody.

Mwalimu Nyerere did not even force his children to toe the party line. One of his sons, Charles Makongoro - different from another Makongoro who attended school with us at Tambaza and who was sometimes mistaken for President Nyerere's son - left the ruling party founded by his father and, with the blessings of his family, joined what then was the country's leading opposition party on Tanzania mainland; the Civic United Front (CUF) was the main opposition party in Zanzibar, not on the mainland, as it still is today.

In 1995, Charles Makongoro Nyerere was elected as one of the few opposition members of parliament, but lost his seat following a court ruling before his five-year term expired. He then rejoined the ruling party. He returned to parliament in February 2004 after President Benjamin Mkapa appointed him a member;

one of the 10 members the president is empowered to appoint to the national legislature at his discretion as stipulated by the constitution of the United Republic of Tanzania.

Our school was also fully integrated. We lived in the same hostel with Asian and Arab students. We also had African, Asian and European teachers, most of them Tanzanian citizens. Other schools across Tanzania were also fully integrated - student and faculty. At our school, students came from all parts of the country and from many different tribes. We were not encouraged to attend school - except at the primary school level - in our home districts, which were usually inhabited by members of our own tribes. We were, in fact, assigned to schools and jobs after graduation far away from our tribal homelands in order to live and work with members of other tribes.

It was a deliberate effort by the government to break down barriers between members of different tribes and races in order to achieve national unity. And it worked. This was probably Nyerere's biggest achievement - the creation of a cohesive political entity unique on a continent rife with ethnic tensions and torn by conflict caused and fueled by ethno-regional rivalries in the struggle for power and for the nation's resources. Our schools were a microcosm of what Tanzania became: a united, integrated, peaceful and stable nation.

It was also when I was in high school at Tambaza that I first got hired in June 1969 as a reporter by the *Standard*, which became the *Daily News* the following year. I started working full-time in 1971 after I finished high school (Form VI or standard 14) the previous year. Our managing editor was Brendon Grimshaw, a British, and the news and deputy editor was David Martin, also British, who also worked for the London *Observer* for many years after he left Tanzania. David Martin also worked for the BBC and even covered the Angolan civil war. I remember listening to him in a live report from Angola on the CBC (Canadian Broadcasting Corporation, Toronto) radio when I lived in Detroit, Michigan, USA, in the seventies.

President Nyerere was our editor-in-chief. But he never served in an executive capacity at the *Daily News*. As an overall guardian of this publicly owned institution - the paper, the *Standard*, was renamed *Daily News* in 1970 when it was nationalized - he gave us the freedom to say what we wanted to say and even encouraged us to criticize the government and its policies. And he meant what he said.

We wrote what we wanted to write without any fear of retribution or censorship. Others also testify to that. As Philip Ochieng', probably Kenya's best known journalist and political commentator who was attracted to Tanzania by Nyerere's leadership and policies and joined our editorial staff at the *Daily News*, stated in a tribute to Mwalimu, "There Was Real Freedom in Mwalimu's Day," in *The East African*:

> I never really covered Mwalimu Nyerere. By the time I got to Tanzania to work for *The Standard Tanzania*, I had been an editorial pontiff in Nairobi's *Sunday Nation* for upwards of two years. And that was what I continued to do in Dar-es-Salaam....
>
> Working for the president, between September 1970 and January 1973, was probably the most enjoyable period of my entire journalistic career. There were at least two reasons for this. The first was that ours was a community of ideas. The second, contrary to what was constantly claimed here in Nairobi and by the Western press, was that the Dar-es-Salaam newspapers enjoyed a high level of freedom to publish. This reflected the fact that Tanzania enjoyed an unprecedented freedom of speech. But it was never licentious freedom of the kind with which Nairobi's alternative press assails our eyes every morning.
>
> Following the Arusha Declaration of 1967, Julius Kambarage Nyerere had, early in 1970, nationalised *The Tanganyika Standard* from Lonhro and rechristened it *The Standard Tanzania* (sic) as the official print organ of the government. *The Nationalist* and its Kiswahili sister *Uhuru* already existed as the organs of the ruling Tanganyika African National Union (TANU), with Ben Mkapa as its editor. Brought in from London as Managing Editor of *The Standard* was a tough-talking South African woman of Asian origin called Frene Ginwala. Ginwala, who is now the Speaker of the South African Parliament in Cape Town, was a woman of strong left-wing convictions. She very soon collected around men and women from the international community with equally strong socialist views.
>
> This was the context in which I left Nairobi for Dar-es-Salaam, invited by Ginwala. Mwalimu Nyerere acted as our - non-executive - Editor-in-Chief. And yet every Friday I published an opinion column highly critical of his system.
>
> I waxed critical especially of the recent nationalised commercial and industrial houses: the corruption that was beginning to invade them and their umbrella organisations, the ineptitude, the apparent absence of development ideas. Yet never once did Ginwala or myself receive a telephone call from or a summons to Ikulu - State House - complaining about anything we had written. Of course, there were many murmurs in the corridors of power against us. They accused us of being a bunch of communists, though we never were. But they

dared not call a press conference to attack us. Nyerere simply would not have allowed them to do so....

Kambarage Nyerere remained one of Africa's quintessential men of the 20th century. His personal probity was unequalled...(as was) his refusal to use his immense power to enrich himself or his family.

It was his intellectual strength and moral fiber that enabled him, when he saw that his (socialist) experiment could not succeed, to admit openly that his life career had been a failure. When he nationalised *The Tanganyika Standard*, he gave us a charter, which expressly challenged its news editors to criticise all social failings by whomever they are committed. I had never been and would never be freer than when I worked in Dar.... This freedom of the press...was only a mirror-reflection of the much more important freedom of ideas throughout the country. Though Nyerere believed more than 100 per cent in Ujamaa, he never tried to force it down anybody's throat. Nor did he ever issue *The Standard*, *The Nationalist* or the latter's Swahili daily and weekly counterparts *Uhuru* and *Mzalendo*, with any instruction to print only Nyerereist ideas or to slant news in favour of that ideology and its exponents.

If that had been the case, Tanzania's amazing pluralism of ideas at that time would not have reached the world. Yet it did reach the world, attracting into that country hundreds of intellectuals from all over the world. The University of Dar-es-Salaam at Ubungo was Africa's, perhaps the world's, intellectual Mecca. Dar-es-Salaam harboured all the radical liberation movements in Africa, Latin America, the Middle East, Ireland, South-East Asia, even the United States. It was a crossroads of such celebrated freedom fighters as Agostinho Neto, Samora Machel, Marcelino dos Santos, Jorge Rebello, Janet Mondlane, Yoweri Museveni, Sam Nujoma, Thabo Mbeki, Oliver Tambo, Gora Ebrahim, Amilcar Cabral, Angela Davis and others, changing ideas with us, often hotly.... There were intellectuals - both native and alien - who expressed ideas so far to the right that they bordered on fascism. Others expressed ideas so far to the left that again they bordered on fascism.... For these were not uniform minds.... The humdinger, however, was that all these ideas were expressed freely and printed in the party and government newspapers with little attempt at editorial slanting and chicanery....

Until his death, Nyerere, who was humble, self-effacing and selfless, continued to serve humanity on many capacities - particularly his promotion of mutual South-South assistance to reduce dependence on Western alms and his attempt to bring about order in Burundi.

An intellectual of immense stature, a man of great personal integrity, a paragon of humanism, Julius Kambarage Nyerere will be hard to replace in Tanzania, in Africa and on the globe. I was privileged to know and work with such a man. That is why, as I mourn, I ask, with Marcus Antonius, whence cometh such another?[15]

Members of the entire editorial staff were fully aware of the kind of freedom we had to criticize the government, although we worked for a government-owned newspaper. But the government owned it on behalf of the people, *wananchi*. Therefore we were free to criticize leaders and policies and express our views across the spectrum without being censored. President Nyerere established that as a policy.

Our editors, first Sammy Mdee who later became President Nyerere's press secretary, and next Ben Mkapa who was elected president of Tanzania in 1995 and won a second five year-term in 2000, did not violate this policy which was adopted after the newspaper was nationalized. They sometimes even invited reporters to write or contribute to editorials. Self-criticism was also routine. Every morning before we went out on assignments, we had a post-mortem of the paper presided over by the editor, dissecting the stories we wrote the previous day.

Such was the camaraderie, the ambience and egalitarian disposition, and freedom, we enjoyed at our newspaper; the largest English daily in Tanzania and one of the three largest and most influential in East Africa.

Although we were independent and wrote whatever we wanted to write, we were also at the center of a maelstrom because of the ideological ferment that the country was undergoing during that period in its quest for socialist transformation in pursuit of the egalitarian ideals of *Ujamaa* (which means familyhood in Kiswahili) espoused by Nyerere: a political theorist and philosopher, scholar and politician, without an equal on the continent in terms of intellectual depth and prowess and pursuits among leaders with the exception of President Leopold Sedar Senghor of Senegal, a poet-philosopher - "I feel, therefore I am," he mused, reminiscent of Rene Descartes, "I think, therefore I am"; and Dr. Kwame Nkrumah, president of Ghana and revolutionary thinker and theoretician.

But Nkrumah was overthrown in February 1966 in a CIA-engineered coup before Nyerere enunciated his socialist ideology in the Arusha Declaration almost exactly one year later in February 1967 after the Ghana coup. So, with Nkrumah gone - he died in April 1972, six years after he was overthrown - only Nyerere and Senghor remained on the scene as the leading political thinkers among leaders on the continent.

I remember when Nkrumah died. I was at work on that day at the *Daily News* when the bulletin about his death came in on the telex in the evening in our editorial office. One of the first persons to express profound shock was Karim Essack, about whom more later, but Dr. Nkrumah's death equally affected the rest of us who read the news bulletin that evening. The other reporters were gone by then.

Although Nkrumah's death left on the scene two towering intellectual presidents, Nyerere and Senghor, it was Nyerere who was the far more influential between the two on the continent and in the international arena. Senghor was also seen as a white man in a black skin. But his unabashed Francophilia did not diminish his stature as an intellectual, especially among his admirers, and even among some of his critics who saw him as a black Frenchman who should have been born white and brought up in France.

In 1980, he stepped down as president of Senegal and went to live in France where he died in December 2001 at the age of 95.

He was one African leader - and there were many others - who was not admired by many reporters on our editorial staff, anymore than Dr. Hastings Kamuzu Banda, the president of Malawi, was. I didn't know any on our staff who admired Banda.

Our newspaper, like the country itself, attracted not only reporters and revolutionary thinkers from different parts of Africa and beyond but also reporters of different ideological interests within Tanzania itself. There was, for instance, Karim Essack - a Tanzanian of Asian (Indian) origin - who was a leftist revolutionary and, like the rest of us on our editorial staff who were not leftist although some were, also an uncompromising foe of apartheid and other oppressive regimes. He also wrote a book about Dr. Eduardo Mondlane and the liberation struggle in Mozambique and maintained, until his death in 1997, close ties with revolutionaries and radical thinkers around the world including many in Latin America. As the socialist-oriented International Emergency Committee (IEC) - founded to defend the life of Dr. Abimael Guzman, a Peruvian Marxist philosophy professor and leader of the revolutionary group Shining Path, captured and imprisoned in Peru in 1992 - stated in October 1997 in its eulogy, "In Memory of Karim Essack":

> The IEC coordinating committee was saddened to learn that Karim Essack died this summer. He was a Tanzanian anti-imperialist who, for several

decades, actively supported national liberation movements across the world. Karim Essack was a friend of the Peruvian people and a supporter of the People's War in Peru who dedicated some of his writings to Dr. Guzman and other PCP fighters. He was a signatory to the IEC Call and helped propagate the campaign in Africa. He will be missed.[16]

Karim Essack was just one of the reporters of Asian descent on our staff, which was fully integrated: black African being in the majority; Asian, mostly of Indian and Pakistani origin; Arab; and British. This also reflected Nyerere's ideals. As Tanzania's president and editor-in-chief of our newspaper, he would not have tolerated an editorial team that was exclusivist and intentionally did not reflect the racial and ethnic composition of our society - although, for practical purposes, not every tribe could have been represented on our staff or any anywhere else in the country.

But the bedrock principle on which our society was built under Nyerere was that no one should be discriminated against. And he meant what he said. Few countries in the world can match Tanzania's record of inclusion. And it is not uncommon to hear people from other countries who have lived in Tanzania say, "There is no racism and tribalism in Tanzania"; "Tanzania is the only country in Africa that has conquered tribalism," as Keith Richburg says in his book *Out of America: A Black Man Confronts Africa*;[17] "There is very little tribalism - and racism - in Tanzania"; "Tribalism and racism are not major problems in Tanzania." The last statement is closest to reality.

And in keeping with Tanzania's policy of welcoming refugees and promoting Pan-African solidarity as enunciated by Nyerere, members of our editorial staff from other African countries were not only guaranteed equal rights and accorded full protection like the rest of us, but also career advancement like everywhere else in Tanzania. So were other non-citizens from outside Africa.

In fact, in the 1970 general elections, people from other African countries who were not citizens of Tanzania were allowed to vote. President Nyerere allowed that as one of the ways of promoting African unity. And it is possible some of them even voted against him. But his gesture of goodwill was highly appreciated and resonated far beyond our national borders.

At our newspaper, some of the foreign reporters who held responsible positions included Tommy Sithole, sports editor, who returned to Zimbabwe and became managing editor of the state-owned *Zimbabwe Herald* after his country won independence under the leadership of Robert Mugabe, himself of scholarly bent like Nyerere, although not of the same intellectual stature and influence as a Pan-African leader.

There was also Philip Ochieng', a Kenyan, who wrote a weekly column, "The Way I See It." He also served as a sub-editor, one among several, including Felix Kaiza, Pascal Shija, Robert Rweyemamu, Uli Mwambulukutu, Abdallah Ngororo, Kassim Mpenda, Jenerali Ulimwengu, Emmanuel Bulugu, and a few others. The news editor was Nsubisi Mwakipunda. Two senior reporters, Reginald Mhango - originally from Malawi - who later in 2002 became managing editor of the *Guardian*, one of Tanzania's leading daily newspapers, and Kusai Khamisa, also served as acting news editors in Mwakipunda's absence. All these were Tanzanians.

Philip Ochieng' eventually went back to Kenya - after further studies in Germany - and served as editor of the government-owned *Kenya Times* before returning to the *Daily Nation*, Nairobi, where he worked before he joined our editorial staff at the *Standard*, later *Daily News*, in Dar es Salaam. He also wrote a book, *I Accuse the Press: An Insider's View of the Media and Politics in Africa*.[18]

We also had sub-editors from South Africa, Nigeria, and Britain. The Nigerian sub-editor came from Biafra and fled his country during the civil war and was one of the many Eastern Nigerians, mostly Igbos, who sought asylum in Tanzania after the Eastern Region seceded from the Nigerian Federation. They included judges and professors, many other professionals and others who came to live in Tanzania during that critical period. And many remained in Tanzania after the war.

It was Nyerere who extended such hospitality to them after Tanzania became the first country to recognize Biafra. And in Dar es Salaam even today, there is a place called Biafra Grounds where mass rallies are held. There are also many Nigerian doctors and other professionals in Tanzania.

They would not have been able to live and work in Tanzania in such large numbers had it not been for Tanzania's track record of hospitality initiated by Nyerere way back in the sixties soon after

Tanganyika won independence from Britain on December 9, 1961. And as Dr. M.O. Ene, chairman of the Enyimba Pan-Igbo Think Tank, said about Nyerere when he died: "I saw the legend in 1966, and the memory still lives with me."

His Pan-African commitment and achievements were internationally acknowledged, despite his failed socialist policies. As Professor Harvey Glickman who made a study tour of Tanzania stated in his article, "Tanzania: From Disillusionment to Guarded Optimism," in *Current History: A Journal of Contemporary World Affairs*:

> Tanzania's profile, in the life and career of President Julius Nyerere, was poor, earnest, caring, and honest - at least until 1985, when Nyerere formally stepped aside in a peaceful constitutional transition (which is extremely rare in Africa). Tanzania's government was stable while other African governments succumbed to coups and civil wars.
>
> The country conducted consecutive national elections at regular five-year intervals. Other one-party states ignored mass participation; Nyerere's Tanzania devised a system of constituency primaries under the party umbrella, controlled at the center, but offering a voice for localism.
>
> Other African governments extolled the virtues of Pan-Africanism; Nyerere engineered the union of his own country and an offshore neighbour. Other African governments denounced white racist governments on the continent; Tanzania took action, cutting off relations with Britain over the issue of African rule in Rhodesia in 1965 (the first country to do so), and offering shelter to the liberation parties and guerrilla forces of southern Africa.
>
> While most African governments rejected the secession of Biafra from Nigeria in 1967, Tanzania recognized Biafra's short-lived government on moral grounds (and was the first to recognize the secessionist region), arguing it was an act of self-defence against ethnic pogroms. While other African countries merely denounced Idi Amin in Uganda in the 1970s, Tanzania's army defeated him in battle in 1979 and drove him from the country.[19]

And Nyerere's policy of good neighbourliness and Pan-African solidarity was also clearly evident at our newspaper which had an exchange programme with neighbouring Zambia and whose president, Dr. Kenneth Kaunda, was Nyerere's ideological compatriot and very close personal friend. A reporter from the *Times of Zambia*, Francis Kasoma, joined our editorial staff while our news editor Nsubisi Mwakipunda went to Zambia to work at the *Times*. Kasoma covered some of the most important political events in the country just as we did. It didn't matter he and a number of other reporters were not Tanzanians.

After working at the *Daily News* for quite some time, Kasoma – now dead - returned to Zambia and years later became a professor and head of the mass communications department at the University of Zambia. He also wrote some books including *The Press and Multiparty Politics in Africa.*[20]

Another member of our editorial staff who also wrote a book was deputy editor Hadji Konde, deceased, who was one of the most renowned Tanzanian journalists with vast experience in the profession. He wrote *Press Freedom in Tanzania.*[21] His work was preceded only by Karim Essack's among those written by newsmen who worked at the *Daily News*, Dar es Salaam, Tanzania.

Another reporter on our editorial staff, Clement Ndulute, also became an author with the publication of his book, *The Poetry of Shaaban Robert,*[22] published in 1994 by the Dar es Salaam University Press. It is a translation of the works of Tanzania's eminent poet from Kiswahili into English. Ndulute went on to pursue further studies at the University of Indiana in the United States where he obtained his PhD in literature. He returned to Tanzania and became a lecturer in literature at the University of Dar es Salaam, Tanzania.

He returned to the United States and became an associate professor of African literature at Mississippi Valley State University and later at Tuskegee University in Alabama.

Another member of our editorial staff who became a professor is Issa Kaboko Musoke. He attended Michigan State University in the United States during the seventies when I was also a student in the same state. He returned to Tanzania and joined the academic staff at the University of Dar es Salaam teaching sociology. He also taught in Botswana for some time.

Yet another reporter from the *Daily News* who also attended school in Michigan around the same time I did, was Deogratias Michael Masakilija. Both of us were sponsored by the Pan-African Congress-USA, an organization based in Detroit and founded by a group of African-Americans in that city to strengthen ties between Black America and Africa and promote African unity.

Their Pan-African philosophy was based on the teachings of Kwame Nkrumah and Julius Nyerere who were the ideological mentors of the organization. They even had the pictures of the two leaders on the wall in their conference hall, together with those of Ahmed Sekou Toure, Malcolm X and Patrice Lumumba. These were the five leaders they admired the most and whose writings they studied for ideological guidance and inspiration.

Tanzania's national dress, the dark suit with a collar-less jacket worn by President Nyerere and other Tanzanian leaders, was the official attire of the male members of the organization. Many Pan-African Congress members also took lessons in Kiswahili which they regarded as a Pan-African language.

Some of the members of the organization went to live or work in Tanzania, while others simply visited the country, one of their favourites, together with Ghana. And a number of others attended the Sixth Pan-African Congress under the stewardship of President Julius Nyerere held at the University of Dar es Salaam in Nkrumah Hall in 1974.

It was the first one held on African soil. The last one, the Fifth Pan-African Congress, was held in Manchester, England, in 1945, and was attended by a number of future African leaders including Kwame Nkrumah, Jomo Kenyatta, Nnamdi Azikiwe, and Dr. Hastings Kamuzu Banda. It galvanized the African independence movement.

Dr. Banda's residence in England became a meeting place for African nationalists including Nkrumah whom Dr. Banda cordially called, "My boy." And Nkrumah and others called Banda "Doc."

After Ghana won independence and Nkrumah became president, Banda went to live and work in Ghana before returning to Nyasaland.

Other students who were sponsored or supported by the Pan-African Congress-USA and attended Wayne State University in Detroit during the same time I did were Kojo Yankah from Ghana who became a member of parliament and cabinet member under President Jerry Rawlings in the 1990s; Amadou Taal and Mamadou Sohna, both from the Gambia.

When Amadou Taal returned to the Gambia, he became a high government official and the country's leading economist appointed by President Dawda Jawara, Gambia's first president. He held the following posts consecutively: Principal Planner in the Ministry of Economic Planning and Industrial Development; Permanent Secretary in the Ministry of Agriculture, and Permanent Secretary in the Ministry of Local Government and Lands. Coincidentally, one of his closest friends, Hassan Jallow who got his law degree from the University of Dar es Salaam in Tanzania in the early seventies, became Gambia's attorney-general and later minister of justice under President Jawara. In 2003, Jallow was appointed by UN Secretary-General Kofi Anan and by the Security Council as the UN chief prosector of the International Criminal Tribunal for Rwanda (ICTR) based in Arusha, Tanzania.

And throughout his tenure, Amadou Taal represented the Gambia at international conferences in many countries including Tanzania. He served until Jawara was overthrown in a military coup in July 1994. He was not sponsored by the Pan-African Congress-USA but was supported by the organization, as was Mamadou Sohna who later became a professor at a university in Virginia in the United States.

Another student who was sponsored by the Pan-African Congress-USA but did not attend Wayne State University and entered public life when he returned home was Kwabena Dompre from Ghana. He was the third student to be sponsored by the organization after Kojo Yankah; and Olu Williams from Sierra Leone who attended the University of Nebraska and obtained a doctorate in agricultural economics. Kwabena went to Western Michigan University. After he returned to Ghana, he entered politics and worked as a high ranking official for President Hilla Limann. He later became a lawyer in Ghana and in the United States.

We all lived in the same house owned by the Pan-African Congress-USA which was also a meeting place for Pan-African Congress members, a number of African students and others including members of the Republic of New Afrika, engaged in lively conversations about the liberation struggle in southern Africa, African politics in general, the civil rights struggle in the United States and other subjects. It was an environment highly conducive to cross-fertilization of ideas across the spectrum, and it left a lasting impression on me and others.

My other schoolmates at Wayne State University who went

into public life, but who were not sponsored by the Pan-African Congress-USA, included Raphael Munavu who became a professor at Nairobi University and then vice-chancellor of Moi University after he returned to Kenya. Although an academic, his position as vice-chancellor of one of Kenya's universities made him a leading educational authority and a public figure.

Another graduate of Wayne State University who was in a similar position but who went to school there long before I did was Dr. Philemon Msuya from Tanzania, assistant dean of Muhimbili Medical School in Dar es salaam headed by Dr. Nhonoli when I was a reporter at the *Daily News*. I once interviewed him and wrote a feature article about our country's medical school in our newspaper; that's how I learned that he was a graduate of Wayne State University Medical School, the largest in the United States.

My interview with Dr. Msuya had to do with high-level manpower and how we would meet our country's needs in the medical field. The projections by the Tanzanian government that we would have enough doctors by 1985 did not correspond to reality; a point I underscored in my article. Wayne State University also had ties to Tanzania in other ways. Tanzania's junior minister of health and - together with Bibi Titi Mohammed - one of the first two female cabinet members in Tanganyika soon after independence, Lucy Lameck, also attended Wayne State University.

And there were two professors from Tanzania, Mark Kiluma and Mayowera, who taught Kiswahili at Wayne State University when I was a student there in the seventies. And the head of the linguistics department, Professor Sorensen, lived in Tanzania - what was then Tanganyika - for 25 years, and first went there before I was born. He was, all those years, a Catholic priest in Morogoro where I also lived when I was under five years old.

Besides the two Tanzanians teaching Kiswahili, other African professors at Wayne State University included Mxolisi Ntlabati from South Africa. An associate of Nelson Mandela and others who ended up in the dock in the Rivonia Trial, he would have been one of them had he not fled the country via Tanganyika and gone to the United States for further studies.

Tragically, he was killed in 1979 by the same apartheid regime he fled from, after he left Detroit, Michigan, and returned to South Africa and was banished to a remote part of Ciskei, one of the homelands, where the only job he could find was teaching at a secondary school and which severely limited his career opportunities in a deliberate effort by the white racist government to destroy him. He died at the hands of the authorities.

A strong admirer of President Julius Nyerere and his policies, he named one of his children Ujamaa in honour of Mwalimu Nyerere for his Pan-African solidarity and commitment to the liberation struggle. Dr. Ntlabati also served as pastor of the People's Community Church, one of the largest black churches in Detroit which was only a few yards away from the Pan-African Congress house where we lived. The church also sponsored one student from Ghana who lived in the church building, with all his tuition and living expenses paid by the church members.

Another fellow African student at Wayne State University, Emmanuel Sendezera from Malawi, also ended up in South Africa as a physics professor at Witwatersrand University and at another university in Kwazulu/Natal Province. He and John Muhanji from Kenya were the only two black PhD students in physics at Wayne State University in the seventies. They were also among the few students from East Africa on campus besides me, a few Kenyans, Ethiopians, and one Ugandan nun. And like Raphael Munavu, John Muhanji also returned to Kenya.

Wayne State University also had students from many other African countries. And our organization on campus, the Organization of African Students (OAS) of which I was president, had a monthly publication called *Ngurumo*, which was also the name of a Swahili newspaper in Tanzania. The students, most of whom came from West Africa, chose the name because they were attracted by its literal meaning, Thunder. And probably just as many said they liked the name because it reminded them of Nkrumah, an embodiment of Pan-Africanism, which our organization also embraced as a unifying ideology.

My association with this publication was the last I would have as a journalist. After I left Wayne State University, my life veered in another direction in terms of academic pursuits and career advancement. Years later, I ended up writing books, mostly academic works.

While Musoke and I never returned to journalism after finishing our studies in Michigan, Masakilija did. After he returned to Tanzania, he not only continued to work as a journalist but went on to pursue other interests as well in the private sector. And one of our colleagues on the editorial staff at the *Daily News*, Abdallah Ngororo, who joined the government and became permanent secretary - head of the ministry's civil service - at different ministries under President Benjamin Mkapa, our former editor, died in 2002.

And I came up way down the road as an author with my first book published in 1999, 27 years after I left the *Daily News*. And unlike the works of my colleagues all of which dealt with the press, except Ndulute's about poetry, mine was about economics, entitled, *Economic Development in Africa*,[23] which also came to be used as a college textbook mainly for graduate (post-graduate) studies in colleges and universities in the United States, Canada, Britain, Australia, South Africa and other countries, as have a number of other books I have written including *The Modern African State: Quest for Transformation*,[24] and *Africa and the West*.[25]

Although they are mostly found in university libraries around the world, and in a number of public libraries, they are also intended for members of the general public. I never intended to write them exclusively for the academic community. And I have taken the same approach in writing this book.

In *Economic Development in Africa*, I do acknowledge that our socialist policies failed, as President Nyerere himself admitted when he stepped down in November 1985 as much as he did on other occasions in the following years. But I also do know that Nyerere's economic policies were *not* - total failure. We had significant achievements in a number of areas. As I state on Amazon.com in my review of a book by George Ayittey, A Ghanaian professor of economics at The American University, *Africa in Chaos*:

> Ayittey has written an excellent book. In fact, I'm just as critical of Africa's despotic and kleptocratic regimes in all the books I have written. But I don't entirely agree with his assessment of Kwame Nkrumah, Julius Nyerere, and Kenneth Kaunda.
>
> He says his focus is not on the leadership qualities of any of the African

leaders but on their policies. It is true that socialism failed to fuel economic growth. But an objective evaluation of what Nkrumah, Nyerere, and Kaunda did, shows that they had some success in a number of areas. Yet, Ayittey has almost nothing good to say about them in his book, *Africa in Chaos*. In fact, these are the three leaders of whom he's most critical in his book, devoting several pages to them more than any other African leader.

Under Nkrumah, Ghana had the highest per capita income in sub-Saharan Africa. It was Nkrumah who laid the foundation for modern-day Ghana. He built the infrastructure that has sustained and fuelled Ghana's economic development through the years. It is true that there were also many failures under Nkrumah, and after he was gone; for example, institutional decay and crumbling infrastructure. But who built those institutions and the infrastructure?

Nkrumah built schools, hospitals, roads, factories, dams and bridges, railways and harbours. Tens of thousands of people in Ghana who are lawyers, doctors, engineers, nurses, teachers, accountants, agriculturalists, scientists and others wouldn't be what they are today had it not been for the educational opportunities provided by Nkrumah.

Ayittey talks about quality, saying that what mattered during Nkrumah's reign was quantity, not quality. What's the quality of the Ghanaian elite, including Ayittey himself, educated under Nkrumah? Are they not as good as anybody else? What was the quality of education at the University of Ghana, Legon? Did it admit and train students of mediocre mental calibre? Did it have inferior academic programmes? And an inferior faculty? Were more people dying in Ghanaian hospitals than they were being saved? Did the schools, hospitals, factories, roads and other infrastructure Nkrumah built do more harm than good? Would Ghana have been better off without them like Zaire under Mobutu?

In Tanzania, Nyerere also built schools, hospitals, clinics, factories, roads and railways, dams and bridges, hydroelectric power plants and other infrastructure. Although his policy of Ujamaa (meaning familyhood in Kiswahili) was not very successful, it did enable the country to bring the people together and closer to each other in order to provide them with vital social services. The people had easier access to schools, clinics, clean water and other services provided by the government, than they otherwise would have been, because they lived closer to each other; which would have been impossible had they been spread too thin across the country, living miles and miles apart.

Also under Nyerere, education was free, from primary school all the way to the university level. Medical services were also free, in spite of the fact that Tanzania is one of the poorest countries in the world. Still, under Nyerere, it was able to afford all that. Everybody had equal opportunity. Under his leadership, Tanzania also made quantum leaps in education. It had the highest literacy rate in Africa, and one of the highest in the world, higher than India's, which has one of the largest numbers of educated people and the third largest number of scientists after the United States and the former Soviet Union.

One of the biggest achievements under Nyerere was in the area of adult education. Tanzania, on a scale unprecedented anywhere else in the world, launched a massive adult education campaign to teach millions of people how to read and write. Within only a few years, almost the entire adult population of Tanzania - rural peasants, urban workers and others - became literate. Almost everybody in Tanzania, besides children not yet in school, was able to read and write. And the University of Dar es Salaam in Tanzania became one of the most renowned academic institutions in the world, in less than ten years, with an outstanding faculty including some of the best and internationally acclaimed scholars from many countries.

Provision of vital services even to some of the most remote parts of the country - far removed from urban and social centers - was not uncommon although the services were, I must admit, curtailed through the years because of economic problems. Yet, all that was achieved under Nyerere who sincerely believed, and made sure, that everybody had equal access to the nation's resources. I know all this because I am a Tanzanian myself, born and brought up in Tanzania, and was one of the beneficiaries of Nyerere's egalitarian policies.

Tanzania has come a long way, and still has a long way to go. But give credit where credit is due, in spite of failures in a number of areas, and which must be acknowledged by all of us. I even admit that in my books. But also look at where we were before: At independence in 1961, Tanganyika (before uniting with Zanzibar in 1964 to form Tanzania) had only 120 university graduates, including two lawyers who had to draft and negotiate more than 150 international treaties for the young nation and handle other legal matters for the country. With 120 university graduates, Tanganyika was, of course, better off than the former Belgian Congo which had only 16 at independence in 1960, and Nyasaland (now Malawi) with only 34 at independence in 1964. Still, that was nowhere close to what Tanganyika would have been had the British tried to develop the colony; which was never their intention. None of the 120 university graduates got their degrees in Tanganyika. There was no university in the country. The British never built one, and never intended to build one. Tanganyika built one after independence, and it became internationally renowned as an excellent academic institution in less than a decade.

The 120 university graduates Tanganyika had at independence was nothing in terms of manpower for a country; not even for a province or region. As Julius Nyerere said not long before he died:

'We took over a country with 85 percent of its adults illiterate. The British ruled us for 43 years. When they left, there were two trained engineers and 12 doctors. When I stepped down there was 91 percent literacy and nearly every child was in school. We trained thousands of engineers, doctors, and teachers.'

Nyerere stepped down in 1985. And all that was achieved within 24 years since independence. No mean achievement.[26]

The cornerstone of his economic policy for Tanzania's development was Ujamaa. And it was supported by the majority

of Tanzanians, even if grudgingly by a significant number of them. But even some of the skeptics wanted to give it a chance. And when it failed, even Nyerere's harshest critics admitted that he meant well; which explains his enormous popularity across the country even after he stepped down, although the economy virtually came to a grinding halt especially during the last several years of his presidency.

He remained as popular as he was through the decades since independence, and was even admired by some of his most ardent critics. As Jonathan Power, who was highly critical of Nyerere's policies and one party-rule, stated in his article, "Lament for Independent Africa's Greatest Leader":

Tanzania in East Africa has long been one of the 25 poorest countries in the world. But there was a time when it was described, in terms of its political influence, as one of the top 25. It punched far above its weight. That formidable achievement was the work of one man, now lying close to death in a London Hospital....

His extraordinary intelligence, verbal and literary originality... and apparent commitment to non-violence made him not just an icon in his own country but of a large part of the activist sixties' generation in the white world who, not all persuaded of the heroic virtues of Fidel Castro and Che Guevara, desperately looked for a more sympatheitc role model.

Measured against most of his peers, Jomo Kenyatta of Kenya, Kwame Nkrumah of Ghana, Ahmed Sekou Toure of Guinea, he towered above them. On the intellectual plane only the rather remote president of Senegal, the great poet and author of Negritude, Leopold Senghor, came close to him.

Not only was Nyerere financially open, modest and honest, he was uncorrupted by fame or position. He remained throughout his life, self-effacing and unpretentious. Above all, he inspired his own people to resist the tugs of tribalism and to pull together as one people. To this day Tanzania remains one of the very few African countries that has not experienced serious tribal division. Its continuously fraught relationship with the Arab-dominated off-shore island of Zanzibar is another matter.

Later, discarding his earlier more pacifist convictions, he was to become the eminence rise of the southern African liberation movements in Angola, Zimbabwe, Namibia and South Africa extending a wide open embrace to their operations. For this his country paid a heavy price, in material terms, but also because Nyerere's role as interlocutor with the West demanded enormous amounts of time and energy that often led him to neglect his domestic responsibilities....

Nyerere was not an egomaniac who banged the table and surrounded himself only with sycophants. He was simply the self-assured headmaster that he had been since his teaching days....

Tanzania remains one of the very poorest countries in the world.... Whereas a once equally poor nearby country, Botswana, has progressed rapidly to the point where it is barely recognizable as the impoverished backwater it was only thirty years ago, Tanzania remains mired in the rut of underdevelopment and only recently, since Nyerere voluntarily retired in 1985, has begun to make up for lost time.

For most of Nyerere's long period in office his country was in economic difficulties. Inherited poverty, appalling weather, world recessions, crazed neighbours and war in southern Africa were all parts of the problem, but in the end there was not a good excuse for such continuous failures....

Nyerere's Christian socialist ideology dreamed of new ways of organizing society when there were hardly the rudiments of modern structures.... His biggest mistake of all was what he called 'ujamaa' - a kind of African, Israeli kibbutz-inspired collectivisation....

Later Nyerere was to admit that even in his home village (Butiama), which he often liked to visit, ujamaa had not really taken hold. In the end he was forced to put ujamaa on a back burner, but the damage had been done.

Many of us will mourn Julius Nyerere when he is gone. He was, without any doubt, second only to Nelson Mandela, the most inspiring African leader of his generation.[27]

Although most Tanzanians - and millions of other Africans - were indeed inspired by Nyerere, there were many who disagreed with him and did not like his policies, especially socialism and one-party rule. And like the general population, our editorial staff at the *Daily News* was not a monolithic whole. Many reporters professed to be socialist or supported Tanzania's socialist policies. But some were clearly at the other end of the ideological spectrum, including a number of those who claimed to be socialist and strong supporters of Nyerere's ujamaa policies.

This dichotomy or ambivalence is probably best explained by Nyerere's sincerity and enormous popularity among the masses. Reporters were part of the elite. So, going against the president who was the embodiment of the wishes and aspirations of the poor peasants and workers, and who articulated their sentiments, would have been "treacherous" and "unpatriotic," some of them felt; in spite of the fact that he encouraged us to be critical and freely express our views.

Yet few people - anywhere across the country - wanted to be seen as uncaring, betraying the masses. Therefore for some on our editorial staff, it was self-censorship, to identify themselves with the poor peasants and workers who constituted the vast majority of the population and the backbone of our economy. They were the nation.

Many people including reporters found it hard to criticize Nyerere. His sincerity, humility, and deep concern for the masses confounded even some of his most persistent critics, as did his disarming and startling candour. Even after he stepped down from the presidency, he did not hesitate to criticize his successor whenever he felt such criticism was warranted. And he was blunt about it, and applauded for his honesty and deep concern for the well-being of the nation. Even newsmen, known for their distrust of politicians, applauded him:

> Former Tanzanian president Julius Nyerere on Tuesday (March 13, 1995) accused the government of President Ali Hassan Mwinyi of corruption and violating the constitution and urged Tanzanians to vote differently in the next elections.
>
> Addressing a gathering of local and foreign journalists at the Kilimanjaro International Hotel here (in Dar es Salaam), Nyerere also accused Mwinyi's administration of condoning religious differences and tribalism.
>
> 'This would not only lead to the collapse of the now-sensitive 30-year-old union between the twin-islands of Zanzibar and Pemba and Tanzania mainland, but would also plunge the country into chaos,' Nyerere warned and urged Tanzanians to ensure that they voted for 'a president able to correct the situation and put the country on the right track.'
>
> Nyerere, who ruled Tanzania for 24 years after independence from British colonial rule in 1961, described Tanzania as a country 'stinking with corruption.'
>
> 'Corruption in Tanzania has no bounds. Every country I visit they talk about corruption in Tanzania. Tanzania is stinking with corruption,' Nyerere told journalists gathered at the Tanzania Press Club.
>
> Referring to a tax fraud in the country that recently led to aid suspension by donor countries and organisations, Nyerere declared: 'This was one quality of corruption. Any government that works for the wealthy does not collect tax, it chooses to harass small-time dealers,' Nyerere charged.
>
> Nyerere, affectionately referred to as 'Mwalimu (Teacher) and Father of the Nation' by Tanzanians, said he was speaking of qualities required of a future president to avoid plunging the country into total collapse.
>
> Comparing Tanzania to 'a house that has just been completed,' Nyerere said 'the country has been hit by a tremor, developing cracks which must be filled,' and said the cracks were 'the political union between Zanzibar and the mainland, corruption, religious tensions, tribalism, the constitutional crisis and lack of rule of law.'
>
> In an apparent reference to President Mwinyi himself, Nyerere told the journalists that Tanzania needed a leader who will defend and promote the national constitution. 'It can't be a person that gets advice from his wife, and tomorrow we see some decision has been made. You can't have such a guy.

You won't know what his wife will advise him,' Nyerere said amid applause from more than 100 journalists attending the gathering.

Tanzania goes to the polls next October (1995) in the first multi-party presidential and parliamentary elections since the country attained independence 34 years ago.[28]

Much as Nyerere was revered, he remained humble until his last days. His humility and genuine compassion for the masses was probably the most prominent quality of his long political career spanning almost half a century.

I particularly remember one incident in 1972 when another reporter, Stanley Kamana, and I were assigned to cover the president. More than 30 years later, Kamana was still a journalist and one of the leading veterans in the profession in the country, together with my other former colleagues at the *Daily News*, including Kassim Mpenda who became director of Radio Tanzania, Dar es Salaam (RTD), and later Tanzania's director of Information Services at the ministry of information and broadcasting, as he still was at this writing. So was Charles Kizigha who was still at the *Daily News*, an enduring phenomenon at the paper for three decades after I left the editorial staff; Reginald Mhango, a senior reporter for 30 years who was appointed editor of the *Guardian*, Tanzania, in 2002; Jenerali Ulimwengu, one of the two lawyers who were reporters on our editorial staff, who became chairman and publisher, Habari Corporation, responsible for the publication of several newspapers in Kiswahili; Pascal Shija who became managing editor of *The Express*; and our former editor Sammy Mdee who was appointed chairman of the Tanzania Broadcasting Services (TBS) by President Mkapa in 2003.

When my colleagues and I were together at the *Daily News* 30 years ago, covering the president with Stanley Kamana on that day was one of the main assignments I was given, besides covering parliament which I did many times, only a few months before I left for the United States to pursue further studies.

President Nyerere addressed a mass rally in Dar es Salaam where he criticized the authorities of the Coast Region (Mkoa wa Pwani, in Kiswahili) for ordering the demolition of stands owned by hawkers on a major street, Ilala, which feeds into Pugu Road that goes all the way to the national airport. Foreign dignitaries from a number of countries were coming to Dar es Salaam in only a few days to attend a major conference. But the regional officials, including Regional Commissioner Mustafa Songambele who was also at the rally, did not want these dignitaries to see the peddlers and their stands on this major route they were going to take on their way into the city from the airport.

They felt ashamed and did not want to "humiliate" and "embarrass" our country. The hawkers and their stands were, in fact, more than any eyesore, according to these officials. Such a spectacle could not be reconciled with our determination to maintain national dignity in spite of all the poverty we had and still have in Tanzania.

That was the twisted logic of these leaders.

In his public address, President Nyerere asked about the peddlers: "What have they done wrong? What do you want them to do without income? What are you going to give them instead, once you demolish the stands? That's the only means they have to earn a living." Some stands had already been demolished, but the rest were not, after Nyerere's speech.

What happened then reminds me of what happened in 1998 when American President Bill Clinton visited Ghana and other African countries. Many government officials in Accra, Ghana's capital, did not want Clinton and his entourage to see the open sewage in the capital. President Jerry Rawlings ordered them to leave everything as it was so that the Americans should "see the way we live." Just covering it up won't solve the problem. Once the Americans are gone, the raw sewage will still be there.

Nyerere, for whom Rawlings had profound respect, had the same attitude. Impressing foreigners was not part of his personality. His biggest concern was the well-being of the poor, the downtrodden, the oppressed. With or without the stands on Ilala Street, the visiting dignitaries would probably not even have noticed any difference, any way, and would not have been impressed either way. Nyerere's response to the callous indifference of the Coast Region government officials is an enduring memory I have always cherished. And it should be a lesson for other African leaders who claim that they care about their people while they are busy doing exactly the opposite.

Another memorable but tragic occasion during my career as a

reporter in Tanzania was when I covered the country's first vice president, Sheikh Abeid Karume, who was also president of Zanzibar. Our constitution allowed that because Zanzibar was an autonomous - not a sovereign - entity within the union. And it still is, although there have been some changes stipulating that the country shall have only one vice president, not two as before (one from the isles and the other from the mainland), and that contenders for the presidency and vice presidency can come from anywhere in the union without any restrictions except those prescribed by law. The changes took place after multiparty democracy was introduced in the early 1990s.

I covered Karume in 1972 not long after I returned to Dar es Salaam from Zanzibar where I had been sent with another reporter, Juma Penza, to cover the eighth anniversary of the Zanzibar revolution of January 1964. A senior reporter at the *Daily News*, Penza later became an information officer of Tanzania's ruling party (CCM) and still held that post in the 1990s and beyond.

We were in Zanzibar for several days. Karume came to Dar es Salaam after we got back from Zanzibar and gave a speech at the Police Officers' Mess in Msasani, an area on the outskirts of the capital where President Nyerere also lived in a simple house, away from his official residence, Ikulu (State House).

Speaking in Kiswahili, Karume told the officers to examine their inner selves in order to conduct themselves in an exemplary manner when performing their duties. That was his last speech in Dar es Salaam. He returned to Zanzibar and, not long afterwards, was assassinated on April 7 in a hail of bullets. He was reportedly shot eight times at close range. Coincidentally or not, he had also been in office for eight years as first vice president of Tanzania. The number of times he was shot may have been deliberately calculated to symbolize the number of years he had been in office - one bullet for each year - if indeed he was hit eight times.

Abdulrahman Mohammed Babu, a Zanzibari from Pemba Island and senior cabinet member in the union government and one of the most prominent Tanzanian leaders, was accused by the Zanzibari authorities of masterminding the assassination and detained on the mainland in connection with the murder. But President Nyerere refused to send him back to Zanzibar where he probably would have been executed, as Kassim Hanga was, under a judicial system that had little regard for justice and individual rights, let alone for those accused of killing the country's first vice president.

As an autonomous entity, Zanzibar also had its own judicial system whose dispensation of justice differed from what we had on the mainland in many fundamental respects.

After Babu was released from detention in 1977, he left Tanzania and became a professor at San Francisco State University, California, in the United States. He died in Britain in 1996 and the Tanzanian government brought his body back home and assumed full responsibility for his funeral expenses in acknowledgment of his status as a national leader, regardless of whatever differences he may have had with his colleagues including President Nyerere himself.

Karume's assassination was the first of a Tanzanian leader since independence, preceded by Tom Mboya's in neighbouring Kenya only three years before in July 1969. Aboud Jumbe succeeded Karume and became Zanzibar's president and Tanzania's first vice president under Nyerere, but resigned in 1984 because of his dissatisfaction with the structure of the union. Rashidi Kawawa, a veteran politician since independence who together with Nyerere and Oscar Kambona constituted a trio and the most influential political team in Tanzania until Kambona went into self-imposed exile in Britain in July 1967, was the country's second vice president.

President Nyerere continued to lead Tanzania until November 1985 when he voluntarily stepped down after being in office for 24 years since independence from Britain on December 9, 1961. It was a long political career, marked by successes and failures.

A lot has been said about the failure of his economic policies. But little has been said about his achievements. As he told the World Bank in 1998: "We took over a country with 85 percent of its adults illiterate. The British ruled us for 43 years. When they left, there were two trained engineers and 12 doctors. When I stepped down there was 91 percent literacy and nearly every child was in school. We trained thousands of engineers, doctors and teachers."[29]

He was painfully aware of our long, tortuous journey since

independence, being one of the few university graduates himself when he assumed stewardship of the nation. He was, in fact, the first African from Tanganyika to obtain a master's degree in 1952 at Edinburgh University in Scotland where he studied economics, history, and philosophy. We had very few trained people and had to rely on expatriates in most fields. But because of his excellent leadership, we were able to achieve a lot in only a few years.

I, myself, would not be what I am today had it not been for his leadership. And you wouldn't be reading this book or any of the others I have written. And the reason is simple: I would not have been able to go to school. Under his leadership, education was free for everybody, unlike today. Medical service was also free, again unlike today.

Even transport for us to go to boarding school, to any part of the country, was free, paid for by the government; which means by the peasants and workers of Tanzania, with their tax money. We all had equal opportunity to be the best we could be. Few countries can claim that, and mean it. Tanzania did that, because of Nyerere.

But none of this would have been possible had the country not been united. There was a strong possibility back in the sixties and even in the seventies that our country could have fallen apart or been plunged into chaos, fractured along tribal and regional and even religious lines, if we had poor leadership; especially under the multiparty system which capitalizes on greed and partisan interests as has happened in Tanzania since the introduction of multiparty politics, although it doesn't have to be that way if the parties involved transcend sectarianism and ethno-regional loyalties. As Nyerere said many years after his retirement:

> I really think that I ran the most successful single-party system on the continent. You might not even call it a party. It was a single, huge nationalist movement....I don't believe that our country would be where it is now if we had a multiplicity of parties, which would have become tribal and caused us a lot of problems. But when you govern for such a long time, unless you are gods, you become corrupt and bureaucratic.... So I started calling for a multiparty system.[30]

Neighbouring Kenya faced the same problem, regional fragmentation, when one of the political parties, the Kenya

African Democratic Union (KADU) led by Ronald Ngala - a former teacher and prominent politician in the Coast Province - pursued a regionalist agenda which could have split the country along ethno-regional lines. Or it could have weakened the central government so much that national leaders would not have been able to exercise any power over the regions. His agenda was also supported by many other Kenyans who were not members of KADU, especially those from smaller tribes.

And there is still strong interest in *majimboism* (regionalism) even today in Kenya, mainly because of the political dominance of the ruling party, the Kenya African National Union (KANU), which seemed to be destined to rule perpetually until it was defeated in the 2002 general election by a coalition of opposition parties, NARC, ending almost 40 years of hegemonic control of Kenya. *Majimbo*, a Kiswahili word, means provinces or regions; *jimbo* being its singular form.

But Jomo Kenyatta succeeded in establishing a unitary state under a strong central government to keep the country united like Nyerere did in Tanganyika, later Tanzania. The difference is that Kenya's ruling party, KANU, was dominated by the Kikuyu, Kenyatta's tribe and the country's biggest; while in Tanganyika, the ruling Tanganyika African National Union (TANU) was pluralistic. No single tribe became dominant; another great achievement by Nyerere.

Yet, Ngala's quest for regional autonomy in Kenya seems to have been vindicated by President Kenyatta himself because of his dictatorial instincts. He was highly sensitive to criticism and neutralized his opponents quickly. That is what he did to his vice president, Oginga Odinga, who resigned and went on to form the opposition party, the Kenya People's Union (KPU), based on egalitarian ideals like Nyerere's to pursue policies which would benefit the masses, not just the elite like KANU's under Kenyatta did. Odinga accused Kenyatta's government of ignoring and exploiting *wananchi*, the people, and was neutralized, with Kenyatta claiming, "I have been kind for too long."[31]

Ronald Ngala also had a taste of Kenyatta's bile in parliament one day in a very distasteful way. As Mundia Kamau stated in his article, "A Nation in Distress," in Kenya's *Mashada Daily*:

> Jomo Kenyatta was not a democrat at all. He was the exemplification and

personification of the African 'Big Man,' a ruthless dictator. Jomo Kenyatta carried on where the British left off, continuing with the plunder of public resources, and theft of public land. He mastered the art of oppression the African way, by ruthlessly exploiting the ignorance, biases, and prejudices of most Africans, a trend that still sadly persists....

An example of Kenyatta's ruthless intolerance comes out in Koigi wa Wamwere's autobiography when he states how Kenyatta once drew his gun in parliament intending to shoot the late Ronald Ngala for criticising his government, and was only restrained by then Speaker, Humphrey Slade. The myth that Kenyatta was a democrat and professional must be dispensed with immediately, if we truly hope to solve the problems of this country. The only essential difference between Kenyatta and his successor Moi, is that Kenyatta was more widely travelled and more eloquent in English.[32]

Kenyatta may have been wrong in silencing Ronald Ngala and his opposition party, KADU, the way he did in parliament by threatening to shoot the opposition leader. Yet, the threat to national unity posed by extensive autonomy (*majimboism*, derived from majimbo) as advocated by Ngala and his party KADU, and by the multiparty system, cannot be ignored if such devolution of power is not implemented within prescribed limits and specifically designated areas of authority; and if multiparty democracy is allowed to thrive on ethno-regional loyalties and partisan interests at the expense of the nation.

But that was not a major problem in Tanzania under Nyerere, although he decentralized power under a unitary state, something rarely done - if at all - in most highly centralized states across the continent.

Tragically, tribalism is beginning to gain a foothold in Tanzania, with tribal organizations emerging on the scene, tolerated or sanctioned by the state by invoking pluralism. And appeal to tribal and regional sentiments has become a feature of national politics since multiparty democracy was introduced in the early nineties.

The resurgence of this ugly phenomenon was underscored by former Vice President Joseph Sinde Warioba, also a distinguished jurist, in a speech in Dar es Salaam in March 2001. President Benjamin Mkapa himself was fully aware of these sectarian threats and won his second term with a promise to keep the country united, transcending ethinc, regional, racial and religious differences.

The introduction of multiparty politics, which has exacerbated the situation prompted many people to re-evaluate the transition from one-partyism to multipartyism. Many Tanzanians are probably having second thoughts about the wisdom of the decision by the national leaders who made this fundamental change against what was generally perceived to be popular will. When the people across the country were asked in the early nineties whether or not Tanzania should adopt the multiparty system, it was reported that the majority of those who participated in the survey were opposed to the change.

This may be one of the reasons - besides poor organization, lack of direction, and personal rivalries - why opposition parties have not been able to win significant support in Tanzania; prompting one prominent opposition leader who rejoined the ruling party, CCM, in 2002 to say that CCM will rule Tanzania for the next 500 years. As the old saying goes, if you can't beat them, join them. A number of other opposition leaders and members have taken this pragmatic approach, which may also help to maintain national unity and stability.

Although I am in favour of multiparty democracy if it works well, I sometimes also have had strong reservations about the functional utility of the multiparty system in the African context because of its divisive tendencies and potential for catastrophe. To contend otherwise, given Africa's experience in many cases, is rank dishonesty or sheer naiveté.

In most cases, the multiparty system tends to fuel tribal and regional rivalries. But the one-party system itself is not above reproach when it discriminates against some groups and individuals as has been the case in most African countries - in Kenya under Kenyatta and Moi, favouring members of their tribes, the Kikuyu and the Kalenjin, respectively; Malawi under Banda whose government was dominated by the Chewa; Ivory Coast which was a *de facto* one-party state under Felix Houphouet-Boigny and Henri Bedie who favoured members of their Baoule tribe, as did President Laurent Gbagbo, another Baoule; Togo under Gnassingbe Eyadema favouring members of his northern tribe, the Kabye, who also constituted 70 percent of the national army, to name only a few.

However, the multiparty system, more than the one-party

system, can promote democracy in Africa if the people vote across tribal and regional lines to advance a common agenda. Yet, few African countries can honestly claim to have a majority of such voters who have transcended ethno-regional loyalties; a strong case for federalism and a limited number of parties as prescribed by law. Their interests are highly partisan. And they are not based on policy differences, bringing together members of different tribes and social and economic classes to pursue common interests. Their interests are defined by tribal and regional identities more than anything else.

The multiparty system is strongly advocated as a safeguard against corruption and dictatorship. It can, indeed, serve as a watchdog for the underdog to expose corruption, ensure transparency, and end dictatorship in African countries; but only if the parties don't, however surreptitiously, appeal to their regional constituencies to win elections.

So, limit the number of political parties to broaden their base across the nation. Have three parties at the most, or may be even two. And this will, in fact, strengthen the opposition because, more often than not, governments thrive on a divided opposition, making it easy for incumbents to win elections by fair means or foul.

Therefore the opposition should be the first to support limiting the number of political parties, since this will help government opponents to mobilize forces into a cohesive bloc even if it is based on a coalition of interests, as is the case in politics in general. Politics is based on compromise.

But dominant political parties which are in power in African countries will probably be the last to support limiting the number of political parties, since this will help unite their opponents; unless a limited number of political parties is going to benefit them somehow, for example, by co-opting the opposition, thus reducing it to nothing.

The argument for a limited number of political parties is validated by experience. There are very few truly national parties in Africa. And if we can't form such parties which attract substantial numbers of people from all the tribes across the country as TANU - and even CCM - did under Nyerere and his successors, without lopsided membership, then only the one-party system can claim to be truly national; but only if it also embraces members of all tribes, is liberalized, and decentralized to curb autocratic instincts.

Under Nyerere, I remember when students openly questioned, without fear of retribution, the merits of the one-party system. For example, at Tambaza High School in Dar es Salaam, we had such free discussion - risky, and even deadly, in most African countries - in class conducted by our headmaster, Mr. Lila (pronounced as Lee-la), a highly articulate man with profound insight into political theory and mass participatory politics. He had thorough command of the subject and explained Nyerere's ideology well. And he supported it, yet was open to criticism; which was very encouraging and reassuring to the students. We were not muzzled.

We also knew the kind of opportunities we had. There were Asian (mostly Indian and Pakistani), Arab, and African students in my class. Yet, despite the fact that Tanzania was under a black majority government, the Asian and Arab students knew they had equal opportunity just like the rest of their fellow countrymen because of the kind of leadership and moral vision provided by Nyerere. He led by example. Many students of different tribes and races went on to lead successful lives in different areas because of the equal opportunities provided by Nyerere. That was not the case in most African countries, including neighbouring Kenya, where discrimination was rampant as it still is today.

In his cabinet since independence - and even before in 1960 when Tanganyika won self-government with Julius Nyerere as chief minister but still under colonial rule - he had members of all races, including women; for example, Derek Bryceson, an Englishman, who came to Tanganyika in 1951; Amir H. Jamal, an Indian; Abdulrahman Mohammed Babu, an Arab; Salim Ahmed Salim, also an Arab; Bibi Titi Mohammed, the first female cabinet member appointed as junior minister of community development soon after independence; Lucy Lameck, appointed as junior minister of health, also in the sixties and, together with Bibi Titi, one of Tanzania's most prominent leaders.

There was also Dr. Leader Stirling who was the oldest cabinet member and who outlived them all - those just mentioned including President Nyerere - and who was one of the first leaders of the independence movement in Tanganyika. Born in Britain in

1906, Dr. Stirling was a missionary doctor who came to Tanganyika in 1935. He worked as a doctor in Masasi - home district of President Benjamin Mkapa - in southern Tanganyika for 24 years before entering politics.

His political career began in 1958 when he became a member of the pre-independence parliament - known as LEGCO (Legislative Council) - as a representative of the Tanganyika African National Union (TANU), the party which led the country to independence. He served as minister of health from 1975 to 1980, and died in Dar es Salaam in February 2003 at the age of 96. And these are only a few examples of the rainbow leadership of Tanzania, and a microcosm of what our country came to be, under President Nyerere.

There were many others - across the racial spectrum - in high government positions including the diplomatic service. In fact, Salim Ahmed Salim, former Tanzania's permanent representative to the United Nations, was recalled by Nyerere and given a succession of senior cabinet posts through the years. He once served as defence minister, minister of foreign affairs, and as prime minister. He then went on to become secretary-general of the Organization of African Unity (OAU) in Addis Ababa, Ethiopia.

He served for 12 years from 1989 to 2001; an unprecedented term, longer than any of his predecessors did, and was the last OAU secretary-general before the organization was transformed into the African Union (AU) at the last OAU meeting in June 2001 in Lusaka, Zambia. But the actual transition was a gradual process, and the AU did not start functioning until later, after being formally launched in Durban, South Africa, in July 2002 under the chairmanship of South African President Thabo Mbeki.

When Salim Ahmed Salim was Tanzania's ambassador to the UN, he was almost elected UN secretary-general and won the support of the majority of the members in the General Assembly. But the big powers had their own agendas and preferences and blocked his election.

The United States did not want him at the helm because of Tanzania's relentless support of the People's Republic of China through the years to get the world's most populous nation admitted into the UN, instead of pretending that it did not exist, with Ambassador Salim being one of the strongest advocates even when he served in a neutral capacity as president of the UN General Assembly - he was still Tanzania's ambassador. And the Soviet Union did not want him because the Russians felt that he was too independent and would not bend to their wishes.

And he could even have been elected president of Tanzania in 2005 had it not been for some of his enemies who undermined his candidacy.

Following the death of Tanzania's Vice President Omar Ali Juma in July 2001, it was reported that Dr. Salim Ahmed Salim was the favourite of the political heavyweights in the country's ruling party, CCM, to succeed him but did not become vice president because he turned down the offer. Others claimed that because of his high international profile, he would have overshadowed President Benjamin Mkapa, and therefore turned down or was not given the post; although it is highly unlikely that Mkapa would have been eclipsed by Dr. Salim.

Mkapa is a man of such high intellectual calibre, strong personality and self-confidence, that it would have been virtually impossible to overshadow him; qualities which helped propel him to the highest position in the country as president with the full support of Nyerere. In fact, it was Nyerere who recommended him to be the presidential candidate of the ruling party, CCM, although he almost lost the nomination to Jakaya Mrisho Kikwete, a favourite among the younger members of the party, and won it by a small margin.

Whatever the case, Salim remained a formidable political personality and had a chance to be elected president.

There is evidence everywhere across Tanzania showing that Nyerere built a truly pluralistic society with equal opportunity for all. My classmates are some of the beneficiaries, regardless of their tribal and racial identities. For example, one of them, Mohammed Chande Othman - he was simply called Chande - of Arab extraction, once served as a senior prosecution attorney and chief prosecutor at the International Criminal Tribunal for Rwanda (ICTR) established by the UN in Arusha, Tanzania.

He earned his law degree at the University of Dar es Salaam, one of the best law schools in Africa, and the first to be established in East Africa. After working at the UN court in

Tanzania, he was assigned to East Timor where he was appointed general prosecutor - UN's chief prosecutor - to help the young southeast Asian nation establish its judicial system under UN auspices.

And there are countless other Tanzanians, of all races and tribes, who have reached the pinnacle of success through the years at home and abroad because of the foundation laid by Nyerere that has sustained Tanzania as a peaceful, stable country, with opportunities for all. And he did that with humility and simplicity which characterized his political career more than any other leader on the continent.

After Nyerere voluntarily stepped down as president of Tanzania in November 1985, it was with a simple bicycle that he returned to his home village of Butiama in northern Tanzania near the southeastern shores of Lake Victoria, to live and work on the farm; and eat simple breakfast of porridge with the children from poor families in the area. He did it every morning. As James Mpinga wrote in *The East African*:

> There is little to show that Butiama, the birthplace of Julius Nyerere, raised one of Africa's greatest sons. Mud huts surround the Catholic Church where Nyerere used to pray, and both the church and the mud huts tell a story. From the mud huts came the children who knew exactly when Mwalimu would have his breakfast, and dutifully came to share it with him every morning, and in the church their parents shared a common faith and prayer.
>
> 'At first it was bread and butter for both Mwalimu and the kids. Soon I couldn't cope with the increasing numbers of children joining him for breakfast, so I downgraded it to porridge and *kande* (a boiled mixture of maize off the cob and pulses),' recalls Mwalimu's former housekeeper, Dorothy Musoga, 74, now living in retirement in Mwanza in a house built for her by Mwalimu....
>
> She was worried...about the future of his family and what she called Mwalimu's 'other children' who loved to share his breakfast. 'With Mwalimu dead, free breakfast for poor villagers will become a thing of the past,' Dorothy reflected.... The poverty of their parents remains, as does the lack of infrastructure at Butiama, which Mwalimu didn't want to transform into an edifice to be envied....
>
> On Saturday, October 23 (1999), when Mwalimu was buried, Butiama may well have started to slip back into oblivion, to become what it once was, an unknown village in the middle of nowhere.... The process may, indeed, have started earlier, with Mwalimu's own house...(which) bears marks of his self-denial. Children fetch water from a public standpipe and their mothers wash clothes in the open. The house itself could do with a fresh coat of paint....

Judging from the relatively wealthier homestead of the chief (nearby), Mwalimu was no more than a peasant....

When I later visited the compound of Mwitongo, where Mwalimu was buried not far from the graves of his parents, only a few insiders and the late Nyerere's close family members had remained, among them his former press secretary Sammy Mdee....

When Chairman Mao was asked what he thought about the French Revolution, a century and a half after it had taken place, he retorted: 'It's too early to say.'

Few in Tanzania can give a better answer about the impact of Nyerere's death. For the poor children of Butiama, however, the days of free breakfast with their beloved grandpa are gone. It is hard to imagine what will follow.[33]

It is indeed hard to imagine what will follow, in a world where there are few such men and women. Nyerere embodied the best that man can achieve in the service of fellow men, but which few are willing to do. He was not a saint, in the religious sense, but may deserve to be called Saint Julius because of his selfless devotion to the poor in the tradition of saints.

He sacrificed so much, yet got so little in return, and did not expect or want anything in return. He just did his job, what he knew had to be done, for his people and others, no matter what the cost. He was the least paid head of state, earning $500 per month, yet one of the most revered; Thomas Sankara of Burkina Faso followed him in his footsteps when he himself became the least paid head of state after Nyerere stepped down. And, instead of living in magnificent splendour, and in the president's official residence, the State House (Ikulu, as we call it), President Nyerere chose to live a humble life in a simple house on the outskirts of the capital in an area called Msasani.

He did not even have a pension to live on when he retired, until parliament hastily voted for one to help sustain him. As *Newsweek* stated soon after he died: "The world has lost a man of principle."[34] Unlike most leaders, including religious leaders, he practiced what he preached. And he admitted his mistakes, a rare quality among leaders, almost all of whom equate such admission with weakness. Yet it's probably the most important quality of leadership on which everything else depends.

Perhaps it is worth remembering that even some of his ardent critics acknowledged his contributions and paid him lasting tribute. Probably no other African scholar kept up a lively debate on the merits of Nyerere's policies as Ali Mazrui did; although he never questioned his commitment and integrity, and powerful intellect, and remained friendly with him until Mwalimu's final days, despite differences between the two. In a tribute to Mwalimu and on the special bonds between the two, Professor Mazrui had a lot to say in his article in *Voices*, Africa Resource Center, entitled, "Nyerere and I":

> In global terms, he was one of the giants of the 20th Century.... While his vision did outpace his victories, and his profundity outweigh his performance, he did bestride this narrow world like an African colossus....
>
> As personalities, what did Julius and I have in common? He was a politician who was sometimes a scholar. I was a scholar who was sometimes a politician.... Nyerere and I were trying to build bridges between Africa and great minds of Western civilisation.... With his concept of Ujamaa, Nyerere also attempted to build bridges between indigenous African thought and modern political ideas....
>
> 'The two top Swahili-speaking intellectuals of the second half of the 20th Century are Julius Nyerere and Ali Mazrui.' That is how I was introduced to an Africanist audience in 1986 when I was on a lecture-tour of the United States to promote my television series: The Africans: A Triple Heritage (BBC-PBS). I regarded the tribute as one of the best compliments I had ever been paid. In reality, Mwalimu Nyerere was much more eloquent as Swahili orator than I although Kiswahili was my mother tongue and not his.
>
> In the month of Nyerere's death (October 1999), the comparison between Mwalimu and I took a sadder form. A number of organisations in South Africa had united to celebrate Africa's Human Rights Day on October 22. Long before he was admitted to hospital, they had invited him to be their high-profile banquet speaker.
>
> When Nyerere was incapacitated with illness, and seemed to be terminally ill, the South Africans turned to Ali Mazrui as his replacement. I was again flattered to have been regarded as Nyerere's replacement. However, the notice was too short, and I was not able to accept the South African invitation.
>
> It is one of the ironies of my life that I have known the early presidents of Uganda and Tanzania far better than I have known the presidents of Kenya (my country). Over the years, Julius Nyerere and I met many times. (Ugandan President) Milton Obote was one of the formative influences of my early life, in spite of our tumultuous relationship....
>
> Let me also refer to Walter Rodney. He was a Guyanese scholar who taught at the University of Dar es Salaam and became one of the most eloquent voices of the left on the campus in Tanzania. When Walter Rodney returned to Guyana, he was assassinated.
>
> Chedi Jagan, on being elected President of Guyana, created a special chair in honour of Walter Rodney. Eventually I was offered the chair and became its first incumbent. My inaugural lecture was on the following topic: 'Comparative Leadership: Walter Rodney, Julius K. Nyerere and Martin Luther King Jr.'

After delivering the lecture, I subsequently met Nyerere one evening in Pennsylvania, USA. I gave him my Walter Rodney lecture. He read it overnight and commented on it the next morning at breakfast. He promised to send me a proper critique on my Rodney lecture on his return to Dar es Salaam. He never lived long enough to send me the critique.

Nyerere's policies of Ujamaa amounted to a case of Heroic Failure. They were heroic because Tanzania was one of the few African countries, which attempted to find its own route to development instead of borrowing the ideologies of the West. But it was a failure because the economic experiment did not deliver the goods of development.

On the other hand, Nyerere's policies of nation-building amount to a case of Unsung Heroism. With wise and strong leadership, and with brilliant policies of cultural integration, he took one of the poorest countries in the world and made it a proud leader in African affairs and an active member of the global community.

Julius Nyerere was my Mwalimu too. It was a privilege to learn so much from so great a man.[35]

A man of high integrity and an enormous and astonishing intellect, he was one of the most exalted, yet extremely humble. He was, indeed, a man of the people. Such is the mark of true genius, a rare breed among men. As former American President Jimmy Carter said: "Julius Nyerere should be remembered as one of the greatest leaders of this century."[36] It is a fitting tribute, although somewhat of an understatement.

The world has, in fact, produced only a few such men and women in a span of centuries. And he had few peers on the African continent who could equal his stature; a point underscored by Ali Mazrui in another tribute to Nyerere at Cornell University, although he disagreed with him on a number of fundamental issues. He last saw Nyerere when both were among the main speakers in different forums during the inauguration of Nigerian President Olusegun Obasanjo in May 1999. As he stated in his lecture at Cornell, also published in Kenya's *Daily Nation*:

> Most Western judges of Julius Nyerere have concentrated on his economic policies and their failures. Ujamaa and villagisation have been seen as forces of economic retardation, which kept Tanzania backward for at least another decade.
>
> Not enough commentators have paid attention to Nyerere's achievements in nation-building. He gave Tanzania a sense of national consciousness and a spirit of national purpose. One of the poorest countries in the world found itself one of the major actors on the world scene. Nyerere's policies of making

Kiswahili the national language of Tanzania deepened this sense of Tanzania's national consciousness and cultural pride....

Above all, Nyerere as president was a combination of deep intellect and high integrity. Leopold Senghor's intellect was as deep as Nyerere's, but was Senghor's integrity as high as Nyerere's? Nelson Mandela's integrity was probably higher than Nyerere's, but was Mandela's intellect as deep as Nyerere's?

Some East African politicians might have been more intelligent than Nyerere. Others might have been more ethical than Nyerere. But Julius K. Nyerere was in a class by himself in the combination of ethical standards and intellectual power. In the combination of high thinking and high ethics, no other East African politician was in the same league.

He and I deeply disagreed on the merits of Ujamaa. He and I once disagreed on East African federation. I thought his socialist policies harmed East African integration. He and I disagreed on the Nigerian civil war. He and I disagreed on the issue of Zanzibar. I thought Zanzibar was forced into a marriage, which was not of its own choosing.

And yet Nyerere and I were committed to the proposition that patriotic Africans could disagree and still be equally patriotic. I saw him in Abuja in Nigeria, just before the inauguration of President Olusegun Obasanjo late in May 1999. Julius Nyerere and I gossiped in Kiswahili. He looked well - deceptively well, considering his illness.

He and I were keynote speakers at a workshop to inaugurate Nigeria to a new era of democracy in 1999. We were voices from East Africa at a major West African event. We were voices of Pan-Africanism on the eve of the new millennium. Nyerere's voice was one of the most eloquent voices of the 20th Century. It was a privilege for me to stand side-by-side with such a person to mark a momentous event in no less a country than our beloved Nigeria.[37]

A man whom Mazrui also once hailed as "the most original thinker in English-speaking Africa," a tribute he also paid to Senghor with regard to Francophone Africa,[38] Nyerere will always remain an inspiration to millions, including some of his critics.

Mazrui, himself a leading critic of Nyerere's policies yet an admirer of Nyerere's intellect and integrity, drew fire through the years from some of the most vociferous defenders of Nyerere and his policies. They included the late Dr. Walter Rodney from Guyana who taught at the University of Dar es Salaam when I was a reporter at the *Daily News*; other professors and students at the university as well as a number of Tanzanians including some reporters at the *Daily News* and *The Nationalist* in Dar es Salaam. To many of them, his criticism of Tanzania's egalitarian policies in a nation of poor peasants and workers amounted to a case of Tanzaphobia by one of Africa's leading academics, and probably the most well-known in international circles besides his nemesis Wole Soyinka.

I also disagreed with Mazrui on a number of issues, although I did not have the visceral hatred for him that was obvious among some of his leftist critics, of which I wasn't one. I was simply a nationalist and Pan-Africanist, neither to the right nor to the left, as I still am today, although I have sympathized with leftist causes more than I have with those on the right, if at all.

When I was a student at Tambaza High School in standard 14 (Form VI) in 1970, I remember reading in one of Tanzania's two major daily newspapers, *The Nationalist*, a letter to the editor - Ben Mkapa, later my editor at the *Daily News*, and president of Tanzania (1995 - 2005) - from Professor Ali Mazrui. It was a passionate defence of his patriotism in response to his critics who felt that he was highly critical of Tanzania's policies out of sheer spite and hatred, and not out of genuine commitment to the well-being of the country.

He responded by saying that he loved Tanzania, and that Tanzania meant a lot to him. He went on say that he spent part of his childhood in Tanzania, in what was then Zanzibar, and partly attended school in Tanzania (then Tanganyika) when he was growing up. He said he went to school in Moshi, in Kilimanjaro Region in northeastern Tanzania, and that Tanzania will always be important to him. The letter may have elicited some sympathy for him from some of the readers, but many of his critics were probably impressed by none of this.

Some of them were brutally frank in their assessment of the renowned Kenyan professor; for example, Kusai Khamisa, a senior reporter at our newspaper, now deceased, said "Mazrui has a pathological hatred of Tanzania." And one senior Tanzanian diplomat whom I knew said "Ali Mazrui has done everything possible to destroy Tanzania. I have been tempted several times to write a crtique of his writings."

I remember talking to Philip Ochieng' - a Kenyan himself - one day in 1972 when we worked together at the *Daily News*, and asking him what he thought about Ali Mazrui. I brought up the subject, and knowing Philip's strong political views, I wanted to hear what he had to say about it.

A fiery Marxist, yet who years later was appointed editor of the capitalist government-owned *Kenya Times* under President Daniel arap Moi after he returned to Kenya, he dismissed Mazrui as a very dangerous academic. No capital offense, but criticism of government, the kind Mazrui was known for even if just as a scholar engaged in objective evaluation and analaysis of ideas, has sent people to the gallows in many African countries. Others have been summarily executed, shot on the spot, or simply "disappeared." As Mazrui himself says, he almost got killed by Idi Amin in Uganda for criticizing him.

I remember reading an article Mazrui wrote after he fled Uganda and when Amin was busy expelling Asians, including Ugandan citizens who just happened to be of Asian origin. It was entitled, "When Spain Expelled the Moors," and incurred the wrath of the dictator, obviously after someone read it to him and told him what Mazrui meant by that. Amin had only a standard two - second grade - education and could hardly read or write. Mazrui taught at Makerere University in Kampala, Uganda.

But such blunt assessment of pro-capitalist academics like Mazrui and others was not unusual in socialist-oriented Tanzania among leftists like Philip Ochieng'. Nor was criticism of the West. Although I myself was a strong admirer of Nyerere and other African leaders such as Nkrumah because of their egalitarian policies and Pan-African commitment, and was not enamored of the West, I was sometimes criticized by some of my colleagues on the editorial staff at the *Daily News* for wearing a necktie almost everyday; as did two other reporters, Judicate Shoo and Emmanuel Lenga. One day, Philip, who always wore a short-sleeved shirt or a dashiki, lifted my tie and said, half-jokingly, "Godfrey, you're tied to the West," as he shook it.

That was ridiculous. I was tied to the West as much as he was when he enjoyed drinks imported from the West, which he did, and wore Western clothes, minus a tie; and as much as he enjoyed Western music. Philip loved humming Western tunes including "Guantanamera," his favourite, which he often whistled in our editorial office, punctuating the tune with the song's name. The name Philip itself tied him to the West - not just to the Biblical homeland - just as much, and like mine, of course. So did President Nyerere's first name, Julius!

Just remember Mobutu, with his full African name and

indigenization policy of "Authenticity," complete with a leopard-skin hat, and a traditional cane he carried and which is so common among African chiefs and other traditional rulers as a symbol of authority. In 1971, he ordered all names in the country changed to African names. He also "indigenized" the economy by raiding national coffers for himself and giving property - seized from foreigners - to his cronies and family members who had also amassed wealth by stealing from the masses.

Now, contrast that with Patrice Lumumba who wore Western suits and a necktie. Who was more tied to the West? Leopold Senghor espoused Negritude - about which Wole Soyinka said "a tiger does not have to proclaim its tigritude" - yet he was unabashedly Francophile and proud to be a "black Frenchman." Dr. Milton Obote wore Western suits and a necktie, besides African safari suits also worn by Dr. Kenneth Kaunda who stopped wearing Western suits and replaced them with what came to be popularly known as Kaunda style. Was Obote tied to the West?

What about Robert Mugabe and Samora Machel, admirers of Chairman Mao, and Marxist firebrands until they were tempered by harsh economic realities, who also wore Western suits and neckties? Were they tied to the West? During the land crisis in Zimbabwe in the late 1990s and beyond, Mugabe showed the whole world how much he was tied to the West!

But that is the twisted logic of some leftists, although many of their counterparts are Westerners and wear Western suits and neckties, just like the politburo members in the former Soviet Union and her satellites, as well as ordinary citizens in those countries, did.

It is ironic that many people in Third World countries are highly critical of the industrialized West - and for good reasons in many cases, although sometimes out of sheer spite - yet they want to live like Westerners, admire the Western life style, and ape the consumption proclivities of the West.

Critical of the West as Philip was, I still remember that some reporters on our editorial staff did not see much virtue, if any, in such criticism by him because of his Western tastes, including his social life however personal that was; as it indeed was. As senior reporter Reginald Mhango - now managing editor of *The*

Guardian - once asked, loudly, in our editorial office about Philip's dating preferences: "Why just white women?"

Mhango may have had a valid point. So did Philip, of course, who could have retorted had been within earshot: "So what? That's none of your business"; just as it was none of his that I wore a necktie, which "tied me to the West," as he saw it.

Whaever the case, Philip Ochieng', one of Africa's most prominent journalists and Kenya's best known, remained an unrepentant Marxist despite the collapse of communism and renunciation of Marxism-Leninism as a state ideology by almost all the countries which had adopted it, except North Korea, ruled by Stalinist hardliners, and Cuba under the internationalist Castro.

But we agreed on one thing: Nyerere was a great leader. And he was not just Tanzania's, but Africa's leader.

He first wanted to unite East African countries, but failed to do so. Yet that was not his fault. Some of his critics blamed him for that. They include Ali Mazrui who blamed Nyerere's - hence Tanzania's - policies for the failure of the proposed federation. But that is not why the three East African countries of Kenya, Uganda, and Tanganyika did not unite.

They did not unite because of nationalism; which is also the main reason why regional integration in Africa has failed, to answer one of the questions Mazrui raised in his memorial lecture at Cornell University in October 1999, in which he paid tribute to President Julius Nyerere.

Nationalism triumphed over Pan-Africanism in the East African context because Kenya and Uganda did not want to surrender their sovereignties to a macro-national state in which they would be submerged. Only Nyerere, among the three East African leaders, was ready to do so. Nyerere even offered to delay Tanganyika's independence so that the three East African countries could attain sovereign status on the same day and unite under one government. And among the three, Kenya was the least enthusiastic.

At a meeting in Nairobi, Kenya, in June 1963, the three East African leaders - Kenyatta, Nyerere, and Obote - signed a declaration of intent to form a federation before the end of the year. Many people were excited about this, and even songs were composed heralding the dawn of a new era.

I remember a song in Kiswahili which was often played in the early and mid-1960s on the radio in Tanganyika and Kenya, called "Shirikisho la Afrika ya Mashariki," which means the Federation of East Africa. It was sung by one of Kenya's and East Africa's most popular musicians and guitarists, Peter Tsotsi, originally from Northern Rhodesia, which is Zambia today. Others sang the same song. Other famous musicians and guitar players in Kenya included Daudi Kabaka, originally from Uganda, and Fadhili Williams. But the federation was never consummated, in spite of all the optimism we had.

It was expected that the president of the East African Federation - Federal Republic of East Africa or whatever - would be Jomo Kenyatta, in deference to Mzee, the Grand Old Man; and Julius Nyerere would be vice president. But Kenya also wanted the foreign minister of the East African federation to be a Kenyan, probably Tom Mboya.

Uganda would therefore have been frozen out of all the three top positions; hardly a basis for unity. And, obviously, the extortionate demands by Kenya were deliberately intended to frustrate Nyerere's - and to a smaller degree, Obote's - efforts to unite the three East African countries.

Therefore Kenyan leaders would, perhaps, have agreed to unite with Uganda and Tanganyika only if they were going to dominate the federation.

Kenya also did not want to lose its dominant position as the most developed and industrialized country in East Africa. During British colonial rule, Nairobi was virtually the capital of East Africa. It was the headquarters of the East African Common Services Organisation (EACSO) - railways and harbors, posts and telecommunications, airways, currency board, research facilities and much more. It was also the largest and most developed city in East Africa.

And of all the East African countries, Kenya had the largest number of European settlers, about 66,000 and mostly British including members of the British aristocracy. They invested heavily in Kenya and tried to develop its economy because they saw it as an outpost of Britain which one day would become an independent state under white rule like South Africa, Australia and New Zealand; a dream white settlers in Rhodesia, now

Zimbabwe, also tried to pursue. That is why Lord Delamere, Kenya's first governor, called it "White Man's Country."

Had Kenya agreed to unite with Uganda and Tanganyika to form a federation, it would have to be an equal among equals; would have been required to contribute a bigger share to the federal budget because of its relatively strong economy; and would have to make other sacrifices - in terms of revenue sharing and removing tariffs to import more goods from Uganda and Tanganyika - in order to help the two weaker economies catch up. And this was just too much for the Kenyan leadership. Kenya, not East Africa, came first, because of nationalism.

Uganda was also a major problem. Dr. Milton Obote wanted to form the federation probably as much as Nyerere did, and even spoke out against the dissolution of the Central African Federation of Rhodesia (Northern Rhodesia and Southern Rhodesia) and Nyasaland.

He was the only African leader to do so. He believed that had the Central African Federation (which was formed in 1953 and dissolved in 1963) emerged from colonial rule as a single entity, it would have been a powerful African supra-nation and a major step towards continental unity.

But Uganda had serious internal problems because of strong opposition to the national government led by Obote. The strongest opposition came from the Buganda kingdom, vistually a state within a state, whose leaders were determined to reclaim its original glory as an independent nation as it was before the advent of colonial rule like the Ashanti in Ghana.

Other traditional strongholds in Uganda were also opposed to central authority. If all these kingdoms - Buganda, Ankole, Bunyoro, and the princedom of Busoga as well as other traditional centers of authority such as the Teso and the Acholi - were not ready to surrender power to the national government in Kampala; then one would certainly not have expected them to do so to an even more distant authority at the federal level of the three East African countries.

In terms of national integration, Uganda faced the toughest problem among all the three countries. Nyerere himself conceded that much, despite his unflinching determination to unite all the countries in the region, a goal he pursued until his death. Many

Ugandan leaders also invoked the constitution saying it did not allow them to surrender their country's sovereignty to any other authority; a provision that was included to appease the Buganda kingdom and others opposed to any further diminution of their authority. The national government itself was more than enough for them.

Yet, if the Ugandan leaders were serious about forming an East African federation, they could have changed their constitution and included a provision requiring Uganda to renounce her sovereign status in favour of union as the Ghananian constitution of March 1960 did, committing Ghana to full or partial renunciation of her sovereignty to achieve African unity.

Regarding Tanzania's socialist policies as an obstacle to federation, we need not look further to see that it was in fact Kenya, not Tanzania, which was an anomaly among the three countries and therefore the main obstacle to federation. Both Nyerere and Obote were socialist-oriented even far back then, in 1963, before they proclaimed their socialist policies, while Kenyatta was not.

Therefore it was Kenya's capitalist policies, which wrecked the proposed federation, as Nyerere and Obote moved closer ideologically and in terms of policy formulation, eventually promulgating socialist policies. Tanzania issued the Arusha Declaration in February 1967, and Uganda the Common Man's Charter in October 1969. But even they failed to unite, without Kenya, in spite of their common socialist policies and one-party states. Kenya also became a one-party state in 1969 following the banning of the opposition Kenya People's Union (KPU) led by former vice president Oginga Odinga.

The three countries even had a common market, a common currency, and common services - including posts and telecommunications, railways and harbors, the East African Airways (EAA), and research institutes - inherited from the British and which would have formed a solid foundation for a federal state. Still, they failed to unite, because of nationalism.

There was also the Nyerere factor, a potent factor, especially among Kenyans who wanted to dominate the federation but who also feared that the charismatic and highly influential Tanganyikan leader would emerge as the dominant political figure on the scene and become president of the East African Federation; a dreadful prospect for nationalist-minded Kenyans.

There was also, among the national leaders of Kenya and Uganda, fear of losing power and status to a higher authority at the federal level. For example, not all the cabinet members in the three national governments would have become cabinet members in the federal government, or even ambassadors. This was one of the strongest disincentives to consummation of the union, and all professions by them in different forums - including diplomatic conclaves - in support of East African unity was no more than empty rhetoric.

But in fairness, we must also admit that there were some people in the government of Tanganyika who felt the same way as their counterparts did in Kenya and Uganda. There was, however, one fundamental difference. Tanganyika under Nyerere was committed to federation. Kenya and Uganda were not.

Another reason why the three East African countries did not form a federation was the unwillingness among Kenyan and Ugandan leaders to lose platforms in international forums where their countries would no longer be sovereign entities. They would cease to exist. Thus, instead of having three East African governments, each speaking for its own country at the United Nations, the World Bank and other international organizations and institutions, there would - under federation - be only one government; which was unthinkable.

That is why the federation was never formed. And none of those factors had anything to do with Tanganyika, the strongest proponent of East African integration for which Nyerere was prepared to sacrifice so much, including giving up Tanganyika's status as a separate entity. Even if Tanganyika and Uganda had chosen the capitalist path, capitalist Kenya would still not have united with them. And Uganda would have continued to rationalize her opposition to such a union on constitutional grounds.

Obote supported the unification of the three East African countries, unlike most of his colleagues in Uganda. But when in 1964 the Ugandan government and parliament invoked the constitution to justify their opposition to federation, with Kenya already opposed to such a merger, it became obvious that the union could not be formed even under the best of circumstances: similar political and economic systems - neither Tanzania nor Uganda had gone socialist then, and Tanzania did not become a *de jure* one-party state until 1965. And the constitutional argument advanced by Uganda was not a very clever one, as we showed earlier. Constitutions can be amended and even abrogated.

The failure of the three East African countries to unite was one of the Nyerere's biggest disappointments; a point he underscored in an interview with James McKinley of *The New York Times* in his home village of Butiama in August 1996, more than 30 years after that abortive attempt, and 11 years after he voluntarily stepped down from the presidency.

Looking back on his political career, he said his greatest failure was that although he managed to form a union with Zanzibar in 1964 to create Tanzania, he never succeeded in persuading neighbouring countries to form a larger entity, a move, he said, that would have made the region a powerhouse.[39]

Yet, he succeeded in uniting a country of almost 130 different tribes into a cohesive and stable nation unparalleled on the African continent. And in another unprecedented move, he not only succeeded in uniting two independent countries, but in forming the only union in the history of post-colonial Africa, and which has survived for more than 40 years.

His unsurpassed skills in nation-building were clearly evident, not only across tribal but also racial lines, creating a political entity that is virtually indistinguishable from an organic whole. In terms of racial harmony, Tanzania is one of the very few countries in Africa to have achieved that. And it is probably the only one where non-black candidates - of European, Asian, and Arab descent - never lost elections to black candidates in predominantly black constituencies.

There was, for example, Derek Bryceson, a Tanzanian of British descent who always won elections against black candidates to represent Kilosa District in parliament. He was also the only white elected official on the entire continent representing an overwhelmingly black district in parliament, and held a number of cabinet posts under President Nyerere for many years, mostly as minister of agriculture.

When he died in a British hospital in 1980, his body was flown back to Tanzania for burial after a state funeral. Thousands of people went to the airport to receive the body, and thousands more lined the streets of Dar es Salaam to pay their last respects as the vehicle carrying his body in a convoy of cars passed by. He was one of the most popular and respected leaders of Tanzania.

Amir H. Jamal, of Indian descent, was another very popular and highly respected leader and technocrat who represented Morogoro District in parliament and, like Bryceson, never lost an election against black candidates in a predominantly black constituency. He also held several senior cabinet posts - finance; commerce and industries; development and economic planning, and others including ambassadorial - for many years since independence. He also served as chairman of the Board of Governors of the International Monetary Fund (IMF) when he was Tanzania's minister of economic planning.

He died in 1995 in Vancouver, Canada. Speaking at his funeral in Dar es Salaam, Nyerere remembered him as a colleague and compatriot, in a moving speech, and on one of the saddest occasions in the country's history.

Both Bryceson and Jamal were also veterans of the independence struggle. And there were many others - white, Asian, Arab - in different leadership positions and other posts working together with indigenous Africans, as they still do today including some cabinet members.

None of this would have been possible had it not been for President Julius Nyerere or another leader of such high calibre capable of uniting members of different tribes and races into a cohesive entity.

And he inspired those who followed in his footsteps, President Ali Hassan Mwinyi and President Benjamin Mkapa, to pursue the same policies of tolerance, harmony, and peaceful co-existence; although after his death, agitation for greater autonomy - euphemism for independence in this context - in Zanzibar gained momentum, and ethnoregional rivalries and racial hostilities began to surface on an unprecedented scale. But he still left behind a stable nation, relatively speaking, and continues to inspire millions of Tanzanians to close ranks and maintain national unity.

In the pantheon of African leaders, he is one of those who continue to inspire millions across the continent. And his Pan-African commitment was no mere rhetoric, unlike that of most of his colleagues. He meant what he said, and did it. For example, the liberation struggle in southern Africa would probably have taken a different turn had it not been for his commitment and sacrifice. And tens of thousands of refugees from other African countries were given citizenship through the decades when he was president.

In the early eighties alone, almost 100,000 people, mostly from Rwanda and Burundi, became Tanzanian citizens. And he extended his hospitality to others who were equally embraced with open arms. Thousands of refugees from Mozambique during the liberation war in the Portuguese colony also became citizens of Tanzania because of Nyerere's magnanimous policies.

And he continued to make sacrifices for fellow Africans across the continent until his last days; his relentless effort to help resolve the conflict in Burundi being only one example.

When Dr. Kenneth Kaunda was jailed by President Frederick Chiluba for allegedly plotting to overthrow him, Nyerere intervened and helped get him out of jail. And when Olusegun Obasanjo was imprisoned by Nigerian military dictator Sani Abacha, Nyerere worked relentlessly to help free him. After he was freed, Obasanjo said Nyerere was the first person outside Nigeria to call him, and told him he was sorry he did not work hard enough to help get him out of prison; testament to his humility.

At Nyerere's funeral in Dar es Salaam, President Obasanjo nearly whispered as he recalled how Nyerere worked hard to free him from prison where he was serving a life sentence - reduced to 15 years - for allegedly trying to overthrow the government of military dictator Sani Abacha: "He was the first non-Nigerian who called me when I was freed, and he told me he was afraid he hadn't done enough."[40]

His death will never be forgotten by many people, including me. Nyerere's death will remain memorable to me in another respect, although this is only coincidental. He entered Edinburgh University in Scotland in October 1949 where he earned a master's degree in economics and history, and returned to

Tanganyika in October 1952. That was the same year, 1949, and the same month of October, in which I was born in Kigoma in western Tanganyika under British colonial rule. And he died almost exactly 50 years later, on October 14, 1999, 10 days after my 50th birthday on October 4th.

That is not the best way to remember one's birthday, yet, because of this, I will never forget when he died. He was mourned around the world, by the most humble and the most exalted; true testament to his greatness as a selfless leader who put the people first, including those groaning under apartheid and other oppressive regimes, black and white. Without his commitment and sacrifice, Tanzania would probably not have survived as a stable and united country.

And that pretty much sums up what ails Africa today: lack of good leadership more than anything else. It is lack of effective, dedicated leadership, which led to the destruction of Somalia as a nation, the first African country to "disappear" from the map. It is also lack of good leadership, which explains why other African countries dissolved in anarchy, torn by civil wars: Rwanda, Burundi, Congo-Kinshasa, Congo-Brazzaville, Liberia, and Sierra Leone. That is also why other forms of civil strife in different parts of the continent have become a prominent feature of the political landscape and national life.

One can't help but wonder what would have happened in all these countries if they had leaders of Nyerere's and Mandela's calibre, genuinely committed to the well-being of their people, instead of being only interested in how much they are going to steal from them, and how they are going to oppress them and favour members of their tribes and sell their countries to outsiders. As Nyerere said in Accra, Ghana, where he was invited to participate in celebrations marking the 40th anniversary of Ghana's independence in March 1997:

> We must not allow the future of Africa to be determined by those outside Africa. This is 1997 not 1887 - three years away from the 21st century. We must determine our own destiny. We've got to empower ourselves through unity to determine the fate of our continent...
> Today we have African leaders who have simply looted their countries and their countries have gone to the dogs. We don't need those men...but we do need leadership. We need government that works and we need a hard-core of people who are willing to work hard and contribute to their country's

welfare.[41]

It is a fitting tribute that Africans from different countries across the continent and other people elsewhere decided to institute a continental award known as the Nyerere Prize for Ethics, proposed by the Independent Commission on the Third Millennium for Africa based in Cotonou, Benin.

The award will go to leaders who have demonstrated outstanding ethical conduct, in honour of the late Mwalimu Julius Nyerere because of his exemplary leadership, which earned him the title, "The Conscience of Africa." Supporters of the project include African governments, the United Nations, and other different organizations and institutions.

But, commendable as the project is, who is really going to get this award? Who deserves it on this beleaguered continent of brutal autocrats and kleptocrats who don't mind bleeding their people to death in more than one way? It is a continent mangled, crippled, and bled by the very same leaders who are going to claim the award "in the name of the people." As Nyerere himself said not long before he died: "Africa is in a mess."

The award may, indeed, have been established in vain; hardly a fitting tribute to a man who died trying to bring peace to one of the most embattled parts of our continent, the Great Lakes region of East-central Africa, and elsewhere.

Although he is gone, his ideals will always be with us. And they will continue to inspire us in our quest for peace and stability, justice and equality, for which he lived and died. It is ideals which can be achieved through unity, without which no country can survive, let alone thrive.

But they will remain unattainable ideals if the building blocks for African unity are fragmented by ethnic conflicts and other forms of civil strife.

Many countries have been pulverized from within, and several others continue to sustain crippling blows because of their inability or unwillingness to address one vital issue: There can be no peace without stability, and no stability without justice and equality for all. And that entails, not only guaranteeing freedom of expression as a fundamental democratic right, but equal participation in the political process and in policy formulation and implementation on consensus basis at all levels of government.

It also requires equitable redistribution of wealth to all regions and groups in order to contain and defuse ethnic and regional tensions and rivalries. Most of these are caused by discrimination; hardly a basis for unity. Fortunately, we were able to avoid these problems in Tanzania because of Nyerere's leadership.

Growing up in Tanganyika in the fifties and sixties was a memorable experience for me. I was born under colonial rule 12 years before independence. I grew up not only in an independent but a united republic. When Tanganyika won independence from Britain on December 9, 1961, I was 12 years old and did not have the slightest idea of what was going to happen in only two years. Even grown-ups involved or interested in politics did not have any idea that we would be living in a new country within so short a time. On April 26, 1964, Tanganyika united with Zanzibar. The new country was called the Union of Tanganyika and Zanzibar until October 29 the same year when it was renamed the United Republic of Tanzania.

It has been one long journey since then, and we still have a long way to go towards unity across the continent. But achieving this noble objective entails, first and foremost, conflict resolution in Africa. It is a goal Nyerere was trying to achieve when his life came to an end, an end which also marked the beginning of a new era towards the end of the twentieth century. As he said in Accra, Ghana, on March 6, 1997, in a speech celebrating Ghana's 40th independence anniversary, his generation fought for independence. It is now for this generation to unite Africa. His speech was entitled, "Africa Must Unite":

"Forty years ago the people of Ghana celebrated the raising of the flag of their independence for the first time. Throughout Africa people celebrated - in solidarity with Ghana but also for themselves. For the liberation of Africa was a single struggle with many fronts. Ghana's independence from colonial rule in 1957 was recognised for what it was: the beginning of the end of colonialism for the whole of Africa. For centuries we had been oppressed and humiliated as Africans. We were hunted and enslaved as Africans, as we were colonized as Africans.

The humiliation of Africans became the glorification of others. So we felt our African-ness. We knew that we were one people, and that we had one destiny regardless of the artificial boundaries, which the colonialists had invented. Since we were humiliated as Africans we had to be liberated as Africans.

So forty years ago we recognised your independence as the first triumph in Africa's struggle for freedom and dignity. It was the first success of our demand to be accorded the international respect, which is accorded free peoples. Ghana was the beginning, our first liberated zone. Thirty-seven years later in 1994 - we celebrated our final triumph when apartheid was crushed and Nelson Mandela was installed as the president of South Africa. Africa's long struggle for freedom was over.

But Ghana was more than just the beginning. Ghana inspired and deliberately spearheaded the independence struggle for the rest of Africa.

I was a student at Edinburgh University when Kwame Nkrumah was released from prison to be Leader of Government Business in his first elected government. The deportment of the Gold Coast students changed. The way they carried themselves up - they way they talked to us and others, the way they looked at the world at large, changed overnight. They even looked different. They were not arrogant, they were not overbearing, they were not aloof, but they were proud. Already they felt free and they exuded that quiet pride of self-confidence of freedom without which humanity is incomplete.

And so eight years later when the Gold Coast became independent, Kwame Nkrumah invited us, the leaders of the various liberation movements in Africa, to come and celebrate with you. I was among the many invited. Then Nkrumah made a famous declaration, that Ghana's independence was meaningless unless the whole of Africa was liberated from colonial rule. Kwame Nkrumah went into action almost immediately.

In the following year he called the liberation movements to Ghana to discuss a common strategy for the liberation of the continent from colonialism. In preparation for the African Peoples' Conference, those of us in East and Central Africa met in Mwanza, Tanganyika, to discuss our possible contribution to the forthcoming conference. That conference lit the liberation torch throughout colonial Africa.

Kwame Nkrumah was your leader, but he was our leader too: For he was an African leader. People are not gods. Even the best have their faults, and the faults of the great can be very big. So Kwame Nkrumah had his faults. But he was great in a purely positive sense. He was a visionary. He thought big, but he thought big for Ghana and its people and for Africa and its people. He had a great dream for Africa and its people. He had the well-being of our people at heart. He was no looter. He did not have a Swiss bank account. He died poor. Shakespeare wrote that the evil that men do lives after them, but the good is often interred with their bones.

Five years later, in May 1963, thirty-two independent African states met in Addis Ababa, founded the Organisation of African Unity (OAU), and established the liberation committee of the new organisation, charging it with the duty of coordinating the liberation struggle in those parts of Africa still under colonial rule.

The following year, 1964, the OAU met in Cairo. That Cairo summit is remembered mainly for the declaration of the heads of state of independent Africa to respect the borders inherited from colonialism. The principle of non-interference in the internal affairs of member states of the OAU had been enshrined in the charter itself; respect for the borders inherited from colonialism comes from the Cairo Declaration of 1964 (the resolution was Nyerere's idea and he introduced it at the Cairo summit). In 1965, the OAU met in Accra. That summit is not well remembered as the founding summit in 1963, or the Cairo summit of 1964.

The fact that Kwame Nkrumah did not last long as head of state of Ghana after that summit may have contributed to the comparative obscurity of that important summit. But I want to suggest that the reason why we do not talk much about that summit is probably psychological: it was a failure. That failure still haunts us today.

The founding fathers of the OAU had set themselves two major objectives: the total liberation of our continent from colonialism and settler minorities, and the unity of Africa. The first objective was expressed through the immediate establishment of the Liberation Committee by the founding summit. The second objective was expressed in the name of the organisation - it is the Organisation of African Unity.

Critics could say that the charter itself, with its great emphasis on the sovereign independence of each member state, combined with the Cairo Declaration on the sanctity of the inherited borders, makes it look like the 'Organisation of African Disunity.' But that would be carrying criticism too far and ignoring the objective reasons which led to the principles of non-interference in the Cairo Declaration.

What the founding fathers - certainly a hard-core of them - had in mind was genuine desire to move Africa towards greater unity. We loathed the balkanization of the continent into small non-viable states, most of which had borders, which did not make ethnic or geographical sense. The Cairo Declaration was prompted by a profound realisation of the absurdity of those borders.

It was quite clear that some adventurers would try to change those borders by force of arms. Indeed, it was already happening. Ethiopia and Somalia were at war over inherited borders. Kwame Nkrumah was opposed to balkanization as much as he was opposed to colonialism in Africa. To him and to a number of us, the two - balkanization and colonization - were twins. Genuine liberation of Africa had to attack both twins. A struggle against colonialism must go hand in hand with a struggle against the balkanization of Africa.

Kwame Nkrumah was the great crusader for African unity. He wanted the Accra summit of 1965 to establish a union government for the whole of independent Africa. But we failed. The one minor reason is that Kwame, like all great believers, underestimated the degree of suspicion and animosity, which his crusading passion had created among a substantial number of his fellow heads of state. The major reason was linked to the first: already too many of us had a vested interest in keeping Africa divided.

Prior to independence of Tanganyika, I had been advocating that East African countries should federate and then achieve independence as a single political unit. I had said publicly that I was willing to delay Tanganyika's independence in order to enable all three-mainland countries to achieve their independence together as a single federated state. I made the suggestion because of my fear, proved correct by later events, that it would be very difficult to unite our countries if we let them achieve independence separately.

Once you multiply national anthems, national flags and national passports, seats at the United Nations, and individuals entitled to 21-gun salute, not to speak of a host of ministers, prime ministers, and envoys, you will have a whole army of powerful people with vested interests in keeping Africa balkanized. That was what Nkrumah encountered in 1965.

After the failure to establish the union government at the Accra summit of 1965, I heard one head of state express with relief that he was happy to be returning home to his country still head of state. To this day I cannot tell whether he was serious or joking. But he may well have been serious, because Kwame Nkrumah was very serious and the fear of a number of us to lose our precious status was quite palpable.

But I never believed that the 1965 Accra summit would have established a union government for Africa. When I say that we failed, that is not what I mean, for that clearly was an unrealistic objective for a single summit. What I mean is that we did not even discuss a mechanism for pursuing the objective of a politically united Africa. We had a Liberation Committee already. We should have at least had a Unity Committee or undertaken to establish one. We did not. And after Kwame Nkrumah was removed from the African political scene nobody took up the challenge again.

So my remaining remarks have a confession and a plea. The confession is that we of the first generation leaders of independent Africa have not pursued the objective of African unity with the vigour, commitment and sincerity that it deserves. Yet that does not mean that unity is now irrelevant.

Does the experience of the last three or four decades of Africa's independence dispel the need for African unity? With our success in the liberation struggle, Africa today has 53 independent states, 21 more than those, which met in Addis Ababa in May 1963. If numbers were horses, Africa would be riding high! Africa would be the strongest continent in the world, for it occupies more seats in the UN General Assembly than any other continent. Yet the reality is that ours is the poorest and weakest continent in the world. And our weakness is pathetic. Unity will not end our weakness, but until we unite, we cannot even begin to end that weakness.

So this is my plea to the new generation of African leaders and African people: Work for unity with firm conviction that without unity there is no future for Africa. That is, of course, assuming that we still want to have a place under the sun.

I reject the glorification of the nation-state, which we have inherited from colonialism, and the artificial nations we are trying to forge from that inheritance. We are all Africans trying very hard to be Ghanaians or Tanzanians. Fortunately for Africa we have not been completely successful. The outside world hardly recognises our Ghanaian-ness or Tanzanian-ness. What the outside world recognises about us is our African-ness.

Hitler was a German, Mussolini was an Italian, Franco was a Spaniard, Salazaar was a Portuguese, Stalin was a Russian or a Georgian. Nobody expected Churchill to be ashamed of Hitler. He was probably ashamed of Chamberlain. Nobody expected Charles de Gaulle to be ashamed of Hitler. He was probably ashamed of the complicity of Vichy. It is Germans, and Italians and Spaniards and Portuguese who feel uneasy about those dictators in their respective countries.

Not so in Africa. Idi Amin was in Uganda, but of Africa, Jean Bokassa was in Central Africa, but of Africa. Some of the dictators are still active in their respective countries, but they are all of Africa. They are all Africans, and all are perceived by the outside world as Africans. When I travel outside Africa the description of me as former president of Tanzania is a fleeting affair. It does not stick. Apart from the ignorant who sometimes asked me whether Tanzania was Johannesburg, even to those who knew better, what stuck in the minds of my hosts was the fact of my African-ness. So I had to answer questions about the atrocities of the Amins and the Bokassas of Africa.

Mrs. Gandhi did not have to answer questions about the atrocities of Asia. Nor does Fidel Castro have to answer about the atrocities of the Somozas of Latin America. But when I travel or meet foreigners, I have to answer questions about Somalia, Liberia, Rwanda, Burundi and Zaire, as in the past I used to answer questions about Mozambique, Angola, Zimbabwe, Namibia or South Africa.

And the way I was perceived is the way most of my fellow heads of state were perceived. And that is the way you are all being perceived. So accepting the fact that we are Africans gives you a much more worthwhile challenge than the current desperate attempts to fossilize Africa into the wounds inflicted upon it by the vultures of imperialism....

Reject the return to the tribe. There is richness of culture out there, which we must do everything we can to preserve and share. But it is utter madness to think that if these artificial, non-viable states, which we are trying to create, are broken up into tribal components and we turn those into nation-states, we might save ourselves.

That kind of political and social atavism spells catastrophe for Africa. It would be the end of any kind of genuine development for Africa. It would fossilize Africa into a worse state than the one in which we are. The future of Africa, the modernization of Africa that has a place in the 21st century is linked up with its decolonization and detribalization. Tribal atavism would be giving up any hope for Africa. And of all the sins that Africa can commit, the sin of despair would be the most unforgivable.

Reject the nonsense of dividing African people into Anglophones, Francophones and Lusophones. This attempt to divide our people according to the language of their former colonial masters must be rejected with the firmness and utter contempt that it richly deserves. The natural owners of those wonderful languages are busy building a united Europe. But Europe is strong, even without unity. It has less need for unity and strength that comes from unity than Africa....

The second phase of the liberation of Africa is going to be much harder than the first. But it can be done. It must done. Empower Africa through unity, and Africa shall be free, strong and prosperous....

A new generation of self-respecting Africans should spit in the face of anybody who suggests that our continent should remain divided and fossilized....in order to satisfy the national pride of our former colonial masters.

Africa must unite! This was the title of one of Kwame Nkrumah's books. That call is more urgent today than ever before. Together, we the people of Africa will be incomparably stronger internationally than we are now with our multiplicity of non-viable states. The needs of our separate countries can be, and are being, ignored by the rich and powerful. The result is that Africa is marginalised when international decisions affecting our vital interests are made.

Unity will not make us rich, but it can make it difficult for Africa and the African people to be disregarded and humiliated. And it will therefore increase the effectiveness of the decisions we make and try to implement for our development.

My generation led Africa to political freedom. The current generation of leaders and the people of Africa must pick up the flickering torch of African freedom, refuel it with their enthusiasm and determination, and carry it forward."[42]

His death was indeed a significant event in the history of Africa. It marked the end of an era in which African countries won independence, and in which the African founding fathers left an indelible mark on the young nations they helped to nurture during the post-colonial period.

In spite of the failures they had in a number of areas, especially in the economic arena, they will always be remembered as the leaders who not only led our countries to independence but who also helped end white minority rule in southern Africa by supporting liberation movements waging guerrilla warfare against the racist regimes in the region.

This concerted effort culminated in the collapse of apartheid in the citadel of white supremacy and the last bastion of white minority rule on the continent, and whose demise was witnessed by Nyerere when he attended the inauguration of Nelson Mandela as the first democratically elected president of South Africa.

The struggle for African liberation had finally come to an end. It was a struggle to which Nyerere dedicated his life. And he will always be remembered for that. Always.

Chapter Six:

Tanzania after Nyerere

A number of significant changes have taken place in Tanzania since Nyerere left office. And they are fundamental changes in many respects.

Socialism has been renounced as a state ideology, even if not in so strident a tone in deference to Mwalimu probably more than anything else. And capitalism has returned with a vengeance.

The one-party system has also been abandoned, although Tanzania remains a *de facto* one-party state for all practical purposes. Multiparty democracy has been introduced, although it has had little impact on the political scene because of the weakness of the parties and their leaders. They have offered nothing new. They have also been compromised by their partisan nature by appealing to ethnoregional loyalties.

And Zanzibar remains a tinderbox, with the opposition in the former island nation determined to wreck the union, having been emboldened by Nyerere's departure from this world.

But none of this has seriously affected the domestic tranquility the country has enjoyed since independence as one of the most peaceful and stable in the entire world; also one of the most united, although there have been some disturbances now and then, here and there, through the years since the introduction of multiparty politics in 1992, much of this being attributed to mischief-making within the opposition camp to score political kudos where other means - of fair play - have failed to win them support among the masses, in spite of their legitimacy as alternative forums for ventilation of grievances and articulation of new ideas in the political arena.

Where Tanzania is headed in this post-Nyerere and post-Cold War era of global capitalism and multiparty democracy is an entirely different matter. But it requires serious thinking among all Tanzanians about the destiny of this island of peace and stability on a turbulent continent, lest disruptive elements and unscrupulous politicians somehow manage to mislead a signficant number of people into believing what they are being told in order to promote their own interests at the expense of the nation.

And there are indications that is indeed the case. There are a number of political parties that are unabashedly regionalist in orientation. The main opposition party in Zanzibar, the Civic United Front (CUF), which is strongest on Pemba island, has made it clear that it is not interested in maintaing the union. As its leader Shariff Hamad bluntly stated in October 2000 just before the general election in an interview with *Time*: "If we win, I see no reason to stay in the Union. Zanzibaris have not benefited from it one bit. I would go to the mainland and start talks on a program to move toward full independence."[1]

Zanzibar's former Attorney-General and later Chief Justice Wolfgang Dourado who once was detained for more than 100 days for criticizing the union and calling for a three-government federation during Nyerere's presidency, articulated similar sentiments, probably echoed by many Zanzibaris, when he was also interviewed in October 2000 by *Time*: "The millions and billions of aid and development money that comes into Tanzania, do your research into how much of it comes here. Nothing. We try to talk to them, but it's a dialogue with the deaf and dumb."[2]

Tanzania's former first vice president who also was the president of Zanzibar, Aboud Jumbe, was just as blunt about his disenchantment with the union. He resigned – there were reports that he was forced to resign - in 1984 because of his opposition to the structural arrangements of the union and wanted Tanzania to have three governments, instead of two as is the case today.

There is a union government for the united republic which is also the government of the Tanzania mainland, the former independent country of Tanganyika, and a separate government for Zanzibar. Aboud Jumbe wanted three governments: one for

181

the union, one for Zanzibar, and one for Tanganyika; a move that was strongly opposed by President Nyerere who said it would lead to the break-up of the union.

Jumbe even wrote a book about the problem, *The Partnership: Tanganyika-Zanzibar Union: 30 Turbulent Years*, published in 1994, ten years after he resigned, in which he contends that Zanzibar has not benefited from the union since it was formed in 1964. As he stated at a press conference in Dar es Salaam in January 1998 on the 34th anniversary of the Zanzibar revolution, he did not understand why the government continued to maintain the rigid structure of the union and refused to have three governments in spite of the desire for such change among many people in the country. As he put it: "I don't understand why the government should cling to this stand, but I suspect it is for the same reasons that my book, *The Partnership*, has been ignored since the era of the single party system."[3]

On whether or not the union was beneficial, and if it had in any way benefited Tanzania mainland since he said it had not benefited Zanzibar, he bluntly stated: "Ask Nyerere, because he is the one who went to Zanzibar. He is the one who wanted the union. He must have had goals. Has he achieved them? I cannot speak for mainlanders on the achievement of the union."[4]

Aboud Jumbe also went on to say that he believed the shortcomings of the union of Tanganyika and Zanzibar had played a major role in delaying the establishment of an East African federation.

Nyerere played a critical role in maintaining a stable union because of his great influence. People on both sides listened to him. His formidable influence was also clearly evident in other areas; for example, when he helped Dr. Eduardo Mondlane to win the leadership of FRELIMO; in fact it was said that Mondlane was "handpicked" by Nyerere to lead the Mozambican liberation movement.

He also played a critical role in helping Samora Machel, a much more capable leader than his opponents, to become the next president of FRELIMO after Dr. Mondlane was assassinated in February 1969. It is said that some Tanzanian cabinet members during that time wanted FRELIMO's vice president, Uria Simango, to be the next leader. As Professor John Saul, who taught at the University of Dar es Salaam and worked closely with some Tanzanian government officials when Nyerere was president, stated:

> Certainly I recall, from reasonably close at hand, the struggle in the late 1960s over the sucession to Mondlane within FRELIMO, the Mozambican liberation movement still primarily domiciled on Tanzanian soil.
> The outcome, that saw the far more worthy Samora Machel defeat the Simango faction, was won primarily because Nyerere had the political will and craft to back down the 'cultural nationalist' triumvirate, so strong within TANU at that time, of (Bhoke) Munanka, (Lawi Nangwanda) Sijaona, and (Saidi) Maswanya, a group who sought, initially, to have the Tanzanian state guarantee Simango's ascendancy....
> This example...demonstrates the kind of power Nyerere could exercise when he cared to do so.[5]

Nyerere also strongly supported Robert Mugabe, helping him to consolidate his position in ZANU (Zimbabwe African National union) and become the most influential leader of the liberation struggle in Zimbabwe overshadowing the veteran politician Joshua Nkomo. He played the role of king maker, not only in those two countries but elsewhere including Uganda after the ouster of Idi Amin.

Therefore, he exerted even more influence in his own country, and the Zanzibar crisis was just one of those he managed skillfully. That is why there was speculation that the union would not survive after he died. But it has survived.

Still, there is no question that there are serious problems in the union. And they have assumed another dimension, threatening to destroy it, since Nyerere died. There is no guarantee that if a referendum were held today, the majority of the people of Zanzibar would vote in favour of the union as it is currently structured; although many of them don't want to see it destroyed because of the benefits they get from being a part of a larger economically secure political entity.

The union should be renegotiated and restructured to accommodate the interests of Zanzibaris and ventilate their grievances. And they do have grievances. That is why Tanzania's ruling party, CCM, is not very popular in Zanzibar. The union can and should be saved. The question is how.

Continue to talk to the people of Zanzibar. Listen to their

grievances. Give them meaningful concessions including cabinet posts. Otherwise we are going to have an eruption which could threaten and even destroy the union. Formation of coalition government, which should include leading opposition members, is one of the best solutions to this crisis.

Giving some cabinet posts to members of the opposition, on the mainland and and in Zanzibar, may seem to be too much of a concession; it is as if the government is capitulating to extortionist demands by the opposition. But that is not the case. It is consensus building critical to peace and stability, without which it is impossible to maintain a stable union.

It has been done elsewhere, and it can also be done in Tanzania. For example, when John F. Kennedy, a Democrat, was president, he appointed some Republicans to his cabinet. And they held some of the most prominent cabinet posts. They were Dean Rusk who was secretary of state; Robert McNamara, secretary of defense; and Douglas Dillon who served as secretary of the treasury under two Democratic administrations of Kennedy and Lyndon Johnson.

This is not to say that because it has been done in the United States and other countries, it should also be done in Tanzania. It is simply to say that if the opposition is not given a prominent role to play in national affairs, and is not included in decision making at the highest level, it will be almost impossible to build consensus across the spectrum so critical to maintaining a stable union.

The opposition has its own weaknesses. It has failed to mobilize support across the nation. But this should also be looked at in its proper historical context.

The people of Tanzania have lived under one-party rule for more than 40 years since independence; the same party that won independence is the same party that is in power today. And they know what this party has done for them in terms of maintaining peace and stability and providing services, especially under Nyerere when education was free and medical service was also free. Therefore they are not used to changing national leadership along party lines, and they don't know what will happen if the opposition gets power.

But for democracy to survive, and thrive, you need a strong

opposition. The opposition parties need to merge and form one strong political party. There are just too many of them and they are not united behind a single candidate who can be a credible challenge to the presidential candidate of the ruling party in the general election.

But the government also has a duty to strengthen the opposition by increasing the number of opposition members in parliament on the basis of proportional representation. Every vote counts. Therefore the people who vote for the opposition should also be represented in parliament.

The constitution should also be re-written to reflect new realities and accommodate conflicting interests. It should be re-written not just by the members of parliament but by representatives of different interest groups - opposition parties, labour organizations, students, professionals, women, religious bodies, regional groups and others - whose recommendations by a special constitutional commission *must* be taken into account when re-writing the constitution.

That is the only way the constitution can reflect the will of the people and acquire legitimacy as the embodiment of their aspirations.

All this should be done only after the constitutional proposals have been discussed at a national convention attended by representatives of *all* interest groups across the nation; the new constitution to be ratified by a constituent assembly specifically convened for this purpose.

A constitution is not holy writ, like the Bible or the Koran. It is written by man, and it can be re-written by man. It is not an infallible document like the word of God.

Nyerere's era of one-party rule is gone forever, although Tanzania is now a *de facto* one-party state because of the weakness of the opposition. But challenge to its leadership is something that should be expected to continue now that the country has adopted multiparty democracy. Yet, multiparty democracy has no functional utility without a two-party system. Third parties are a nuisance. They never win elections.

But it will be a long time before Tanzania has a credible opposition. The ruling party, CCM, will probably remain in power for a long time because of its track record. It has impeccable - and formidable - credentials as a nationalist and Pan-Africanist movement, one of the most successful in the entire Third World because of the leadership provided by Nyerere for almost half a century since TANU was founded in 1954.

It led the struggle for independence and won. It promised to deliver goods and services to the people, and it did, especially under Nyerere. And it has continued to advance its populist agenda under his successors and the people have responded positively to that, although much remains to be done especially in this era of globalization dominated by greed at the expense of the masses.

It will be extremely difficult to dislodge CCM from power. It is highly unlikely that the opposition will win the next general election or any other in the next twenty or thirty years. As one opposition leader said in 2000, CCM is going to remain in power for 500 years.

The future was never meant for us to see. But he could be vindicated by history.

Appendix I:

Nyerere: Reflections

YOU WANTED me to reflect. I told you I had very little time to reflect.

I am not an engineer (reference to the vice-chancellor of the University of Dar es Salaam who identified himself as an engineer in his introductory remarks) and therefore what I am going to say might sound messy, unstructured and possibly irrelevant to what you intend to do; but I thought that if by reflecting, you wanted me to go back and relive the political life that I have lived for the last 30, 40 years, that I cannot do.

And in any case, in spite of the fact that it's useful to go back in history, what you are talking about is what might be of use to Africa in the 21st century. History's important, obviously, but I think we should concentrate and see what might be of use to our continent in the coming century.

What I want to do is share with you some thoughts on two issues concerning Africa. One, an obvious one; when I speak, you will realise how obvious it is. Another one, less obvious, and I'll spend a little more time on the less obvious one, because I think this will put Africa in what is going to be Africa's context in the 21st century. And the new leadership of Africa will have to concern itself with the situation in which it finds itself in the world tomorrow - in the world of the 21st century. And the Africa I'm going to be talking about, is Africa south of the Sahara, sub-Saharan Africa.

I'll explain later the reason why I chose to concentrate on

Africa south of the Sahara. It is because of the point I want to emphasise.

It appears today that in the world tomorrow, there are going to be three centers of power: some, political power; some, economic power, but three centers of real power in the world. One center is the United States of America and Canada; what you call North America. That is going to be a huge economic power, and probably for a long time the only military power, but a huge economic power.

The other one is going to be Western Europe, another huge economic power. I think Europe is choosing deliberately not to be a military power. I think they deliberately want to leave that to the United States.

The other one is Japan. Japan is in a different category but it is better to say Japan, because the power of Japan is quite clear, the economic power of Japan is obvious.

The three powers are going to affect the countries near them. I was speaking in South Africa recently and I referred to Mexico. A former president of Mexico, I think it must have been after the revolution in 1935, no, after the revolution; a former president of Mexico is reported to have complained about his country or lamented about his country. "Poor Mexico," said the president, "so far from God yet so near the United States."

He was complaining about the disadvantages of being a neighbour of a giant. Today, Mexico has decided not simply to suffer the disadvantages of being so close to the United States. And the United States itself has realised the importance of trying to accommodate Mexico.

In the past there were huge attempts by the United States to prevent people from moving from Mexico *into* the United States; people seeking work, seeking jobs. So you had police, a border very well policed in order to prevent Mexicans who *seek*, who *look* for jobs, to *move* into the United States. The United States discovered that it was not working. It *can't* work.

There is a kind of economic osmosis where whatever you do, if you are rich, you are attractive to the poor. They will come, they'll even *risk* their own lives in order to come.

So the United States tried very hard to prevent Mexicans going into the United States; they've given up, and the result was

NAFTA. It is in the interest of the United States to try and create jobs in Mexico because, if you don't, the Mexicans will simply come, to the United States; so they're doing that.

Europe, Western Europe, is very wealthy. It has two Mexicos. One is Eastern Europe. If you want to prevent those Eastern Europeans to come to Western Europe, you jolly will have to create jobs in *Eastern* Europe, and Western Europe is actually *doing* that. They are *doing* that. They'll help Eastern Europe to develop. The whole of Western Europe will be doing it, the Germans are doing it.

The Germans basically started first of all with the East Germans but they are spending lots of money also helping the other countries of Eastern Europe to develop, including unfortunately, or *fortunately* for them, including Russia. Because they realise, Europeans realise including the Germans, if you don't help *Russia* to develop, one of these days you are going to be in trouble.

So it is in the interest of Western Europe, to help Eastern Europe including Russia. They are pouring a lot of money in that part of the world, in that part of Europe, to try and help it to develop.

I said Western Europe has two Mexicos. I have mentioned one. I'll jump the other. I jump Europe's second Mexico. I'll go to Asia. I'll go to Japan. Japan - a wealthy island, *very* wealthy indeed, but an *island*. I don't think they're very keen on the unemployed of Asia to go to Japan. They'd rather help them where they are, and Japan is spending a lot of money in Asia, to help create jobs *in* Asia, prevent those Asians dreaming about going to Japan to look for jobs. In any case, Japan is too small, they can't find wealth there.

But apart from what Japan is doing, of course Asia *is* Asia; Asia has *China!* Asia has *India*, and the small countries of Asia are not very small. The population of Indonesia is twice the population of Nigeria, your biggest.

So Asia is virtually in a category, of the Third World countries, of the Southern countries; Asia is almost in a category of its own. It is developing as a power, and Europe knows it, and the United States knows it. And in spite of the *huge* Atlantic, now they are talking about the Atlantic *Rim*. That is in recognition of the importance of Asia.

I go back to Europe. Europe has a second Mexico. And Europe's second Mexico is North Africa. North Africa is to Europe what Mexico is to the United States. North Africans who have no jobs will not go to Nigeria; they'll be thinking of Europe or the Middle East, because of the imperatives of geography and history and religion and language. North Africa is part of Europe and the Middle East.

Nasser was a great leader and a great *African* leader. I got on extremely well with him. Once he sent me a minister, and I had a long discussion with his minister at the State House here, and in the course of the discussion, the minister says to me, "Mr. President, this is my first visit to Africa."

North Africa, because of the pull of the Mediterranean, and I say, history and culture, and religion, North Africa is pulled towards the North. When North Africans look for jobs, they go to Western Europe and southern Western Europe, or they go to the Middle East. And Europe has a specific policy for North Africa, specific policy for North Africa. It's not only about development; it's also about security. Because of you don't do something about North Africa, they'll come.

Africa, south of the Sahara, is different; *totally* different. If you have no jobs here in Tanzania, where do you go? The Japanese have no fear that you people will flock to Japan. The North Americans have no fear that you people will flock to North America. Not even from West Africa. The Atlantic, the Atlantic as an ocean, like the Mediterranean, it has its own logic. But links North America and Western Europe, not North America and West Africa.

Africa south of the Sahara is isolated. That is the first point I want to make. South of the Sahara is totally isolated in terms of that configuration of developing power in the world in the 21st century - on its own. There is no centre of power in whose self-interest it's important to develop Africa, *no* centre. Not North America, not Japan, not Western Europe. There's no self-interest to bother about Africa south of the Sahara. Africa south of the Sahara is on its own. *Na si jambo baya.*

Those of you who don't know Kiswahili, I just whispered, "Not necessarily bad."

That's the first thing I wanted to say about Africa south of the Sahara. African leadership, the coming African leadership, will have to bear that in mind. You are on your own, Mr. Vice President.

You mentioned, you know, in the past, there was some Cold War competition in Africa and some Africans may have exploited it. I never did. I never succeeded in exploiting the Cold War in Africa. We suffered, we suffered through the Cold War. Look at Africa south of the Sahara. I'll be talking about it later. Southern Africa, I mean, look at southern Africa; devastated because of the combination of the Cold War and apartheid. Devastated part of Africa. It could have been *very* different. But the Cold War is gone, thank God. But thank God the Cold War is gone, the chances of the Mobutus also is gone.

So that's the first thing I wanted to say about Africa south of the Sahara. Africa south of the Sahara in those terms is isolated. That is the point I said was not obvious and I had to explain it in terms in which I have tried to explain it. The other one, the second point I want to raise is completely obvious. Africa has 53 nation-states, most of them in Africa south of the Sahara. If numbers were power, Africa would be the most powerful continent on earth. It is the weakest; so it's obvious numbers are not power.

So the second point about Africa, and again I am talking about Africa south of the Sahara; it is fragmented, fragmented. From the very beginning of independence 40 years ago, we were against that idea, that the continent is so fragmented. We called it the Balkanisation of Africa. Today, I think the Balkans are talking about the Africanisation of Europe. Africa's states are too many, too small, some make no logic, whether political logic or ethnic logic or anything. They are non-viable. It is not a confession.

The OAU was founded in 1963. In 1964 we went to Cairo to hold, in a sense, our first summit after the inaugural summit. I was responsible for moving that resolution that Africa must accept the borders, which we inherited from colonialism; accept them as they are.

That resolution was passed by the organisation (OAU) with two reservations: one from Morocco, another from Somalia. Let me say why I moved that resolution. In 1960, just before this country became independent, I think I was then chief minister; I received a delegation of Masai elders from Kenya, led by an American missionary. And they came to persuade me to let the Masai invoke something called the Anglo-Masai Agreement so that that section of the Masai in Kenya should become part of Tanganyika; so that when Tanganyika becomes independent, it includes part of Masai, from Kenya.

I suspected the American missionary was responsible for that idea. I don't remember that I was particularly polite to him. Kenyatta was then in detention, and here somebody comes to me, that we should break up Kenya and make part of Kenya part of Tanganyika. But why shouldn't Kenyatta demand that the Masai part of Tanganyika should become Masai of Kenya? It's the same logic. That was in 1960.

In 1961 we became independent. In 1962, early 1962, I resigned as prime minister and then a few weeks later I received Dr. Banda. *Mungu amuweke mahali pema* (May God rest his soul in peace). I received Dr. Banda. We had just, FRELIMO had just been established here and we were now in the process of starting the armed struggle.

So Banda comes to me with a big old book, with lots and lots of maps in it, and tells me, "Mwalimu, what is this, what is Mozambique? There is no such thing as Mozambique." I said, "What do you mean there is no such thing as Mozambique?" So he showed me this map, and he said: "That part is part of Nyasaland (Malawi was still Nyasaland at that time). That part is part of Southern Rhodesia, that part is Swaziland, and this part, which is the northern part, Makonde part, that is *your* part."

So Banda disposed of Mozambique just like that. I ridiculed the idea, and Banda never liked anybody to ridicule his ideas. So he left and went to Lisbon to talk to Salazar about this wonderful idea. I don't know what Salazar told him. That was '62.

In '63 we go to Addis Ababa for the inauguration of the OAU, and Ethiopia and Somalia are at war over the Ogaden. We had to send a special delegation to bring the president of Somalia to attend that inaugural summit, because the two countries were at *war*. Why? Because Somalia wanted the Ogaden, a *whole* province of Ethiopia, saying, "That is part of Somalia." And Ethiopia was quietly, the Emperor quietly saying to us that "the whole of Somalia is part of Ethiopia."

So those three, the delegation of the Masai, led by the American missionary; Banda's old book of maps; and the Ogaden, caused me to move that resolution, in Cairo 1964. And I say, the resolution was accepted, two countries with reservations, and one was Somalia because Somalia wanted the Ogaden; Somalia wanted northern Kenya; Somalia wanted Djibouti.

Throw away all our ideas about socialism. Throw them away, give them to the Americans, give them to the Japanese, give them, so that they can, I don't know, they can do whatever they like with them. *Embrace* capitalism, fine! But you *have* to be self-reliant.

You here in Tanzania don't dream that if you privatise every blessed thing, including the prison, then foreign investors will come rushing. No! No! Your are dreaming! *Hawaji*! They won't come! (*hawaji!*). You just try it.

There is more to privatise in Eastern Europe than here. Norman Manley, the Prime Minister of Jamaica, in those days the vogue was nationalisation, not privatisation. In those days the vogue was *nationalisation*. So Norman Manley was asked as Jamaica was moving towards independence: "Mr. Prime Minister, are you going to nationalise the economy?" His answer was: "You can't nationalise *nothing*."

You people here are busy privatising not *nothing*, we did *build* something, we built *something* to privatise. But quite frankly, for the appetite of Europe, and the appetite of North America, this is privatising nothing. The people with a really good appetite will go to Eastern Europe, they'll go to Russia, they'll not come rushing to Tanzania! Your blessed National Bank of Commerce, it's a branch of some major bank somewhere, and in Tanzania you say, "It's so big we must divide it into pieces," which is *nonsense*.

Africa south of the Sahara is isolated. Therefore, to develop, it will have to depend upon its own resources basically. Internal resources, nationally; and Africa will have to depend upon Africa. The leadership of the future will have to devise, try to carry out policies of *maximum* national self-reliance and *maximum* collective self-reliance. They have no other choice. *Hamna*! (You don't have it!)

And this, this need to organise collective self-reliance is what moves me to the second part. The small countries in Africa must move towards either unity or co-operation, unity of Africa. The leadership of the future, of the 21st century, should have less respect, less respect for this thing called "national sovereignty." I'm not saying take up arms and destroy the state, no! This idea that we must *preserve* the Tanganyika, then *preserve* the Kenya as they *are*, is nonsensical!

The nation-states we in Africa, have inherited from Europe. They are the builders of the nation-states par excellence. For centuries they fought wars! The history of Europe, the history of the *building* of Europe is a history of war. And sometimes their wars when they get hotter although they're European wars, they call them *world wars*. And we all get involved. We fight even in Tanganyika here, we *fought* here, one world war.

These Europeans, powerful, where little Belgium is more powerful than the whole of Africa south of the Sahara put together; these *powerful* European states are moving towards unity, and you people are talking about the atavism of the tribe, this is nonsense! I am telling *you* people. How can anybody think of the tribe as the unity of the future? *Hakuna!* (There's nothing!).

Europe now, you can take it almost as God-given, Europe is not going to fight with Europe anymore. The Europeans are not going to take up arms against Europeans. They are moving towards unity - even the little, the little countries of the Balkans which are breaking up, Yugoslavia breaking up, but they are breaking up at the same time the building up is taking place. They break up and say we want to come into the *bigger* unity.

So there's a *building* movement, there's a *building* of Europe. These countries which have old, old sovereignties, countries of hundreds of years old; they are forgetting this, they are *moving* towards unity. And you people, you think Tanzania is sacred? What is Tanzania!

You *have* to move towards unity. If these powerful countries see that they have no future in the nation-states - *ninyi mnafikiri mna future katika nini?* (what future do you think you have?). So, if we can't *move*, if our leadership, our future leadership cannot move us to bigger nation-states, which I *hope* they are going to try; we tried and failed. I tried and failed. One of my biggest failures was actually that. I tried in East Africa and failed. But don't give up because we, the first leadership, failed, no!

Unajaribu tena! (You try again!). We failed, but the idea is a good idea. That these countries should come together.

Don't leave Rwanda and Burundi on their own. *Hawawezi ku survive* (They cannot survive). They can't. They're locked up into a form of prejudice.

If we can't move towards bigger nation-states, at least let's move towards greater co-operation. This is beginning to happen. And the new leadership in Africa should encourage it.

I want to say only one or two things about what is happening in southern Africa. Please accept the logic of coming together. South Africa, small; South Africa is very small. Their per capita income now is, I think $2,000 a year or something around that. Compared with Tanzanians, of course, it is very big, but it's poor. If South Africa begins to tackle the problems of the legacy of apartheid, they have no money!

But compared with the rest of us, they are rich. And so, in southern Africa, there, there is also a kind of osmosis, also an economic osmosis. South Africa's neighbours send their job seekers *into* South Africa. And South Africa will simply have to accept the logic of that, that they are big, they are attractive. They attract the unemployed from Mozambique, and from Lesotho and from the rest. They have to accept that fact of life. It's a problem, but they have to accept it.

South Africa, and I am talking about post-apartheid South Africa. Post-apartheid South Africa has the most developed and the most dynamic private sector on the continent. It is white, so what? So forget it is white. It is South African, dynamic, highly developed. If the investors of South Africa begin a new form of trekking, you *have* to accept it. It will be ridiculous, absolutely ridiculous, for Africans to go out seeking investment from North America, from Japan, from Europe, from Russia, and then, when these investors come from South Africa to invest in your own country, you say, "a! a! These fellows now want to take over our economy" - this is nonsense.

You can't have it both ways. You want foreign investors or you don't want foreign investors. Now, the most available foreign investors for you are those from South Africa.

And let me tell you, when Europe think in terms of investing, they *might* go to South Africa. When North America think in terms of investing, they *might* go to South Africa. Even Asia, if they want to invest, the first country they may think of in Africa *may* be South Africa.

So, if *your* South Africa is going to be *your* engine of development, accept the reality, accept the reality. Don't accept this sovereignty, South Africa will reduce your sovereignty. What sovereignty do you have?

Many of these debt-ridden countries in Africa now have no soverignty, they've lost it. *Imekwenda* (It's gone). *Iko mikononi mwa IMF na World Bank* (It's in the hands of the IMF and the World Bank). *Unafikiri kuna sovereignty gani?* (What kind of sovereignty do you think there is?).

So, southern Africa has an opportunity, southern Africa, the SADC group, *because* of South Africa.

Because South Africa now is no longer a destabiliser of the region, but a partner in development, southern Africa has a tremendous opportunity. But you need leadership, because if you get proper leadership there, within the next 10, 15 years, that region is going to be the ASEAN (Association of South-East Asian Nations) of Africa. And it is possible.

But forget the protection of your sovereignties. I believe the South Africans will be sensitive enough to know that if they are not careful, there is going to be this resentment of big brother, but that big brother, frankly, is not very big.

West Africa. Another bloc is developing there, but that depends very much upon Nigeria my brother (looking at the Nigerian High Commissioner - Ambassador), very much so. Without Nigeria, the future of West Africa is a problem.

West Africa is more balkanised than Eastern Africa. More balkanised, tiny little states. The leadership will have to come from Nigeria. It came from Nigeria in Liberia; it has come from Nigeria in the case of Sierra Leone; it will have to come from Nigeria in galvanising ECOWAS. But the military in Nigeria must allow the Nigerians to exercise that vitality in freedom. And it is my hope that they will do it.

I told you I was going to ramble and it was going to be messy, but thank you very much.

Source:

Mwalimu Nyerere Memorial Site: Written Speeches, South Centre, Geneva, Switzerland, 2001.

This is an abridged version of Nyerere's speech at an international conference at the University of Dar es Salaam, Tanzania, December 15, 1997. The transcription of the non-written speech came from Mrs. Magombe of the Mwalimu Nyerere Foundation, Dar es Salaam.

Translation of Kiswahili words, phrases and sentences in Nyerere's speech into English in the preceding text, done by the author, Godfrey Mwakikagile.

Appendix II

The Legacies of Julius Nyerere: An Economist's Reflections by Professor Gerry Helleiner, University of Toronto

I spent some of the best years of my life working in Dar es Salaam in the late 1960s when Mwalimu Julius Nyerere was its inspiring young President.

In later years, I worked for shorter periods in Tanzania - under each of its Presidents - and had many occasions to reflect on the longer-term role that Nyerere played in his own country. Internationally, too, I have frequently had the honour and privilege of working in Mwalimu's ambit, most notably through the South Commission and the South Centre.

I believe I may be the only economist to speak at this conference. (In fact, it is quite possible that I am the only economist in attendance.) Much of the economics profession has taken rather a dim view of the legacy of Julius Nyerere. (I won't dignify with quotation or repetition some of the things I have heard said about him in the World Bank.)

It is precisely *because* I am an economist - and Mwalimu so evidently was not - that I want to put my profound admiration of his record and his legacy on the record.

It is undoubtedly in the field of economics that Julius Nyerere has received his worst press, and in which his legacy has been seen as most negative. The heading for his obituary in the (London) *Financial Times* read "Man of integrity whose policies hurt his country". That in *The Economist*, while generally friendly, concluded: "He was a magnificent teacher: articulate, questioning, stimulating, caring. He should never have been given charge of an economy."

Personally, I see his legacy in the realm of economic and development policy rather differently.

Mwalimu's grasp of the traditional tenets of economic theory was probably weak and so was that of his closest advisors and speechwriters (although there were those within government of whom this could certainly not be said).

Most of the criticism coming from economists relates to his "socialist" policies. But his government's most damaging economic policy errors, in my view, had little to do with socialism *per se*. They came relatively late in his Presidency and were on the relatively non-ideological issue of exchange rate policy; they were errors shared by many other low-income countries in the early 1980s.

As for his "socialism", some elements can be faulted as far more serious in their negative economic consequences than others. Nationalizations and restrictions on competition (including price controls) in the trading, industrial, agricultural and financial sectors were far beyond governmental management capacities and proved costly. Widespread (and even forced) "villagization" in the rural sector was not only economically costly but also deeply unpopular.

The "basic industry" policy - to the extent that it was part of Nyerere's "socialism" - was also mistaken in that it was premature and inappropriate for so economically small a country; it too proved costly.

All of these "socialist" policies could be foreseen (and were) as likely to slow overall economic growth and development both immediately and over the longer run. (My personal anxieties in this regard, circa 1969-70, may be found in an article in the *Journal of Development Studies*, Vol. 8, no. 1, January, 1972.) Arguably, none seemed likely, of themselves, however, to create the degree of economic collapse that occurred in the early 1980s. Nor, in my view, did they. Severe macroeconomic shocks - oil prices, weather, and war against Amin - and their serious domestic mismanagement were required for that.

In the early 1980s, as the UK White Paper on international development put it in its commentary on African experience, the "worldwide international climate ... left little margin for policy errors" (*Eliminating World Poverty: A Challenge for the 21st Century, White Paper on International Development*, November 1997, p. 9).

In Tanzania, there undoubtedly were such policy errors. Again, my view is that Tanzania's economic dislocations in the early 1980s were only partially attributable to its efforts to restructure the economy towards socialism. Far more serious were the errors in macroeconomic policy in the face of severe shocks (as well as, of course, the shocks themselves).

It is important for critical economists (and others) to recall that there were other elements in Nyerere's socialist programme - increased equity in the distribution of income; an attempt at a direct assault on bottom-end poverty (including provision of primary education and clean water); a "leadership code" for politicians and civil servants; major reform of the educational syllabus; and (at least rhetorical) emphasis on self-reliance and reduced aid dependence.

These elements of Nyerere's "socialist" programme excited widespread admiration and support (ultimately too much support of an unhelpful kind) from many academics and policymakers in the capitalist West, particularly in the Nordic countries and the Presidency of the World Bank. So compelling was this side of his socialist aspirations and practice that, for some time, admirers were prepared to give Tanzania the benefit of the doubt on the less propitious elements of its "socialist" development policy and its economic sustainability.

Sadly, as Tanzania's resource constraints tightened and macroeconomic policies faltered in the late 1970s and early 1980s most of these supporters lost confidence in the overall Nyerere socialist vision. Their withdrawal of financial support then worsened what had already become a crisis situation.

The first serious external pressures upon the Government of Tanzania to reform its economic policies were related primarily to its macroeconomic management policies, *not* to its socialism, and they came, of course, from the IMF. According to the IMF tenets of the times, what Tanzania most required in the late 1970s and early 1980s was cross-the-board governmental austerity and severe currency devaluation.

It was the effort at imposition of such IMF conditionality that prompted Nyerere's famous public outburst (in 1981): "Who elected the IMF to be the Finance Ministry for every country in the world?" (or words to that effect).

There followed an almost total breakdown in Tanzania-IMF relations. Julius Nyerere may be said to have fired the first African salvo in the great debate over the role of the IMF in Africa. (By a quirk of chance, it was at about the same time, 1980 that the annual meetings of the IMF were to be chaired by Amir Jamal, Tanzania's then Minister of Finance. I remember his recounting his surprise when, upon his arrival in Washington for the meetings, IMF staff presented him with a draft of his introductory remarks. He thanked them for their thoughtfulness he delighted in recalling, but told them he had brought his own speech.)

At this point (1980-81), Nyerere and Tanzania were still sufficiently respected that the then-President of the World Bank, Robert McNamara, initiated a mediation effort to seek an accommodation between the IMF and the Tanzanians. This was to be attempted through the provision of technical assistance for the preparation, in Tanzania, of an alternative to the IMF's stabilization and structural adjustment plan; the Government of Tanzania was given a voice (and indeed veto power) over the composition of the three-person team which was given the ultimate responsibility for the task.

With both expatriate and local staff working together in Dar es Salaam for a year, an alternative structural adjustment programme was tortuously constructed. Anticipating later African debates, it called for much greater emphasis upon supply-side expansion than demand-side restraint; much greater care over the distributional effects of required macroeconomic adjustment (with conscious effort to maintain equity of sacrifice); and a more gradual programme for the implementation of reforms.

The effort failed, however, when neither the Government of Tanzania nor the IMF found the programme satisfactory. (This is probably the appropriate point to recount another anecdote, one of my favourite Mwalimu stories.

Upon personally welcoming the agreed three-person team to Tanzania as it embarked on its task, the President followed his initial niceties to the group, each of whom he knew, with the prescient introductory substantive comment: "You know, gentlemen, I asked for money, not advice!" A more succinct statement of the problem of conditionality has probably never been made.)

A major "sticking point" in the failure to agree on what was, for its time, a highly innovative programme (as well as a potentially important model for IMF-member country dispute resolution), though not the only one, was the Government's (mistaken) reluctance sufficiently to devalue its currency. I am personally convinced that, like so many laymen, Mwalimu did not understand the role of the exchange rate; some (not all) of his advisors gave him very bad advice.

As the Government went ahead on its own more and more donors (including now the World Bank) lost faith in Tanzanian macroeconomic management, the economy spiralled further downward, corruption grew, and all-around confidence in the entire Nyerere vision was lost.

The advent of Reagan-Thatcher influences on economic policy throughout the world and in the Bretton Woods institutions (McNamara left the World Bank in 1981) furthered darkened external views of the Tanzanian situation.

The necessary policy turnaround - now in much more dire economic circumstances, and with both much more external policy leverage and, significantly, a degree of non-governmental (mainly university) technical influence - finally began in 1986, *after* Nyerere's departure.

When the turnaround came, except for exchange rate action, which, by its nature, had to come more swiftly (in effect, it began with the "own funds" import programme in 1984), it came fairly *gradually* and slowly. By the mid-1990s, the economy had significantly recovered and donors had returned. Remarkably, political stability had been a constant.

By this time, however, Tanzania was in trouble over other issues. Corruption had reached the highest levels of the

Government and party (attracting public criticism from, among others, the now-retired Mwalimu, who now also supported competitive elections in a multi-party system); the central economic policymaking machinery was demoralized and in disarray; and, partly in consequence, aid donors were almost totally "driving" such development efforts as were under way (outside the private sector).

Economic growth was taking place but there was a notable absence of any public "vision", such as had characterized the Nyerere years, as to where the country was going and why. Economic policy was seen as dictated by the international financial institutions and the aid donors. (For an account, see the Helleiner Report, *Report of the Group of Independent Advisers on Development Cooperation Issues Between Tanzania and Its Aid Donors*, Gerald K. Helleiner, Tony Killick, Nguyuru Lipumba, Benno J. Ndulu and Knud Erik Svendsen, Royal Danish Ministry of Foreign Affairs, June 1995.)

The Government of Benjamin Mkapa, newly elected in 1995, set out with the encouragement of some of the major aid donors, to restore ownership of its own development programmes, fight corruption, and recreate a sense of vision of the country's direction.

While much remains to be done, to a remarkable degree, it seems to me, it has been succeeding. It reached an important agreement, in principle, with the aid donor community on appropriate aid relationships - and, again, while much remains to be done, there can be no doubt that ownership of economic policy and programmes is returning to Tanzania.

The Government has prepared its own policy framework paper (PFP) and its own long-term vision statement (both with non-governmental inputs), led its own public expenditure review (PER) and the new Tanzania Assistance Strategy (TAS), and will now develop its own Poverty Reduction Strategy Paper (PRSP). Increasing (though still too small) proportions of aid expenditure are flowing through (or at least reported in) the national budget as the central economic administration strengthens.

Tanzanian-led sectoral strategies and policies are being developed and implemented in health, roads and education. Prime emphasis throughout these efforts is to address the principal problems of poverty and to do so under Tanzanian, not donor, leadership. (More details on all this can be found in a paper prepared for the May 1999 meeting of the Consultative Group for Tanzania: Gerry Helleiner, "Changing Aid Relationships in Tanzania, December 1997 through March 1999", Dar es Salaam, mimeo, 1999.)

One senior (and informed) World Bank official has remarked (to me privately) that, despite all the favourable press on Uganda, Tanzania is actually about four years or more ahead of it in terms of truly nationally-owned (and thus sustainable) economic policy for overall development. Tanzania may seem to move more slowly, he noted (and I agree), but it does so on a firmer and more stable base.

This base was established, I would argue, in the time of Julius Nyerere - a politically unified country; shared values as to equity in income distribution and political participation; and determination to develop and implement one's own policies and programmes.

Because Tanzania now has in place all of the key elements for sustained development - macroeconomic stability; broadly sensible incentive structures; broad political participation and stability; growing national self-confidence, ownership and capacity - I believe it is likely that, barring calamities of weather or the terms of trade, Tanzania will soon be everyone's favourite African "success story" (and model).

It is now "conventional wisdom" in Washington (even in the IMF, at least in terms of its rhetoric) and in donor capitals that poverty needs to be addressed as a matter of highest priority; that political stability and good governance (notably reduced corruption) are prerequisites for development; and that national ownership of programmes is critical to their success.

It has taken them a long time to reach these positions. But Julius Nyerere was espousing them and trying to build practice upon them 30 years ago. His slogan of "socialism and self-reliance", if transmitted today as "equity, honesty and ownership", would win universal assent. He was decades ahead of his time in these matters.

Today's key Tanzanian policymakers - both politicians and technocrats - grew up and were educated in the Nyerere years.

They have undoubtedly learned from earlier economic and other policy mistakes. (Mwalimu was himself a learner and pragmatist, who often changed policy positions when the evidence as to the failure of previous approaches seemed clear.)

I believe that the respect, which Mwalimu enjoyed in his own country right up until his death indicates that they also retained much that Mwalimu had taught. They now can build "humane governance" on the political and value base he constructed. (The apt concept of "humane governance" has recently been developed to encompass sound and equitable economic *and* political governance, including responsive and participatory institutions, respect for human rights, and special provision for the most needy and most vulnerable. See *Human Development in South Asia, 1999*, Mahbub ul Haq, The Human Development Centre and Oxford University Press, Pakistan, 1999.)

Whatever his other mistakes in the realm of economics, in one area of economic policy Mwalimu was dead right - and, again, ahead of his time.

Both in his anguished cry about the IMF in 1981 and in his subsequent work in the South Commission and the South Centre, he steadily maintained the need for fairer international (or global) systems of economic governance, particularly in the financial sphere. It is important to underline his consistent emphasis upon *equity* in global economic governance arrangements because there is every sign that current reform efforts in the international financial arena are overly focussed upon efficiency considerations and the avoidance or minimization of the effects of systemic crises.

This focus has resulted in some effort to incorporate some of the interests and concerns of the newly emerging countries and the largest of the poor countries and this certainly constitutes important progress in global economic and financial governance; but it leaves out the poorest and weakest. The latter are unrepresented - either in the new Financial Stability Forum or in the even newer Group of Twenty (G20), chaired by the Canadian Finance Minister. (The G20 has also contrived to exclude all of the so-called "like-minded" countries, who might be expected to take a deeper interest in the problems of the poorest countries and peoples, as they have done in the past on debt relief and other issues.)

Nyerere's activities in the international/global sphere included efforts to bolster analysis, both economic and political, to inform those who speak for the developing countries, especially the poorest among them, in international negotiations and organizations. The developing countries are still woefully weakly equipped to deal with the batteries of well-funded economists, lawyers and lobbyists who defend Northern interests in international discussions and the media.

He was among those who saw, far ahead of others, that there is ultimately no substitute for one's own technical, professional and institutional strength. Today it is known as "capacity building", and it has entered "conventional wisdom" as to what is to be done not only in Africa but throughout the developing world.

Yes, Julius Nyerere made some economic policy mistakes. In this he was certainly not alone. He also left a country capable of learning from its experience with a minimum of political ruckus, a country now moving forward economically on a firm political and value base. That is a significant legacy.

At the international level the fruits of his efforts are probably more distant. I expect, however, that one day they too will come.

Notes

Chapter One

1. Erika Johnson, *The Other Side of Kilimanjaro* (London: Johnson Publications Ltd., 1971), p. 16. See also, Donald Cameroon, *My Tanganyika Service and some in Nigeria* (London: Allen and Unwin, 1939; Lanham, Maryland: The University Press of America, second edition, 1982).

2. Godfrey Mwakikagile, *Nyerere and Africa: End of an Era: Expanded Edition* (Atlanta, Georgia: Protea Publishing Co., 2004).

3. Andrew Nyerere, in a letter to the author, 2003.

4. Erika Johnson, *The other Side of Kilimanjaro*, op. cit.

5. Abdallah Said Fundikira, quoted in *Africa News Online*, November 8, 1999.

6. Julius Nyerere, quoted, ibid.

7. Nyerere's mother, quoted, ibid.

8. Nyerere, quoted in *The New York Times*, March 31, 1957.

9. Nyerere's libel case, reported by *Drum*, November 1958, Dar es Salaam, Tanganyika.

10. Nyerere, upon hearing that TANU had won the 1958 - 1959 general election; also quoted by Nathanel Turner, "Julius Kambarage Nyerere: Statesman and Pan-African Leader," in *Chickenbones: A Journal for Literary @ Artistic African-American Themes*, 1999.

11. Nyerere, interviewed by *Drum*, Dar es Salaam, Tanganyika, March 1959.

12. Nelson Mandela, *Long Walk to Freedom: The Autobiography of Neslon Mandela* (New York: Little, Brown & Co., 1994).

1. Nyerere, in his speech in the Tanganyika colonial legislature, LEGCO, in October 1959.
2.

Chapter Two

1. Julius Nyerere, in an interview with Ikaweba Bunting in Nyerere's home village of Butiama near the southeastern shores of Lake Victoria in northern Tanzania, in the *New Internationalist*, December 1998.
2. Nyerere, quoted by Rolf Italiaander, *The New African Leaders* (New York: Prentice Hall, 1961).
3. Jomo Kenyatta, in Nairobi, Kenya, October 14, 1961, quoted by Ali A. Mazrui, *Towards A Pax-Africana* (London: Weidenfeld & Nicolson, 1967), p. 254. Kenyatta remarks sparked a lot of debate on what he really meant, whether or not he was demanding servility from Europeans and other non-Africans. The controversy was reported in British newspapers, including the London *Times* during that period. See also an article by Tom Stacey on the subject in the *Sunday Times*, London, June 3, 1962; and Ali A. Mazrui, "Consent, Colonialism and Sovereingty," in *Political Studies*, Vol. II, No. I, February 1963.
4. Kenyatta, ibid.
5. Julius K. Nyerere, *Freedom and Socialism: A Seelection from Writings and Speeches 1965 - 1967* (Dar es Salaam, Tanzania: Oxford University Press, 1968), p. 30.
6. Julius K. Nyerere, *Freedom and Unity: A Selection from Writings and Speeches* (Dar es Salaam: Oxford University Press, 1966), p. 77.
7. *The Arusha Declaration*, Arusha, Tanzania, February 1967.

Chapter Three

1. Julius Nyerere, quoted by James C. McKinley, "Tanzania's Nyerere Looks Back: Many Failures, and One Big Success - Bringing a Nation to Life," in the *International Herald Tribune*, September 2, 1996, p. 2. See also, James C. McKinley, on Nyerere and tanzania, in *The New York Times*, September 2, 1996. On Nyerere's retirement as president in November 1985, see *Daily News*, Dar es Salaam, Tanzania, November 1985.
2. Cranford Pratt, *The Critical Phase in Tanzania, 1945 to*

1968: Nyerere and the Emergence of a Socialist Strategy (Cambridge: Cambridge University Press, 1976).

3. Cranford Pratt and Bismarck Mwansasu, editors, *Towards Socialism in Tanzania* (Toronto: Toronto University Press, 1979).

4. Cranford Pratt, "Julius Nyerere: The Ethical Foundation of His Legacy," University of Toronto, Ontario, Canada. See also, Cranford Pratt, "Julius Kambarage Nyerere, 1922 - 1999: Reflections on His Legacy," in *Southern Africa Report*, vol. 15, no. 1, December 1999.

5. Julius Nyerere, quoted by Chris Bazier, in "The Lion Lies Down: Julius Nyerere Comes to the End of an Anti-Colonial Life," in the *New Internationalist*, Issue 319, December 1999.

6. Nyerere, quoted by James McKinley, "Tanzania's Nyerere Looks Back...," in *The New York Times*, loc.cit.

7. Nyerere, ibid.

8. Tanzania, in "World Bank Report," 1995.

9. Chinua Achebe, in his Presidential Fellow Lecture to the World Bank Group, Washington, D.C., 1998.

10. Nyerere, in an interview at the State House in Dar es Salaam, quoted in "Mwalimu Explains Stand on IMF, " in *Tanzania Embassy Newsletter*, Washington, D.C., January 1985, p. 8.

11. Nyerere, ibid.

12. Ibid.

13. Ibid.

14. Ibid.

15. Ibid.

16. "Tanzania," in *Reader's Digest 1986 Almanac and Yearbook* (Pleasantville, New York: Reader's Digest Association, 1985), p. 665.

17. Ibid.

18. Nyerere, quoted in the *Tanzania Embassy Newsletter*, loc.cit.

19. Cranford Pratt, "Julius Kambarage Nyerere, 1922 - 1999: Reflections on His Legacy," in *Southern Africa Report*, op. cit.

20. Harvey Glickman, "Tanzania: From Disillusionment to Guarded Optimism," in *Current History: A Journal of Contemporary World Affairs*, May 1997, p. 219; with the assistance of Raymond Hopkins; and Richard Mshomba, Elaine

Mshomba, and Victor Kimesera, all the last three from Tanzania. See also, Harvey Glickman, *Ethnic Conflict and Democratization in Africa* (Atlanta, Georgia: African Studies Association Press, 1995).

21. Adebayo Adedeji, interviewed by Margaret A. Novicki, in *Africa Report*, September-October 1983, p. 14.

Chapter Four

1. Julius Nyerere, quoted in *Sunday Independent*, Johannesburg, South Africa, October 17, 1999; and by R.W. Johnson, "Nyerere: A Flawed Hero," in *The National Interest*, Washington, D.C., No. 60, Summer 2000, p. 73.

2. Nyerere, in an interview with Tanzanian journalists, Dar es Salaam, Tanzania, 21 February 1990. The interview was published in two parts; the first, in the *Sunday News*, Dar es Salaam, Tanzania, 25 February 1990; and the second one, in the *Daily News*, Dar es Salaam, 26 February 1990. Both articles included editorial statements at the beginning stating: "Readers are invited to contribute ideas to issues raised by Mwalimu." See also, Daniel Zirker, "The Executive Origins of Multiparty Democracy in Tanzania," in the *Martin Journal of Peace Research*, No. 1, 1997, University of Idaho, USA.

3. Nyerere, *Sunday News*, ibid. He noted that "even discussing the possibility of more than one party becomes treason"; Daniel Zirker, ibid.

4. Ali Hassan Mwinyi, quoted in the *Daily News*, Dar es Salaam, Tanzania, 11 April 1990.

5. Benjamin Mkapa, quoted in the *Daily News*, Dar es Salaam, Tanzania, 16 May 1990.

6. Nyerere, quoted in the *Daily News*, Dar es Salaam, Tanzania, 30 May 1990.

7. Idris Wakil, quoted by Abdallah Yakuti, "We Can't Be Cowed," in the *Daily News*, Dar es Salaam. Tanzania, June 3, 1990.

8. Oscar Kambona, from exile in Britain, in his letter to the editor of the *Daily News*, Dar es Salaam, Tanzania, 2 August 1990.

9. Nyerere, in his last speech as chairman of the ruling party,

CCM, quoted in the *Daily News*, Dar es Salaam, August 17, 1990.

Chapter Five

1. Julius K. Nyerere, quoted by Michael T. Kaufman, "Julius Nyerere of Tanzania Dies; Preached African Socialism to the World, " in *The New York Times*, October 15, 1999, p. B1.
2. Nyerere in an interview in December 1998 with the *New Internationalist*, January-February 1999.
3. Oginga Odinga, *Not Yet Uhuru* (London: Longmans, 1967).
4. Kenneth Kaunda, *Zambia Shall Be Free* (London: Heinemann, 1962).
5. Kaunda, quoted in Colin Legum and John Drysdale, *Africa Contemporary Record: Annual Survey and Documents 1968 - 1969* (London: Africa Research Ltd., 1969), p. 250. See also *Times of Zambia*, Lusaka, Zambia, September 1968.
6. Nyerere, quoted in *Africa Contemporary Record*, ibid., p. 220.
7. Nyerere, in an address to the Tanganyika Legislative Council (LEGCO), Dar es Salaam, Tanganyika, October 22, 1959.
8. David Martin, "A Candle on Kilimanjaro," in *Southern African Features*, December 21, 2001.
9. Nelson Mandela, *Long Walk to Freedom: The Autobiography of Nelson Mandela* (New York: Little Brown & Co., 1995).
10. Yoweri Museveni, in Elizabeth Kanyogonya, editor, *Yoweri K. Museveni: What Is Africa's Problem?: Foreword by Mwalimu Julius K. Nyerere* (Minneapolis: University of Minnesota Press, 2000); Museveni, cited by Lara Santoro, "West Cheers Uganda's One-Man Show," in *The Christian Science Monitor*, March 2, 1999; Peter Graff, "Ex-Leninist Leads Uganda to Prosperity: Single-Party Rule Troubles Free-Market Admirers," in *The Boston Globe*, December 7, 1997, p. A44:

"Museveni is a guerrilla leader who spent much of his life in exile in socialist Tanzania and received his education at the University of Dar es Salaam, then a hotbed of post-colonial leftist radicalism. At the time, Tanzania's patriarch, Julius Nyerere, was a hero to most students for implementing the policy of 'ujamaa' (African socialism)... Museveni still considers himself a disciple of Nyerere."

See also Museveni, in Godfrey Mwakikagile, *Economic Development in Africa* (Commack, New York: Nova Science Publishers, Inc., 1999), p. 142.

11. Che Guevara, *Congo Diaries*.

12. P. W. Botha, in *Africa Contemporary Record*, op.cit., p. 291.

13. Walter Rodney, *How Europe Underdeveloped Africa* (Dar es Salaam, Tanzania: Tanzania Publishing House, 1972).

14. Colin Legum, "The Goal of an Egalitarian Society," in Colin Legum and Geoffrey Mmari, editors, *Mwalimu: The Influence of Nyerere* (Trenton, New Jersey: Africa World Press, 1995), p. 187.

15. Philip Ochieng', "There Was Real Freedom in Mwalimu's Day," in *The East African*, Nairobi, Kenya, October 20, 1999.

16. "In Memory of Karim Essack," the International Emergency Committee (IEC) to Defend the Life of Dr. Abimael Guzman, London, October 1997.

17. Keith B. Richburg, *Out of America: A Black Man Confronts Africa* (New York: Basic Books, 1998), p. 241. As he put it:

"One of my earliest trips was to Tanzania, and there I found a country that had actually managed to purge itself of the evil of tribalism....But after three years traveling the continent, I've found that Tanzania is the exception, not the rule."

18. Philip Ochieng', *I Accuse the Press: An Insider's View of the Media and Politics in Africa* (Initiatives Press: ACT Press).

19. Harvey Glickman, "Tanzania: From Disillusionment to Guarded Optimism," in *Current History: A Journal of Contemporary World Affairs*, May 1997, p. 217.

20. Francis Kasoma, *The Press and Multiparty Politics in Africa* (University of Tampere); F.P.Kasoma, *Communication Policies in Botswana, Lesotho, and Swaziland* (University of Tampere); F.P. Kasoma, *Communication Policies in Zambia* (Tempereen Yliopisto); F.P. Kasoma, *The Press in Zambia: The Development, Role, and Control of National Newspapers in Zambia 1906 - 1983* (Multimedia Publications).

21. Hadji Konde, *Press Freedom in Tanzania* (Nairobi, Kenya: Eastern Africa Publications).

22. Clement Ndulute, *The Poetry of Shaaban Robert* (Dar es Salaam, Tanzania: University of Dar es Salaam Press, 1994).

23. Godfrey Mwakikagile, *Economic Development in Africa* (Commack, New York: Nova Science Publishers, Inc., 1999).

24. Godfrey Mwakikagile, *The Modern African State: Quest for Transformation* (Huntington, New York: Nova Science Publishers, Inc., 2001).

25. Godfrey Mwakikagile, *Africa and the West* (Huntington, New York: Nova Science Publishers, Inc., 2000).

26. Godfrey Mwakikagile, book review of George B.N. Ayittey, *Africa in Chaos* (New York: St. Martin's Press, 1998), on Amazon.com, December 2001.

27. Jonathan Power, TFF Jonathan Power Columns, "Lament for Independent Africa's Greatest Leader," London, October 6, 1999.

28. Julius Nyerere, in "Julius Nyerere Press Conference," Dar es Salaam, AFP, 14 March 1995.

29. Nyerere, remarks to the World Bank, quoted in the *Sunday Times*, October 3, 1999.

30. Nyerere, in the *Sunday Independent*, Johannesburg, October 17, 1999.

31. Jomo Kenyatta, quoted in *Africa Contemporary Record*, op. cit., p. 157. See also *Kenya Weekly News*, Nairobi, Kenya, June 21, 1968:

"How will KPU contest the elections if it is not allowed to be organised on a country-wide basis like KANU?... In its brief, but turbulent history, Kenya has had numerous political parties, which in many cases died a natural death. Let KPU follow them into the grave if the Wananchi do not support its programme after a fair and full hearing of its case...." See also, same quotation, in *Africa Contemporary Record*, ibid.

32. Mundia Kamau, "A Nation in Distress," in *Mashada Daily*, Nairobi, Kenya, November 13, 1999.

33. James Mpinga, "With Mwalimu Gone, Free Bread for Butiama Children Goes Too," in *The East African*, Nairobi, Kenya, November 3, 1999.

34. "Newsweek," October 1999.

35. Ali A. Mazrui, "Nyerere and I," in *Voices*, Africa Resource Center, October 1999.

36. Jimmy Carter, on Nyerere's death, quoted in "Tanzania: Former President Julius Nyerere Dies at 77," in *UN Wire*, New York, October 15, 1999.

37. Ali A. Mazrui, "Mwalimu's Rise to Power," in *Daily Nation*, Nairobi, Kenya, October 17, 1999; "Africa's Mwalimu: Ali Mazrui Pays Tribute to Julius Nyerere," in *Worldview Magazine*, Washington, D.C., Vol. 12, No. 4, Fall 1999.

38. Ali A. Mazrui, *On Heroes and Uhuru-Worship: Essays: Independent Africa* (London: Longmans, 1967).

39. Nyerere, in an interview with James McKinley, "Tanzania's Nyerere Looks back: Many Failures, and One Big Success - Bringing A Nation to Life," in *International Herald Tribune*, September 2, 1996. See also Godfrey Mwakikagile, *Economic Development in Africa*, op. cit., p. 62. As Nyerere stated:

"I felt that these little countries in Africa were really too small, they would not be viable - the Tanganyikas, the Rwandas, the Burundis, the Kenyas. My ambition in East Africa was really never to build a Tanganyika. I wanted an East African federation. So what did I succeed in doing? My success is building a nation out of this collection of tribes."

40. Olusegun Obasanjo, at Nyerere's funeral, Dar es Salaam, Tanzania, quoted by Susan Linnee, "Tanzanian Leader's Funeral Marks End of Era," Associated Press (AP), October 22, 1999.

41. "Look Beyond Mobutu, Nyerere Tells Zaireans," in Features Africa Network, Africa Online, March 12, 1997.

42. Julius K. Nyerere, "Africa Must Unite," his speech in Accra, Ghana, March 6, 1997, marking Ghana's 40th independence anniversary; edited excerpts published by New Africa International Network (NAIN): Debate: www.nain.unitedafricastar.com/html/africa.htm. See also *Daily Graphic*, Accra, Ghana, March 1997; *Daily News*, Dar es salaam, Tanzania, March 1997.

See also Bill Sutherland and Matt Meyer, foreword by Archbishop Desmond Tutu, *Guns and Gandhi in Africa: Pan-African Insights on Nonviolence, Armed Struggle and Liberation in Africa* (Trenton, New Jersey: Africa World Press, Inc., 2000).

See also M.O. Ene, chairman, Enyimba Pan-Igbo Think Tank, on his remarks about Nyerere when he died: "I saw the legend in

1966, and the memory still lives with me."

Chapter Six

1. Shariff Hamad, quoted in *Time*, October 2000.
2. Wolfgang Dourado, quoted in *Time*, ibid.
3. Aboud Jumbe, at a press conference in Dar es Salaam, Tanzania, January 1998.
4. A. Jumbe, ibid.
5. John S. Saul, "Julius Nyerere: The Theory and Practice of (Un)democratic Socialism in Africa," York University, Ontario, Canada, 2000.

About the Author

GODFREY MWAKIKAGILE has written a number books about Africa. They include *Nyerere and Africa: End of an Era* and *Africa After Independence: Realities of Nationhood.*

He has also written some books about the United States and Africa: *Relations Between Africans and African Americans: Misconceptions, Myths and Realities*; and *Africa and America in The Sixties: A Decade That Changed The Nation and The Destiny of A Continent.*